THE DEVELOPMENT OF THE
ENGLISH NOVEL

THE DEVELOPMENT

OF

THE ENGLISH NOVEL

BY

WILBUR L. CROSS

ASSISTANT PROFESSOR OF ENGLISH IN THE
SHEFFIELD SCIENTIFIC SCHOOL
OF YALE UNIVERSITY

GREENWOOD PRESS, PUBLISHERS
NEW YORK

Originally published in 1889
by The Macmillan Co.

Reprinted with the permission
of Wilbur L. and S. Avery Cross

First Greenwood Reprinting 1969

Library of Congress Catalogue Card Number 78-90494

SBN 8371-2204-X

PRINTED IN UNITED STATES OF AMERICA

TO

M. FERDINAND BRUNETIÈRE

This Book

IS INSCRIBED

BY THE AUTHOR

NOTE TO THE SECOND EDITION

WHATEVER may be the value of the opinions expressed in this book, I have spared no pains to be accurate in all statements of fact. The interim between the first and the second impression has been hardly long enough for the discovery of all errors that are sure to creep into a book of this kind. A few, however, have been observed, and are now corrected. They occurred on pages 12, 29, 40, 66, 283, and 289. Undoubtedly there are others; and that they may be eliminated, I invite the coöperation of my readers.

THE AUTHOR.

YALE UNIVERSITY,
Nov. 13, 1899.

CONTENTS

PAGE

INTRODUCTION XI

CHAPTER I

FROM ARTHURIAN ROMANCE TO RICHARDSON

SECT.
1. The Mediæval Romancers and Story-tellers. . . 1
2. The Spanish Influence 6
3. The Elizabethans 10
4. The Historical Allegory and the French Influence . 13
5. The Restoration 18
6. Literary Forms that contributed to the Novel . . 22
7. The Passing of the Old Romance 25
8. Daniel Defoe 27

CHAPTER II

THE EIGHTEENTH-CENTURY REALISTS

1. Samuel Richardson 31
2. Henry Fielding 42
3. The Novel versus the Drama 57
4. Tobias Smollett 63
5. Laurence Sterne 69
6. The Minor Novelists: Sarah Fielding, Samuel Johnson, Oliver Goldsmith 76

vii

CHAPTER III

From ' Humphry Clinker ' to ' Waverley '

SECT.   PAGE
1. The Imitators 82
2. The Novel of Purpose 84
3. The Light Transcript of Contemporary Manners   . 93
4. The Gothic Romance 98
5. The Historical Romance 110
6. Jane Austen — the Critic of Romance and of Manners 114

CHAPTER IV

Nineteenth-century Romance

1. Sir Walter Scott and the Historical Novel .   .   . 125
2. Scott's Legacy 136
3. The Romance of War 149
4. James Fenimore Cooper and the Romance of the
        Forest and the Sea 150
5. The Renovation of Gothic Romance 158

CHAPTER V

The Realistic Reaction

1. The Minor Humorists and the Author of ' Pickwick ' 168
2. Charles Dickens and the Humanitarian Novel .   . 180

CHAPTER VI

The Return to Realism

1. William Makepeace Thackeray 197
2. Bulwer-Lytton in the Rôle of Realist, George Borrow,
        Charles Reade   208

SECT. PAGE
3. Anthony Trollope 215
4. Charlotte Brontë 224

CHAPTER VII

THE PSYCHOLOGICAL NOVEL

1. Elizabeth Gaskell — the Ethical Formula of the Psychologists 234
2. George Eliot 237
3. George Meredith 252

CHAPTER VIII

THE CONTEMPORARY NOVEL

1. Henry James and Impressionism 263
2. Philosophical Realism : Mrs. Humphry Ward and
   Thomas Hardy 268
3. Robert Louis Stevenson and the Revival of Romance 280
4. Rudyard Kipling 290
   Conclusion 293

APPENDIX

1. A List of Twenty-five Prose Fictions 297
2. Bibliographical and Other Notes 300

INDEX 315

INTRODUCTION

This book aims to trace in outline the course of English fiction from Arthurian romance to Stevenson, and to indicate, especially in the earlier chapters, Continental sources and tributaries. I hope that the volume may be of service to the student as a preliminary to detailed investigation in special epochs; and of interest to the general reader, who may wish to follow some of the more important steps whereby a fascinating literary form has become what it is through modifications in structure and content.

The apparent law that has governed these changes is the same as is operative in all literary development: the principle of action and reaction in the ordinary acceptation of the terms. This law has a psychological basis. We are by nature both realists and idealists, delighting in the long run about equally in the representation of life somewhat as it is and as it is dreamed to be. There is accordingly no time in which art does not to some extent minister to both instincts of human nature. But in one period the ideal is in ascendency; in another the real. Why this is so we have not far to seek. Idealism in course of time falls into unendurable exorbitancies; realism likewise offends by its brutality and cynicism. And in either case there is a recoil, often accompanied, as will be noted, by unreasonable criticism, even by parody and burlesque. The reaction of the public is taken advantage of by a man of letters; it is enforced by him and may be led by him. Fielding was such a man, and so was Thackeray. And if, as was true in these two cases, the leader is a man of genius, he can for a period do what he pleases with his public. Now what is the procedure of the man of letters who has assented to a reactionary creed? He reverts to some earlier form or method, and modifies and develops it; in the language of science, he varies the type. Not to go for illustration beyond the two novelists just cited, Fielding set the Spanish rogue story over against Richardson; and Thackeray professedly took Fielding as his model in his reaction against Dickens. Both were, according to their light, realists; but their works are different. No one would confound the authorship of 'Tom Jones' with that of 'Vanity Fair.' Why? Besides the strictly personal element, there are differences in literary antecedents and divergences in public taste. For realism, Fielding had behind him, for the most part, only picaresque fiction and the comedy of manners. Thackeray had behind him not only Fielding, but a line of succeeding novelists — romancers and realists. For example, between Fielding and Thackeray is Scott; and with what result? There is no history in 'Tom Jones'; if 'Vanity Fair' does not have a background in actual historical incident, it has at least the show of history. There is thus never a full return to the past; romance learns from realism; and realism learns from romance. In this way literature is always moving on, and to something that can never be predicted. In the details of my work, in determining the antecedents of a writer and what he added that is new and original in form and content to the art of fiction, I have found that there are modes or processes of change and development best expressed in the terms that natural science has made familiar, — modification, variation, deviation, persistence, and transformation. These are perhaps only analogies. That the material of literary history can be treated with the exactness of science I have, after some experimenting, no disposition to maintain.

The terms 'romance' and 'novel,' which in themselves are a summary of the two conflicting aims in fiction, require at the outset brief historical and descriptive definition. The former is in English the older word, being in common use as early as the fourteenth century. Our writers then meant first of all by the romance a highly idealized verse-narrative of adventure or love translated from the French, that is, from a romance language; they also extended the term to similar stories derived from classic and other sources, or of their own invention. For a verse-narrative approaching closer to the manners of real life — its intrigues and jealousies, — the Provençal poets had employed the word *novas* (always plural); for a like narrative in prose, always short, Boccaccio and his contemporaries were using the cognate word *novella*. Of stories of this realistic content, many were written in English in the fourteenth century, but they were called tales, — a word of elastic connotation, which Chaucer made to comprehend nearly all the different kinds of verse-stories current in his time.

During the two centuries following Boccaccio the
Italians continued to compose books of *novelle*, and in
very great numbers. In the age of Elizabeth they
came into English in shoals, and with them the word
'novel,' as applicable to either the translation or an
imitation. It was a particularly felicitous make-believe
designation, for it conveyed the notion that the incidents and the treatment were new. It however had
a hard struggle to maintain itself, for the Elizabethans
preferred to it the word 'history,' which they applied
to all manner of fictions in verse and prose, as may
be seen from such titles as 'The Tragical History of
Romeus and Juliet' and 'The History of Hamlet,
Prince of Denmark.' This, too, was a happy designation, for it implied a pretended faithfulness to
fact. Richardson and Fielding, after some vacilla-
tion, settled upon the word 'history' for their fictions,
though they both refer to them as novels. From the
invention of printing down to this time the word
'romance,' by which our mediæval writers denoted adventures in verse or in prose, had not been common
in the titles and the prefaces of English fictions,
though many romances had been written. But when
in the last half of the eighteenth century wild and
supernatural stories came into fashion, the word was
often placed upon title-pages. At this time Clara
Reeve, in an exceedingly pleasant group of dialogues,
drew the line of distinction between the romance and
the novel. She says in 'The Progress of Romance'
(1785) : —

The Novel is a picture of real life and manners, and of
the times in which it is written. The Romance, in lofty

and elevated language, describes what never happened nor
is likely to happen. The Novel gives a familiar relation of
such things as pass every day before our eyes, such as may
happen to our friend or to ourselves; and the perfection of
it is to represent every scene in so easy and natural a manner and to make them appear so probable as to deceive us
into a persuasion (at least while we are reading) that all is
real, until we are affected by the joys or distresses of the
persons in the story as if they were our own.

Scott was a disturbing element to the critic's classi-
fication, for he combined the novel and the romance
as defined by Clara Reeve. What name shall the
amalgamation bear? It was at this time that the
word 'novel' became the generic term for English
prose fiction. But while this is mainly true, our no-
menclature continues somewhat uncertain. In a not
very precise way the novel and the romance are still
brought into an antithesis similar to Clara Reeve's.
That prose-fiction which deals realistically with actual
life is called, in criticism and conversation, preëminently the novel. That prose-fiction which deals with
life in a false or a fantastic manner, or represents it
in the setting of strange, improbable, or impossible
adventures, or idealizes the virtues and the vices of
human nature, is called romance.

The expression 'the English novel,' in common
speech, means the novel written in Great Britain.
For reasons that will appear very obvious, I shall
regard the novel written in the United States as a
constituent part of English fiction.

All dates placed in parentheses after novels are of
publication. Where a novel has appeared as a serial
and afterward as a whole the date of the latter pub-

lication is given, unless an express statement is made
to the contrary. Such a date as 1871–72 for 'Middlemarch' means that the novel was published in
parts during those years. Title-pages in most instances are of necessity much abridged. Immediately
after the main text I have placed a list of twenty-
five novels which will show the general progress of
English fiction. This in turn is followed by bibliographical and other notes for the use of more advanced
students. In both instances I have indicated recent
editions available to those who do not have easy access
to large libraries.

It would be impracticable to enumerate here the
sources drawn upon for this volume. J. C. Dunlop's 'History of Prose Fiction' and Professor Walter
Raleigh's 'English Novel' should be expressly mentioned, for, in guiding my reading down to Scott, they
were of great aid. Though I cannot hope to have
detached myself from opinions and estimates now
prevailing, I have striven to gain a new standpoint;
consulting to this end, from Scott onward, current
reviews of novels as they were appearing. As so little
has been attempted thus far in the history of the
English novel, I have been able to present in outline
considerable new material : the far-reaching influence
of Spanish fiction from Fielding to Thackeray; the
historical romance as an offshoot of the historical
allegory; the relation of Richardson and Fielding to
the drama; the beginnings of the Gothic romance in
Smollett; and the immediate source of George Eliot's
ethical formula. Access to the library of the British
Museum has also enabled me to put the origin of the
novel of letters in a new light. What has most im-

pressed me is the intimate connection between English and French fiction. This might be expected in the centuries immediately following the Norman Conquest. The relationship, however, is very close from Richardson to Hardy. So far as I have been able I have given organic treatment to my subject. The book is not a series of independent essays, but one essay, divided here and there for convenience.

While the volume has been passing through the press, I have received much aid from two students in the graduate department of the University, — Mr. A. H. Bartlett and Mr. J. M. Berdan. To Professor Charles Sears Baldwin, who has read all the proof-sheets, I am greatly indebted for unsparing criticism. I have also to thank Professor Henry A. Beers for the encouragement he has given me from the beginning of the work to its publication.

THE DEVELOPMENT OF THE ENGLISH NOVEL

CHAPTER I

FROM ARTHURIAN ROMANCE TO RICHARDSON

1. *The Mediæval Romancers and Story-tellers*

NORMAN England came into possession of an immense body of fictitious narrative. Learned societies have edited and published some of it, but there still remain unedited hundreds of manuscripts, for a knowledge of which we are compelled to have recourse to imperfect bibliographies. The heroes of these tales were taken from Teutonic, Celtic, French, Classic, and Eastern tradition. It was especially around Charlemagne, Arthur, Alexander the Great, and the siege of Troy, that epic and mythological incident gathered, assuming the form of histories and biographies, now called cycles of romance. On their appearance first in French and then in English, these adventures were usually in verse, composed by minstrels and trouvères for recitation and reading at court and in the castles of the nobility; later they were turned into prose. First in popularity and first in interest to him who is seeking the antecedents of the modern novel are the legends of King Arthur and the Round

Table; the scope of which is represented, though not in its fulness, by Tennyson's 'Idylls of the King.' As early as 1139, there was circulating a curious hero-saga, written in Latin by Geoffrey of Monmouth and professing to be a translation from the Welsh. This famous 'History of the British Kings,' reflecting vaguely the struggles of Roman, Celt, and Saxon for supremacy in Britain, becomes in its later parts a splendid romance of Arthur's ancestry, marriage, coronation, conquests, and passage to Avallon to be healed of his wounds. This so-called 'Celtic matter' proved most attractive to the French and Anglo-Norman poets, who reared upon it a vast superstructure. Thus, as might be illustrated by many similar examples,[1] fiction freed itself from the restraint of fact, and the **romance** came into being. Long after this event had taken place, a certain Sir Thomas Malory made a graceful redaction of the stories about Arthur and his knights in a book entitled 'Morte Darthur' (1485), which is for the general reader the first easily accessible prose romance in English.

The Arthurian romances do not consist merely of improbable adventures. It is true that they sought to interest, and did interest, by a free employment of the marvellous, fierce encounters of knights, fights with giants and dragons, swords that would not out of their scabbards, and the enchantments of Merlin. But these romances were also analytical. In those brilliant assemblages of lords and ladies at the Norman and French courts of the twelfth century, conversation turned for subject to the nature of love, and the proper conduct of the lover toward his mis-

[1] 'Epic and Romance,' W. P. Ker, Lond. and N.Y., 1897.

tress; and, as a result, the courtly philosophers, working on Ovid's 'Art of Love' as a basis, formulated a code of passion which rivalled, in minute detail, the metaphysical distinctions of the Schoolmen.   There were major precepts and minor precepts, showing the processes by which a knight might win the heart of the lady of the castle; the symptoms of love were noted and recorded, and nice questions of conduct — for example, the circumstances under which the lady might become 'the fair dear friend' of a knight not her husband — were put into syllogistic form. This casuistry is the basis of the stories of Tristram and Iseult, and of Lancelot and Guenevere.[1]   Other conceptions of passion also found their way into Arthurian romance : in Cameliard, Arthur had the first sight of Guenevere, and ever after he loved her; the fair maid of Astolat swooned and died when abandoned by Lancelot of the Lake; and in course of time, the ethics of the court clashing with the ethics of the cloister, there was conceived Sir Galahad's quest of the Holy Grail.   This formal analysis of love winds its way through Spanish, French, and English romance down to the eighteenth century; and becomes in Richardson a starting-point for a less scholastic dissection of the heart.   The main situations in the great stories of Arthurian romance in which one is asked to sympathize with guilty passion have appeared again and again in the modern novel.   Lancelot and Guenevere, Tristram and Iseult, have proved to be permanent types.

Side by side with the Arthurian cycle, though the period of their popularity was somewhat later,

[1] 'Romania,' xii. 516–534.

were the verse-tales called by the French, who first composed them, romances of adventure. Some of them, as the English alliterative poem 'Gawain and the Green Knight,' are Celtic in incident. Others are episodes of the Charlemagne cycle. Still others, indistinct echoes of Greek and far Eastern fable, are throughout professedly fictitious, and thus have an important significance. Fiction is expanding and taking a step toward the freedom of the modern novel. Its ethics are also undergoing change; for the exaltation of illegitimate passion or of asceticism is not so frequent as in Arthurian romance. The prevailing theme is now the constancy of young lovers, separated by accident or design, and united after shipwreck, capture by pirates, and servitude. Beautiful renderings of this situation are 'Florice and Blancheflour,' and the story of Aucassin, who for his love of Nicolette would sacrifice his kingdom, his knighthood, and Paradise.[1] As verse-tales the romances of adventure disappeared toward the close of the fourteenth century, when Chaucer in 'The Rime of Sir Thopas' ridiculed them as undeservedly as delightfully. But their incidents in many cases survived the wreck of their form. There were Tudor prose versions of the two favorites, 'Guy of Warwick' and 'Robert the Devil'; and the Elizabethan love stories are romances of adventure with pastoral decorations.

The delicate poetry and analysis of courtly romance could hardly have been appreciated by the rude mediæval barons and the common folk. They naturally had their own stories, in verse and prose, which

---

[1] English translation: 'The Lovers of Provence,' N.Y., 1890.

were more in accord with their own lives, feelings, and ways of looking at things.   These stories, of which the finished types are the French *fabliau* in octosyllabic rhyming couplets and the Italian *novella* in prose, have for subject striking and humorous incidents of ordinary life.   They are not, in content, all indigenous. Many of them are the common property of mankind, and have been traced in their germinal form to India. But what originally came from the East was almost invariably so modified and enriched that it seemed to spring from mediæval soil.   Widely diffused were developments of Æsopian fable, such as the story of 'Reynard the Fox,' in which animals are made to talk and reason, and comment in a gay satirical vein on human life and its affairs.   The clergy catered to the popular taste for this kind of story, making, as Wyclif accused them, the basis of the sermon an Eastern tale, from which was drawn a new and fantastic moral.   For the vulgar, the minstrels degraded what had once been a noble art, singing their songs of humorous incident at street corners and at the wassails of the barons.   They held up to cynical ridicule the intrigues and frailties of the clergy ; and gave a coarse realistic touch to Arthurian fable, tearing the mask from the courteous knights and the glittering ladies at Caerleon on Usk, and exposing amid peals of laughter from their hearers the cowardice and unfaithfulness beneath.   In these popular songs and stories, frequently composed with an eye upon the characteristic weaknesses of human nature, are the beginnings of the realistic novel.

During the reign of Richard the Second, John Gower collected and moralized, somewhat after the way of the clergy, many of the tales that had long been current. His great contemporary Chaucer — at will a romancer or a realist — clothed in artistic form the low intrigue, the fable, the adventure, and the romance of chivalry, prefacing them with a group of contemporary portraits. Delightful as are these tales of the Canterbury pilgrims, yet the poem in which Chaucer moved most directly toward the novel is 'Troilus and Cressida.' Its heroine is the subtlest piece of psychological analysis in mediæval fiction; and the shrewd and practical Pandarus is a character whose presence of itself brings the story down from the heights of romance to the plains of real life. Moreover, though written when the dramatic imagination had hardly appeared elsewhere in romance, this tale of illicit passion possesses in a marked degree the structure of Elizabethan tragedy. Less than a century after the death of Chaucer, mediæval and modern England met at the printing-press of William Caxton.

2. *The Spanish Influence*

The first half of the sixteenth century is a dreary waste in the history of English fiction. Its only oasis is Sir Thomas More's ' Utopia,' which, written and published in Latin, may be characterized as the ' Coming Race ' or the ' Looking Backward ' of our learned ancestors. It is true that amid the fierce contest of Romanism and Protestantism for supremacy in English politics, men found time to read stories and romances, but they did not write them. They were content with those that Caxton, Wynkyn de Worde, Pynson, and

Copland edited and printed for them from English mediæval manuscripts, or translated for them from French and German. The direct line in the development of English fiction, though not broken, is at this point worn to a slender thread, which we may neglect. When midway in the reign of Elizabeth creative work began anew, the main impetus came rather from southern Europe, especially from Spain.

The romantic incidents early current in France and England were likewise well known in the Spanish peninsula, where they were moulded into fictions similar to those we have described. From a Portuguese romance of adventure there grew up through the accretions of a long period the famous 'Amadis de Gaula,' which has been preserved in a Spanish prose redaction made by Ordoñez de Montalvo toward the end of the fifteenth century. It is the norm of the romances of chivalry. For its machinery of wonders, hand-to-hand fights with giants, monsters, and devils, the romance dips into mediævalism. Its code of conduct for the knight is likewise essentially the same as in the Arthurian cycle. When Amadis stands before Oriana, he is abashed and silent like Lancelot in the presence of Guenevere; and for her he traverses Europe in search of adventure to prove his worth. But the reader of 'Amadis de Gaula' is at once aware that he is getting away from mediævalism. Its author had some artistic sense of what a novel should be. Its plot for a time has a degree of definiteness, for it drifts toward the marriage of Amadis and Oriana. Magic, which had hitherto been an adornment to please the superstitious, is made to bear an ethical import; and manners are invested with a new and striking dignity. There are appearing also new ideals of character, such as in the course of time Richardson is to fix permanently in the novel : for example, Galaor is the first of the Lovelaces; and Amadis, a figure without taint or speck, is a remote ancestor of Sir Charles Grandison. And lastly, fiction is beginning to have a more serious motive; it would defend the purity of the home, and it would proclaim that right will finally triumph over wrong.

The Spanish romance of chivalry quickly degenerated into grotesque adventure. The reaction against it first took the form of the pastoral. For a long time the poets of southern Europe had been writing series of pastoral poems connected by explanatory prose links; and just as Vergil had in a measure done in his 'Eclogues,' they were accustomed to disguise themselves and their friends under fictitious names. A good example of this kind of work is the 'Arcadia' (1504), written by the Italian Jacopo Sannazaro. But substance was first given to the pastoral in the 'Diana' (1558?) of George of Montemayor, a Portuguese by birth and a Spaniard by adoption, who localized his scene, and wrote mostly in prose. Men and women, who in the romances of chivalry were turned into knights and ladies, now assume the dress and life of shepherds and shepherdesses, wandering along gently flowing streams, sleeping beneath sycamores, and lamenting in madrigals over unrequited loves. To the 'Diana' of Montemayor, which was translated into French and English, even attracting the attention of Shakespeare, is bound most closely all the succeeding pastoral romances of northern Europe.

To Spain, too, the novel owes the development of

another form of fiction. The incident in a popular
mediæval story was frequently a trick or a practical
joke of a witty fellow. The romance of 'Reynard
the Fox' is a collection of such tricks, which Master
Reynard plays upon his brother animals. This kind
of fiction was first turned to good account in prose in
a little Spanish story entitled, 'Lazarillo de Tormes'
(1554), which is the first of the picaresque novels,
or the rogue stories. It differs from its mediæval
prototype in that the tricks are made secondary. A
conspicuous aim of its unknown author was to put a
young scamp behind the scenes of Spanish society,
and let him report and comment upon what was
taking place there. The story was translated into
all the literary languages of Europe, and was followed by a host of imitations down to Fielding and
Smollett. This rogue literature is one of the broadest
avenues through which that license in speech which
characterized the Renaissance in its first stages
entered the modern novel.

Somewhat akin to the Spanish picaresque novel is
'Don Quixote' (1605, 1616). In both, the point of
view is unromantic. The picaresque novel is an
indirect attack upon the romance of chivalry, a shell
or two from the distance; 'Don Quixote' is a bom-
bardment with the intent to demolish utterly 'the
entire mischievous pile of romantic absurdity.' Cervantes accomplished his purpose by placing the
world of romance in the real world, and letting the
characters and sentiments of each mutually play
upon one another. The knight is treated as a madman
and his squire is tossed in a blanket. Along with this
banter Cervantes carried such a careful reproduction

of the language of the aristocracy and the rabble, and
such impressive work in the delineation of character,
that his romance becomes an epoch in the history of
realism. It also marks the appearance in fiction of
a new quality of humor. Europe, ancient and mediæval, had its great humorists long before Cervantes:
they are Aristophanes, Lucian, and Chaucer. But Cervantes' humor goes deeper than theirs. Like theirs,
it is rippling and sparkling on the surface as a
summer sea; as in Chaucer's, there is beneath a warm
stream of kindly feeling; but still deeper there is
a current of the intensest tragedy.   Under the
irresistible sway of this humor, approaching and
receding from pathos, came Fielding, Goldsmith,
Sterne, and Thackeray, and, in a less degree, Smollett,
Scott, Dickens, and Bulwer; with the result that
they created for the continual delight of their audience characters reminding one of Don Quixote.
Among them are Parson Adams, Uncle Toby,
Jonathan Oldbuck, and Colonel Newcome.

3. *The Elizabethans*

Elizabethan England inherited much that was best
in English mediæval fiction: the Arthurian romances,
the moralized stories of Gower, and the highly finished tales of Chaucer.   From Italy came the pastoral
romance in its most dreamy and attenuated form, the
gorgeous poetic romances of Tasso and Ariosto, and
many collections of *novelle*. Some of these *novelle*
had as subject the interesting events of everyday life;
others were of fierce incident and color, and furnished
Elizabethan tragedy with tremendous scenes.   From

Germany came jest-books and tales of necromancy; from France, the Greek story of adventure with its shipwrecks and pirates; from Spain came 'Amadis,' the 'Diana' of Montemayor, and the picaresque novel. And what the noble printers of the Renaissance gave her, England worked over into fictions of her own.

The most characteristic of her adaptations, the one that most fully expressed her restless spirit of adventure and æsthetic restoration of the age of chivalry, was a romance midway between the knightly quest and the pastoral. Of this species, a conspicuous example is Sir Philip Sidney's 'Arcadia' (1590). This romance has in places as background to its pretty wooing adventures the loveliness of the summer scenery about Wilton House, where it was planned, — violets and roses, meadows and wide-sweeping downs 'garnished with stately trees,' — and into it was infused the noble courtesy, the high sense of honor, and the delicate feeling of the first gentleman of the age. Though touching at points the real in its reflection of English scenes and the princely virtues of Sidney and his friends, the 'Arcadia' is mainly an ideal creation. The country it describes is the land of dream and enchantment, of brave exploit, unblemished chastity, constant love, and undying friendship. Villany and profane passion darken these imaginary realms, but they, too, like the virtues, are all ideal. In structure the 'Arcadia' is epic, having attached to the main narrative numerous episodes, one of which — the story of Argalus and Parthenia, faithful unto death — is among the most lovely situations romance has ever conceived and elaborated.

In direct antithesis to its Arcadias, Elizabethan Eng-

land made hasty studies of robbers and highwaymen;
out of which, under the artistic impulse of 'Lazarillo
de Tormes' (translated into English in 1576), were
developed several rogue stories of considerable pre-
tension, such as 'Jack Wilton,' by Thomas Nash,
and 'Piers Plain,' by Henry Chettle. To the same
class of writings belong Greene's autobiographies,
his 'Repentance,' and 'Groat's Worth of Wit,' in
which the point of view is shifted from the comic
to the tragic. Occasionally the Elizabethan romancers
drew their subjects from the bourgeoisie. An amusing instance of this is 'Thomas of Reading,' by
Thomas Deloney, which contains from the picaresque
point of view a graphic picture of the family life of
the clothiers of the West, and of their mad pranks in
London. Its scene is laid in the time of Henry the
First, and it thus becomes historically interesting as
one of the earliest attempts of the modern story-teller
to invade the province of history.

The most immediately popular Elizabethan fiction, whether romantic or realistic, was John Lyly's
'Euphues' (1579–80). In this romance of high life
there are no enchantments and exciting incidents such
as had furnished the stock in trade of Montalvo and
his followers. Lyly sought to interest by his style:
alliteration, play upon words, antithesis, and a revival
of the pseudo-natural history of mediæval fable books.
His characters are Elizabethan fops and fine ladies,
who sit all night at Lady Flavia's supper-table, discussing in pretty phrases such questions as, why
women love men, whether constancy or secrecy is
most commendable in a mistress, whether love in the
first instance proceeds from the man or from the

woman — a dainty warfare in which are gained no
victories. Lyly moralizes like a Gower on the profane passion; he steps into the pulpit and preaches,
telling mothers to suckle their children, and husbands
to treat their wives mildly, for 'instruments sound
sweetest when they be touched softest;' and for young
men he constructs a moral code in minute detail, such as
Shakespeare parodies in Polonius' advice to Laertes.
Weak, puerile, and affected as he was, Lyly wrote with
the best intentions ; he was a Puritan educated in the
casuistry of Rome.

Lyly was the founder of a school of romancers, who,
from their following the affectations of 'Euphues,' are
known as Euphuists. With them all, language was
first and matter secondary : 'A golden sentence is
worth a world of treasure' was one of their sayings.
Of these Euphuists, Robert Greene and Thomas Lodge
excelled their master in the poetic qualities of their
work; witness 'Menaphon' (1589) by the former, and
'Rosalind' (1590) by the latter. In fact 'Rosalind,' a
pastoral composed in the ornate language of 'Euphues,'
is the flower of Elizabethan romance. It satisfies
some of the usual terms in the modern definition of
the novel. For it is of reasonable length; it possesses a kind of structure, and closes with an elaborate
moral.

4. *The Historical Allegory and the French Influence*

From Elizabeth to the Restoration, romancing and
story-telling gradually became a lost art in England.
An imitation of Sidney's 'Arcadia' now and then
appeared, a sketch of a highwayman, and a few strag-

gling imitations of contemporary French romance. That was about all. There was for a time a steady demand for Elizabethan favorites: 'Euphues,' 'Rosalind,' and especially the 'Groat's Worth of Wit,' and the 'Arcadia.' With the excitement that sounded the note of the on-coming civil war — the trial of Hampden and the uprising of the Scots — the English suddenly stopped reading fiction as well as writing it. The one remarkable romance of the period that may be claimed for England is the 'Argenis' (1621), by John Barclay. Born in France of Scotch father and French mother, Barclay lived in France and in England, and finally migrated to Italy, where he wrote the 'Argenis' in Latin. He is thus a real example of the man without a country. His romance was at once diffused through Europe in five Latin editions, and translations into English, French, Spanish, Italian, and Dutch. It is a medley. It resembles the 'Arcadia' in its shipwrecks, pirates, and disguises. In its weighty parts, which recommended it to the learned, it discusses the problems of statecraft, and is thus affiliated to the 'Utopia.' But what gives it a date in the development of fiction is that it is 'a stately fable in manner of a history.' In it Barclay extends to prose romance the allegorical method of Spenser's 'Faery Queen.' First, he reconstructs the political geography of Europe, moving France south to Sicily, Spain to Sardinia, and England to Mauretania. He then rechristens the chief personages of Europe of his own time: Henry the Third of France becomes Meleander; Catherine de Medici, Selenissa; Philip the Second of Spain, Radirobanes; and Queen Elizabeth, Hyanisbe. Under these disguises, he proceeds to relate the history of Europe during the last half of the sixteenth century; describing particularly Henry's troubles with the Guises and the Huguenots, and Philip's attempted invasion of England and the defeat of the Armada. The characters are drawn in rough outline: Philip, proud and arrogant and intriguing with the Guises; Elizabeth, calm and dignified, and almost timid lest she offend her subjects. The romance closes with the marriage of Poliarchus (Henry of Navarre) to Argenis, a daughter of Henry the Third. No attempt is made at exact chronology or accuracy of historical detail. Catherine de Medici is a nurse to Argenis; and Elizabeth is represented as having a husband who died just after she ascended the throne, and a sister Anne who was privately married to Henry the Third. As if to perplex further the imagination of the reader, not only are the scenes of the romance placed in classic countries, but to some extent the story is related in the terms of Roman life and custom. Poliarchus and Argenis are married in a temple dedicated to Juno and Lucina; high priests perform the marriage ceremony, and the bridal party sing hymns to Hymen and pæans to Apollo. This is what the romanticists of later date were to call ' local color.'

Barclay opened the way for a long line of French romances, which, beginning about 1625, extended through the following fifty years. The most popular of these romances were written by Gomberville, La Calprenède, Madeleine de Scudéri, and Madame de la Fayette. And the most famous in its time was Scudéri's ' Grand Cyrus,' which when completed extended over 6679 pages in ten octavo volumes.

Translated into English in ponderous folios and incorporated into Restoration tragedy, these romances left their marks on English fiction down to the publication of 'Sir Charles Grandison.' Gomberville was wild and extravagant. His 'Polexàndre' (1629–37) is a working over of the knightly prowess and the enchantments of 'Amadis de Gaula,' with a slight historical background. La Calprenède emphasized history, which, however, he romanced excessively. His subjects were Cleopatra, Darius, Cyrus, and Pharamond, the legendary founder of the French monarchy. Scudéri's subjects were Solyman the Magnificent, Cyrus, legendary Roman history, and the broils in Granada between the Zegris and the Abencerrages. In dealing with this material, Scudéri forced history to do double duty. The career of Cyrus the Great she brought into harmony with the military exploits of the great Condé; and her heroines bearing Persian or Roman names were adjusted to portraits of her friends. The purpose of Scudéri and her contemporaries was to decorate history with fiction for readers who found history in and of itself dry and uninteresting. However displeasing the means by which they did this may be, the fact remains that they are the founders of historical romance.

Beneath the history is a formal psychology. To the French romancers descended, to be handed over to Richardson, that art of love which underlies mediæval fiction. Again appeared those precepts whereby the lover renounced his individuality and became the slave of his mistress, no longer the lady of the castle but a shepherdess of dishevelled hair and ivory bow. Refinement followed refinement, until Scudéri outdid all her predecessors. For her 'Clélie' she drew a curious allegorical map, known as the *carte de Tendre*, on which is shown the water ways (sighs and tears) by which the traveller, setting out from the town of New Friendship, may reach — if he shun the dead lake of indifference and the wild and angry sea of enmity — one of the cities of Love. To turn the extravagances of Scudéri to finer issues, there were needed a sense for style and proportion and a knowledge of one's self. These essentials were possessed by Madame de la Fayette, who discovered, to translate a phrase from Sainte-Beuve, the border land of romance and reality. With the covering of a brief history, she concealed, without any effort at the hysterical climax, the story of her own heart, which had felt strongly but always sanely. 'La Princesse de Clèves' (1678), true and delicate in its psychology, is one of the classics of European fiction.

Nothing could be easier than to ridicule the French romancers. The realists, as realism was understood in those days, saw their opportunity. Charles Sorel wrote a new 'Don Quixote,' entitled 'Le Berger Extravagant' (1628), in which he burlesqued the pastoral and the ideal treatment of love. What Molière did with Scudéri's love-making in 'Les Précieuses Ridicules' is familiar to all. Boileau sounded the death knell of the old romances, when, in a Lucian dialogue, he marched, in long line, their heroes down to Hades, and consigned them to Pluto to be flogged and cast into Lethe ('Les Héros de Roman,' 1664). But with ridicule there was usually combined, much as in the Spanish picaresque story, scandalous intrigues in low or bourgeois life. Of stories of this kind, the

most worthy of notice are 'Francion' (1622), by
Charles Sorel, 'Le Roman Comique' (1651–57), by
Paul Scarron, and 'Le Roman Bourgeois' (1666),
by Antoine Furetière. These stories were all translated, sometimes curiously mutilated, into English.
Scarron's facetious manner of beginning and ending
his chapters, Fielding has made us familiar with in
'Joseph Andrews' and 'Tom Jones.' The 'Roman
Bourgeois' is the most graphic account of the ways
and doings of the bourgeoisie that had appeared in
fiction. There are scenes in it that might have been
written by Zola. It seems to have given rise to
those numberless sketches, written by Tom Brown
and others, that were soon appearing in London, of
adventures and scenes at Bartholomew Fair, on the
streets, and in the playhouses.

5. *The Restoration*

After the battle of Worcester, the English began
once more to read fiction. Lyly, Greene, and Sidney
all survived the literary wreckage of the civil wars.
From now on the French romances were translated as
fast as they were published in France. And for reading
them and discussing love, friendship, and statecraft,
little coteries were formed, the members of which addressed one another as 'the matchless Orinda,' 'the
adored Valeria,' and 'the noble Antenor.' Best known
in their own time were the groups of platonic lovers,
professing an immaculate chastity, who hovered about
Katherine Philips and Margaret Duchess of Newcastle.
The literary efforts of these romantic ladies and gentlemen were directed to poetry and letter-writing rather

than to fiction. There proceeded from them only one romance, 'Parthenissa' (1664, 1665, 1677), by Roger Boyle, an admirer of Katherine Philips. The most noticeable thing about this inexpressibly dull imitation of Scudéri, is its mixing up in much confusion several great Roman wars. For this, particularly for bringing on the scene together Hannibal and Spartacus, Boyle defended himself in his preface by an appeal to Vergil, who neglected two centuries in his story of Æneas and Dido. For making the same character stand now for one person and now for another in his historical allegory, he gracefully apologized, but he might have cited Barclay as his precedent. Other similar romances were : 'Bentivolio and Urania' (1660), by Nathaniel Ingelo; 'Aretina' (1661), by George Mackenzie; and 'Pandion and Amphigenia' (1665), by John Crowne. The first is a religious fiction ; the second, made up of adventures, moral essays, and disquisitions on English and Scotch politics, was an attempt to revive the conceits of Lyly; the third is an appropriation of Sidney's 'Arcadia.' Like Crowne, the Restoration romancers were generally satisfied to remodel and dress up old material. And what is true of them, is also true of the realists. An odd and wretchedly written production of this period is 'The English Rogue' (1665-71), by Richard Head, and in part by Francis Kirkman. For tricks and intrigues they pillaged Spanish and French rogue stories, Elizabethan sketches of vagabonds, and German and English jest-books; and seasoned their medley with what probably then passed for humor. On the other hand, they wrote much from observation. In their graphic pictures of the haunts of apprentices,

pickpockets, and highwaymen, they discovered the
London slums. Furthermore, unlike their brother
picaresque writers, they sent their hero on a voyage
to the East, and thus began the transformation of the
rogue story into the story of adventure as it was soon
to appear in Defoe.

More original work than this was done by Mrs.
Aphra Behn, who wrote besides many comedies several
short tales, the most noteworthy of which is 'Oroonoko'
(1696). In this story, which is a realistic account of a
royal slave kidnapped in Africa and barbarously put
to death at Surinam, she contrasts the state of nature
with that of civilization, severely reprimanding the
latter. 'Oroonoko' is the first humanitarian novel
in English. Though its spirit cannot for a moment
be compared, in moral earnestness, with 'Uncle Tom's
Cabin,' yet its purpose was to awaken Christendom
to the horrors of slavery. The time being not yet ripe
for it, the romance was for the public merely an
interesting story to be dramatized. The novels of Mrs.
Behn that bore fruit were her short tales of intrigue —
versions in part of her own tender experiences. One
of her successors was Mrs. Mary Manley, who wrote
'The Secret History of Queen Zarah and the Zarazians' (1705), 'The New Atlantis' (1709), and 'The
Power of Love, in Seven Novels' (1720). Mrs. Manley was in turn followed by Mrs. Eliza Haywood, the
author of 'Memoirs of a Certain Island Adjacent to
Utopia' (1725), and 'The Secret Intrigues of the Count
of Caramania' (1727). These productions taken together purport to relate the inside history of the court
from the restoration of Charles the Second to the death
of George the First. To their contemporaries, they

were piquantly immoral; to later times, they are not so amusing. Nevertheless, in the development of the novel, they have a place. They represent a conscious effort to attain to the real, in reaction from French romance. They are specimens, too, of precisely what was meant in England by the novel in distinction from the romance, just before Richardson: a short story of from one hundred to two hundred pages, assumed to be founded on fact, and published in a duodecimo volume.

To John Bunyan the English novel owes a very great debt. What fiction needed, if it was ever to come near a portrayal of real life, was first of all to rid itself of the extravagances of the romancer and the cynicism of the picaresque story-teller. Though Bunyan was despised by his contemporary men of letters, it surely could be but a little time before the precision of his imagination and the force and charm of his simple and idiomatic English would be felt and then imitated. As no writer preceding him, Bunyan knew the artistic effect of minute detail in giving reasonableness to an impossible story. In the 'Pilgrim's Progress' (1678-84) he so mingled with those imaginative scenes of his own the familiar Scripture imagery and the still more familiar incidents of English village life, that the illusion of reality must have been to the readers for whom he wrote well-nigh perfect. The allegories of Barclay and Scudéri could not be understood without keys; Bunyan's 'Palace Beautiful' needed none.

6. *Literary Forms that contributed to the Novel*

Outside the sphere proper of fiction, there was slowly collecting in the seventeenth century material for the future novelist. It was quite the fashion for public and literary men — witness Pepys and Evelyn — to keep diaries and journals of family occurrences and of interesting social and political events. These diaries and journals suggested the novel of family life, and indicated a form of narrative that would lend to fiction the appearance of fact. In 'Robinson Crusoe' and 'Pamela' and hundreds of other novels down to the present, the journal has played a not inconsiderable part. At this time, too, men were becoming sufficiently interested in their friends and some of the great men of the past to write their biographies. In 1640 Izaak Walton published the first of his charming 'Lives.' A quick offshoot of the biography was the autobiography, which, as a man in giving a sympathetic account of himself is likely to run into poetry, came very close to being a novel. Margaret Duchess of Newcastle's 'Autobiography,' published in 1656 in a volume of tales, is a famous account of a family in which 'all the brothers were brave, and all the sisters virtuous.' Bunyan's 'Grace Abounding' is a story of the fierce struggles between the spirit and the flesh, and of the final triumph of the spirit. This autobiographic method of dealing with events, partly or wholly fictitious, has been a favorite with all our novelists, except with the very greatest; and it is employed more to-day than ever before.

It also occurred to several writers after the Restoration that London life might be depicted by a series of imaginary letters to a friend. A most amusing bundle ot two hundred and eleven such letters was published in 1664 by Margaret Duchess of Newcastle. Her object was to transfer to letters, scenes and incidents that had hitherto been the material of the comedy of humor. In 1678 a new direction to this letter-writing was given by a translation from the French of the 'Portuguese Letters.' These letters of a Portuguese nun to a French cavalier revealed to our writers how a correspondence might be managed for unfolding a simple story, and for studying the heart of a betrayed and deserted woman. Edition after edition of the 'Portuguese Letters' followed, and fictitious replies and counter-replies. In the wake of these continuations, were translated into English the letters of Eloisa and Abelard, containing a similar but more pathetic tale of man's selfishness and woman's devotion. They, too, went through many editions and were imitated, mutilated, and trivialized. As a result of this fashion for letter-writing, there existed early in the eighteenth century a considerable body of short stories in letter form. Hardly any of them are readable; but one of them is of considerable historical interest, 'The Letters of Lindamira, a Lady of Quality, written to her Friend in the Country' (second edition, 1713). The author, who may have been Tom Brown 'of facetious memory,' states that, unlike his predecessors, his aim is 'to expose vice, disappoint vanity, to reward virtue, and crown constancy with success.' He accomplishes this 'by carrying Lindamira through a sea of misfortunes, and at last marrying her up to her wishes.' It was in this weak school of fiction,

aiming at something it hardly knew what, that Richardson must in some degree have learned how to man-
age a correspondence.

Moreover, the character-sketch, which was the most
prolific literary form in England and France during the
seventeenth century, has a direct bearing on the novel.
As conceived by Ben Jonson and Thomas Overbury,
who had before them a contemporary translation of
Theophrastus, it was the sketch of some person, real
or imaginary, who embodied a virtue or a vice, or some
idiosyncrasy obnoxious to ridicule.   One character
was set over against another; and the sentences
descriptive of each were placed in the antithesis
which the style of Lyly had made fashionable.   Surely
from this species of literature, the novelist took a les-
son in the fine art of contrast.   The type of sketch
set by Jonson and Overbury was a good deal modified
by the fifty and more character-writers who succeeded
them.   Not infrequently as a frame to the portrait was
added a little piece of biography or adventure; and
there are a few examples of massing sketches in a
loose fiction, as in the continuations of 'The English
Rogue,' and in the second part of the 'Roman Bourgeois.'   The treatment of the character-sketch by
Steele and Addison in the 'Spectator' (1711–12)
was highly original.   They drew portraits of representative Englishmen, and brought them together in
conversation in a London club.   They conducted Sir
Roger de Coverley through Westminster Abbey, to the
playhouse, to Vauxhall, into the country to Coverley
church and the assizes; they incidentally took a retro-
spective view of his life, and finally told the story of
his death.   When they had done this, they had not

only created one of the best defined characters in our prose literature, but they had almost transformed the character-sketch into a novel of London and provincial life. From the 'Spectator' the character-sketch, with its types and minute observation and urbane ridicule, passed into the novel, and became a part of it.

7. *The Passing of the Old Romance*

At the dawn of the Renaissance, verse was usually an embellishment of fiction, and the perfect workman was Chaucer, whose 'Troilus and Cressida' and 'Canterbury Tales' are differentiated from the modern novel mainly by the accident of rhyme. Of the later romances in prose, the two that have gained among all classes a world-wide fame are 'Don Quixote' and the 'Pilgrim's Progress'; and second to them is the 'Princess of Clèves.' Nearly everything else that has been mentioned is to the modern as if it had never been written. That such a fate should have overcome the old romances must be lamented by every one acquainted with their lovely imagery and inspiring ideals of conduct. But it was inevitable, for they almost invariably failed in their art. The great novelists since Fielding have taught the public that a novel must have a beginning and an end. A reader of contemporary fiction, after turning a few pages of Sidney's 'Arcadia,' becomes aware that he is not at the beginning of the story at all, but is having described to him an event midway in the plot. From this point on, the narrative, instead of moving forward untrammelled, except for the pause of an easy retrospect, becomes more and more perplexed by episodes, which are introduced, suspended, resumed, and twisted within one another, according to a plan not easily understood. The picaresque writers, the first of them, adopted the straightforward manner of autobiography; but under the influence of romance, they, too, soon began to indulge in episodes. If at their best the picaresque stories had a beginning, they had no end. They were published in parts; each part was brought to a close with the recurring paragraph that a continuation will be written if the reader desires; and so adventure follows adventure, to be terminated only by the death of the author. It is thus obvious that the romancers and story-tellers had no clearly defined conception of what a novel should be as an independent literary species. They took as their model the epic, not the well-ordered epic of Homer or Vergil, but the prose epic as perverted by the rhetoricians in the decadent period of Greek art.[1]

Moreover, it has come to be demanded not only that a novel must possess an orderly structure, but that it shall be a careful study of some phase of real life, or of conduct in a situation which, however impossible in itself, the imagination is willing to accept for the time being as possible. Accordingly, those who wish to shun the word 'romance' are accustomed to speak of the novel of character and the novel of incident. In the novel of character the interest is directed to the portrayal of men and women, and the fable is a subordinate consideration; in the novel of incident the interest is directed to what happens, and the characters come more by the way. To the former class no one

[1] See the Greek romance, 'Theagenes and Chariclea,' translated, T. Underdown, 1577.

would hesitate to assign 'The Mill on the Floss.' To
the same class might very properly be assigned 'The
House of the Seven Gables,' which, though Hawthorne
called it a romance, is, as he intended it, 'true to the
human heart.' To the latter class belong the Waverley
novels, and to mention an extreme example, 'The
Prisoner of Zenda.' Before Defoe, writers of fiction
did in some degree fulfil the conditions necessary to
a novel in the modern view; but to concoct fantastic
adventures in high or low life, in accord neither with
the truth of fact, nor with the laws of a sane imagination, nor with the permanent motives that sway our
acts — that was the main business of the romancer
and the story-teller. From them to Defoe and Richardson the transition is analogous to that from the
first Elizabethan plays to Shakespeare and his contemporaries; it is the passing from a struggling and
misdirected literary form to a well-defined species.
Nevertheless, a study of European fiction before
Defoe has intellectual, if not æsthetic, compensa-
tions, and to the student it is imperative. It gives
one a large historical perspective. From Arthurian
romance and the *fabliau* downward, in the eternal
swing between idealism and realism, there is a continuous growth — an accumulation of incidents, situations, characters, and experiments in structure, much
of which was a legacy to the eighteenth century.

8. *Daniel Defoe*

'Robinson Crusoe' (1719) is the earliest English
novel of incident. It was at once recognized in
England and throughout literary Europe as some-

thing different from the picaresque story to which it is akin. In what does this difference consist? The situations and jests of Head and Chettle were in some cases as old as Latin comedy; 'Robinson Crusoe' was an elaboration of a contemporary incident[1] that made a fascinating appeal to the imagination. The writer of the rogue story did not expect to be believed. The aim of Defoe was to invest his narrative with a sense of reality; to this end he made use of every device at his command to deceive the reader. He took as a model for his narrative the form that best produces the illusion of truth — that of current memoirs with the accompaniment of a diary. He adroitly remarks in his preface that he is only the editor of a private man's adventures, and adds confidentially that he believes 'the thing to be a just history of fact,' at least, that 'there is no appearance of fiction in it.' He begins his story very modestly by briefly sketching the boyhood of a rogue who runs away to sea — one of thousands — and thus gradually prepares the reader for those experiences which are to culminate in the shipwreck on the Island of Despair. When he gets his Crusoe there, he does not send him on a quest for exciting adventures, but surprises us by a matter-of-fact account of Crusoe's expedients for feeding and clothing himself and making himself comfortable. He brings the story home to the Englishmen of the middle-class, for whom he principally writes, by telling them that their condition in life is most conducive to happiness,

---

[1] See Steele's account of Alexander Selkirk in the 'Englishman,' No. 26.

and by giving expression to their peculiar tenets: their trust in dreams, their recognition of Providence in the fortuitous concurrence of events, and their dogmas of conviction of sin, of repentance, and of conversion. And finally, 'Robinson Crusoe' has its message. Undoubtedly its message is too apparent for the highest art, but it is a worthy one: Be patient, be industrious, be honest, and you will at last be rewarded for your labor. 'Robinson Crusoe' must have seemed to the thousands of hard-laboring Englishmen a symbol of their own lives, their struggles, their failures, and their final rest in a faith that there will sometime be a settling of things justly in the presence of Him 'who will allow no shuffling.' To put it briefly, Defoe humanized adventure.

'Robinson Crusoe' was the most immediately popular fiction that had yet been written. At once it became a part of the world's literature, and it remains such to this day. Defoe took advantage of its vogue to write many other adventures on land and sea. Captain Singleton's tour across Africa is as good reading as Stanley; and to the uninitiated, it seems quite as true to fact. In 'Moll Flanders' is gathered together a mass of material concerning the dregs of London — thieves and courtesans — that remains unequalled even among the modern naturalists. The 'Memoirs of a Cavalier,' once regarded as an actual autobiography, so realistic is the treatment, is the relation of the adventures of a cavalier in the army of Gustavus Adolphus, and later at Marston Moor and Naseby. It is a masterly piece of historical semblance, and it is thus significant. The 'Journal of the Plague Year' is so documentary in appearance that public libraries still class it as a history, though it is fictitious throughout. This verisimilitude which was attained through detail and the unadorned language of everyday life is Defoe's great distinction. Bunyan was in a measure his forerunner, and his immediate successor was Swift, who, under the guise of his delightful voyages among the Lilliputians and Brobdingnagians (1726), ridiculed in savage irony his king, 'his own dear country,' and 'the animal called man.' These three writers who usher in a new era for the novel are the source to which romance has returned again and again for instruction, from Scott to Stevenson.

CHAPTER II

THE EIGHTEENTH-CENTURY REALISTS

1. *Samuel Richardson*

IN 1740 Samuel Richardson, then a well-to-do London printer, fifty years old, published anonymously the first part of 'Pamela; or, Virtue Rewarded.' It is a story of a waiting-maid, who, by her prudent conduct, gains a wild young gentleman for a husband, and reforms him. Richardson was hardly satisfied with his hurriedly written 'Pamela.' It was structurally weak; and its morality was questionable. He now read Addison, and thus indirectly Aristotle, on the principles of dramatic art, and produced the 'History of Clarissa Harlowe' (1747–48). Clarissa, when in imminent danger of being forced by her father and brother to marry a man whom she hates, places herself under the protection of Mr. Robert Lovelace, by whom she is hurried away from Harlowe Place, taken to London, and lodged in the house of a Mrs. Sinclair. She flees from her seducer, is found, brought back, and drugged. Again fleeing, she is maliciously arrested for debt, and imprisoned. At length she dies broken-hearted in a respectable London lodging. Lovelace expiates his crime on the field of honor. This second novel of Richardson's, which is one of the masterpieces of English fiction, was not wholly satisfactory to his friends. Lovelace had been made too attractive, and women

fell in love with him.   It was not quite clear why he
should not have been reclaimed, as was the libertine
Mr. B—— in 'Pamela.'   Richardson saw no way out of
these criticisms, although he believed them to be unjust, except by writing another novel in which he should
embody his ideal of a perfect gentleman.   In special
preparation for this undertaking, he probably read the
'Cyropædia' of Xenophon.   'Sir Charles Grandison'
was published in 1753.   Harriet Byron — an orphan
of rank, very tender and sensitive — is living with her
uncle and aunt in Northamptonshire.   Her provincial
lovers are of course numerous; and of course she
politely but firmly rejects them all.   She is taken to
London by her cousins, Mr. and Mrs. Reeves, on a two
months' visit.   From a masquerade in the Haymarket,
she is carried off by Sir Hargrave Pollexfen.   On
Hounslow heath, Sir Hargrave's chariot and six runs
counter to the chariot and six of Sir Charles Grandison; and Miss Byron throws herself into the arms of
her deliverer.   There are obstacles in the way to the
immediate union of Sir Charles and Miss Byron.   For
should the marriage take place at once, it is certain
half a score of women would break their hearts; and
a very perplexing problem is, what shall be done with
Clementina, a beautiful and passionate Italian to
whom Sir Charles is provisionally engaged.   But the
gentle 'condescending reasonings' of the perfect hero
persuade Clementina to marry some one else and not
ruin the happiness of Miss Byron.

These three novels are mostly in letter form and
of ample extent.   As originally published, 'Pamela'
filled four duodecimo volumes; ' Clarissa,' seven; and
' Grandison,' seven. ` In the first of them — which a

contemporary French translator spoke of as a *petit ouvrage*[1] — there are, according to the author's own lists, forty-two characters; in the second, thirty-eight; and in the third, counting the Italians,[2] whom Richardson by an exquisite blunder placed outside the human pale, there are fifty. Richardson felt, as others[3] have since his time, that his novels were too long, and he often apologized to his audience, telling them how much he had pruned away, and reminding them that the charm of the letter consists in the full utterance of the heart while it is 'agitated by hopes and fears.' By thus letting his characters speak without restraint, he brought the reader into their immediate presence as friend and associate in their daily life His contemporaries talked and wrote about Pamela, Clarissa, and Lovelace, as if they existed in flesh and blood as really as Samuel Richardson himself. Literary pilgrims crossed the Channel, not only to pay their respects to the humble printer at North End and Parson's Green, but also to search out Harlowe Place and the Grandison mansion. The first great imaginative success of the novelist was Defoe's, who made fictitious adventure seem real; the second was Richardson's, who made equally real his men and women, and the scenes in which he placed them. The one thereby discovered the art of the novel of incident; the other, the art of the novel of character.

[1] Preface to French translation of 'Pamela,' by Prévost, 1741.

[2] Richardson divided his characters into three classes: men, women, and Italians.

[3] On the other hand, Tennyson is reported to have said of 'Clarissa Harlowe': 'I like those great *still* books,' and 'I wish there were a great novel in hundreds of volumes that I might go on and on.' — *Alfred Lord Tennyson*, by his son, vol. ii. 372.

The content of Richardson's novels is quite different from that of high romance. They contain no gorgeous descriptions of palaces, no adventures on sea or land, no swimming of broad and angry streams, no earthquakes, no enchanted castles. Their most sensational incident is an abduction. Richardson thus brushed aside the paraphernalia of romance. His plot is always slight, serving merely as a framework for a minute study of the heart. For this work he had forty years of preparation. When a boy he wrote love letters for the country girls in an obscure village somewhere in Derbyshire. When as a successful man of business he took up his residence at North End, Hammersmith, he received into his house for protracted visits of weeks and months, highly moral but rather sentimental young women, whom he called his 'adopted children,' and who in turn addressed him as 'dear papa.' When they go home or are visiting their friends, he sends long letters to them, and they respond in equally wire-drawn replies, scolding him and threatening him with pretty curses because he will not save Lovelace or marry Sir Charles Grandison to Clementina. These self-conscious young women, to whom he acts as a kind of father confessor, he subjects to close scrutiny. He watches their every act and guesses at its motive. Every movement of theirs, every attitude, every trembling of the hand or scraping of the foot, every accent of a word spoken in languor or in fretfulness, every flush of the cheek, every rising tear, every faint gurgling in the throat, has a meaning to him; and in heightened form he registers and interprets what he observes, in imaginary letters. In fiction, movements in thought and feeling — mere flutterings of the heart — have taken the place of adventure. A contemporary poetaster compressed the obvious incidents of 'Grandison' into a poem of a hundred lines. Thus, as is at once evident, the novel of character which Richardson wrote is psychological; it is a revealing of states of feeling in acts.

As a psychologist, Richardson is loosely bound by several threads with romance. Scudéri had her formal analysis of passion, which she received from mediæval metaphysic through the romances of chivalry, and which she in turn handed over to her successors. What Richardson did was to give this old love casuistry a real basis in real life. In this he was in part anticipated by the French novelist and dramatist, Pierre Carlet de Marivaux, whose 'Marianne' (1731–41) is in plot and purpose much like 'Pamela.' For both have a virtuous young woman in distress as the central character, and both are an evolution of the belle âme, an unfolding and triumph of the stainless spirit. There are of course many points of difference between the two novels. Marivaux makes a much larger use than Richardson of the current incidents of contemporary comedy; and love, as he conceived it, is more like the gallantry of the earlier romancers. Though there is very little evidence for the common assertion that Richardson modelled his first novel on 'Marianne,' Marivaux is nevertheless logically the link between him and Scudéri.

There is also in Richardson a lingering on of one form of allegory — the concrete representation of the virtues and the vices. Pamela in the first part of the story is Chastity, and afterward she degenerates into Prudence. Her struggles against the assaults of a debauchee are a survival of purity in the meshes of lust; such, for example, as the disagreeable episode of Una and Sansloy, in 'The Faery Queen.' Sir Charles Grandison is an embodiment of what Spenser meant by Magnificence — a virtue which is the perfection of all the rest and contains them all. He is compassionate, humane, benevolent, kind to his family and friends, truth-loving, steady in his principles, modest, courageous, unreserved, prudent, expeditious in business, manly, nobly sincere, amiable, artless, and handsome. Of him, Miss Byron writes to Lady G——: 'Do you think, my dear, that had he been the first man, he would have been so complaisant to his Eve as *Milton makes Adam ?* . . . No; it is my opinion that your brother would have had gallantry enough to his fallen spouse to have made him extremely regret her lapse; but that he would have done *his own duty* were it but for the sake of posterity, and left it to the Almighty, if such had been his pleasure, to have annihilated his first Eve, and given him a second.'

To the drama, the indebtedness of Richardson is also considerable; somewhat in the way of character, much more in the way of plot and structure. After the famous attack of Jeremy Collier on the immorality of the English stage (1698), playwrights very generally gave a new turn to comedy. The libertine, who in Restoration comedy had quitted the stage in a blaze of glory, was now reclaimed in the fifth act, and his penitence was rewarded by the possession of the fair Victoria. This is the dénouement of 'Pamela.' Comedy underwent further modifications, until it was turned into melodrama; the repentance of the villain in the fifth act was no longer accepted — he was hanged. This is the dénouement — only less violent — of 'Clarissa Harlowe.' In other words, 'Pamela' is bourgeois comedy; 'Clarissa Harlowe' is bourgeois tragedy. Bevil, of Steele's 'Conscious Lovers,' in his Christian feeling against duels and his success in disarming his adversary by his magnanimous conduct, is a rudimentary Sir Charles Grandison. Indiana, in the same comedy, is a slight sketch of a Clementina. Richardson seems also to have derived from the drama a time limit. His ideal is that the occurrences of any one day shall be related on that day. Moreover, although 'Clarissa Harlowe' consists of seven volumes, he is careful to compress the narrative of all the events within the term of one year. This is without doubt a conscious extension of the dramatist's one day to a fixed period more suitable to the novel. Richardson often arranges and conducts his dialogue precisely as if he were writing a play for the closet. 'Clarissa Harlowe' is largely made up of dramatic dialogue within the letters. Indeed, when speaking critically of this novel, Richardson calls it a Dramatic Narrative. One should, however, be on his guard against overestimating this indebtedness. Richardson wrote with little plan; letter grew out of letter naturally; the drama in many ways gave mere direction to his narrative. To his genius alone he owed it that out of the wrecks of a decaying literary form he could construct a 'Clarissa Harlowe,' in which event after event moves forward to the catastrophe with the inevitableness of an 'Œdipus' or of a 'Hamlet.'

Richardson declared over and over again, in his novels, his prefaces, and his postscripts, that the underlying motive of all his work was moral and religious instruction.   In an age (to paraphrase Richardson's own words) when scepticism and infidelity were openly avowed and propagated from the press, when public and domestic morality was blotted from the catalogue of Christian virtues, and even the clergy had become a body of interested men, he thought it his duty to teach the Christian tenets as he understood them.   His sinners who put off repentance to the last moment, die 'in dreadful agonies.'   Pamela is protected and rewarded by that Providence which guards innocence.   The rake who becomes her husband is reformed by the daily sight of the Christian virtues. Clarissa escaping the pollution of her earthly environment becomes as one 'ensky'd and sainted'; and the novel of which she is the heroine is intended as a drama of spiritual triumph, to be contrasted with the fatalism of heathendom.

It was customary in Richardson's time to read his novels aloud in the family circle.   When some pathetic passage was reached, the members of the family would retire to separate apartments to weep; and after composing themselves, they would return to the fireside to hear the reading proceed.   It was reported to Richardson that, on one of these occasions, 'an amiable little boy' sobbed as if his little sides would burst, and resolved to mind his books that he might be able to read 'Pamela' through without stopping. That there might be something in the family novel expressly for the children, Richardson sometimes stepped aside from his main narrative to tell them a moral tale.   Here are two companion pieces, clipped of their decorations.   There were once two little boys and two little girls, who never told fibs, who were never rude, noisy, mischievous, nor quarrelsome; who always said their prayers before going to bed and as soon as they arose. They grew up. The masters became fine gentlemen; and the misses became fine ladies and housewives. There were once three naughty boys who had a naughty sister. They were always quarrelling and scratching, and would not say their prayers. They, too, grew up. One of the boys was drowned at sea, the second turned thief, and the third was forced to beg his bread in a far country. And the naughty girl fell from a tree and broke her arm, and died of fever.

Not only did Richardson aim to teach men and women, boys and girls, that righteousness will be rewarded and sin punished either here or hereafter (with an emphasis everywhere except in the character of Clarissa Harlowe on the here rather than on the hereafter), but he sought to arouse discussion on special cases of conduct. In this he was making a new and skilful use of the disquisitions of the moral romancers, of which Lyly was the Elizabethan type. The questions his characters are made to propose to themselves and answer are such as these: Is first love first folly? What is the distinction between love and liking? Can a man be in love with two women at the same time? At what age ought one to marry? How should a young woman conduct herself when asked in marriage? How should a perfect gentleman behave when she has accepted him? Should he kiss her hand once or twice? Is fear on the part of a woman necessary to true love? Should mothers suckle their children? How far should a wife's worship of her husband interfere with the worship of

God ? How often, to be in good form, should we
attend church ? Should we go to masquerades ? How
early in life ought we to make our wills ? When is a
duel justifiable ? Should we dock the tails of our
horses ? etc. Questions of this kind in the form of
'beautiful and edifying' maxims, collected from his
novels and alphabetically arranged, Richardson published in a duodecimo volume of four hundred pages—
'the pith and marrow' of his teaching. Trivial and
overformal and undignified as the moral code of Richardson may now appear, it excited popular interest
throughout Europe; and that its influence was in
general for good, we have the authority of many,
among whom are Dr. Johnson and Goethe. His friends
and admirers poured letters in upon him, concurring
and disagreeing with him. They called him a 'divine
man,' and felt that he was teaching his generation
'how to live and how to die' more effectively and
more eloquently than Wesley and Whitefield.

Among English writers, only Dickens has received
from his contemporaries the praise Richardson received from his. In his grotto at North End, friends
came to hear him read from his novels as they were
making, or to kiss his inkhorn. A Mr. Edwards,
author of 'Canons of Criticism,' wrote to Richardson,
'I have read, and as long as I have eyes will read, all
your three most excellent pieces at least once a year.'
Two years later the critic died. Young, author of
'Night Thoughts,' wrote, 'As I look upon you as
an instrument of Providence, I likewise look upon
you as a sure heir of a double immortality; when our
language fails, one, indeed, may cease; but the failure
of the Heavens and the Earth will put no period to the

other.' This popularity was not confined to England. Diderot may be regarded as handing down the decision of Prévost, d'Alembert, Rousseau, and literary France, when he placed Richardson's novels on the shelf with Moses, Homer, Euripides, and Sophocles. From Germany, Mrs. Klopstock, wife of the author of the 'Messiah,' sent a letter in this strain after the publication of 'Grandison': 'Having finished your "Clarissa" (oh! the heavenly book!), I would have pray'd you to write the history of a *manly* Clarissa, but I had not courage enough at that time. . . . You have since written the manly Clarissa without my prayer; oh, you have done it, to the great joy and thanks of all your happy readers! Now you can write no more, you must write the history of an Angel.' When his friends ventured to criticise him, this sentence from the Dutch translator of 'Clarissa' indicates the tone: 'I read [your works] with a searching eye, yet not finding any blemishes, but meeting one or two little bright clouds, which, more accurately viewed perhaps, are a collection of shining stars.' This extravagant praise was not insincere, nor was it misplaced. Only the intellect had been addressed by Dryden, Pope, and Swift. Richardson discovered anew the heart. The rise of the humble printer had been sudden and unexpected. Unlearned, he discovered what for a quarter of a century Europe had been looking for, not knowing precisely what it wanted, a form of literature that should adequately present its life as it was, united with an ideal of life as it ought to be.

Richardson added to fiction four full-length portraits: the libertine of hard intellectual polish, the

immaculate gentleman, the chaste woman, and the
Protestant martyr. To him, above all others, the world
is indebted for the novel of letters. He founded a
school which did not become extinct in England till
the publication of 'Jane Eyre.' His influence was at
once felt on the literature of the Continent; his novels
as a whole or in part were translated into French,
Italian, German, and Dutch ; and 'Pamela' was dramatized by Voltaire and by Goldoni. His imitators in
France and Germany may be counted by scores, and the
tremendous latent force which lay hidden in his emotionalism, when cut loose from moral and religious
restraint, was made manifest in Rousseau.

2. *Henry Fielding*

We are not likely to overestimate the historical
position of Richardson; we are more likely to under-
estimate it. Moreover, in the logical sequence of
minor incident, 'Clarissa Harlowe' has been excelled
only by the maturest work of George Eliot. And yet
the weaknesses and shortcomings of Richardson are
apparent, and were apparent in his own time. His
ethical system was based upon no wide observation or
sound philosophy; it was the code of a Protestant
casuist. He was a sentimentalist, creating pathetic
scenes for their own sake and degrading tears and
hysterics into a manner. His language was not free
from the affectations of the romancers; even his
friends dared tell him with caution and circumlocution that he was fond of the nursery phrase. He was
unacquainted, as he said himself, with the high life
he pretended to describe. Never was there a better

opportunity for the ridicule of a Cervantes. And
England had a Cervantes fully equipped. Though he
could not hope to carry with him the great body of
Puritan England, he was sure of finding readers and
applauders among the educated and among those in
whom lived on the spirit of the Cavaliers. When
Richardson published 'Pamela,' Henry Fielding was
in the strong prime of manhood. He had been educated at Eton and had studied law at Leyden. He
was gaining a familiarity with the Greek and Latin
poets, historians, and critics that is very disheartening
to the modern student. He had absorbed the spirit of
the great European humorists 'who laughed satire
into the world,'—Aristophanes, Lucian, Cervantes,
Rabelais, Shakespeare, Molière, Swift, and Lesage.
In the long line, only Chaucer is missing. His comedies
are evidence that he had observed life closely, in
Somersetshire and more especially in the town, in the
region of the Haymarket and Covent Garden. His
experience, probably owing to his own improvidence,
had been hard; and to him the talk about the reward
of the innocent in this life must have appeared amusing. As a playwright he had attacked the rant and
the sentimentalism of the contemporary drama, and
had extended his satire, with the direct thrust of
an Aristophanes, against the political methods and
wholesale bribery of Walpole and his agents. To
ridicule Richardson was simply to turn in another
direction shafts that he had already learned to handle.

'Joseph Andrews' was published in 1742. Fielding began the novel with the intention of writing a
parody on 'Pamela.' The ridicule, boisterous and
recklessly outspoken, made Richardson wince. His

turning Richardson's Lord B—— into Lord Booby, and
his putting into the mouth of Parson Adams a public
rebuke of Pamela and her husband for laughing in
church, were happy strokes. As Fielding went on
with his writing, the occasion of his story slipped
from his memory, and he revealed his inner self, his
high breeding, his fidelity, and his kindness of heart.
He no sooner created Parson Adams than he fell in
love with him, as all the world has done since.

In form 'Joseph Andrews' is a series of adventures
in high and low life, divided into books having mock-
heroic introductions, and diversified by episodes. It
has its prototype in the burlesque adventures by Cervantes and Scarron and in the picaresque novel as refined by Lesage in 'Gil Blas' (1715–35). In bringing his adventures to a close, Fielding burlesqued a
favorite type of the ancient drama — that of recognition and revolution. He marshals his leading characters at Booby Hall, where in the presence of the
Boobys Joseph unbuttons his coat and displays on
his left breast 'as fine a strawberry as ever grew in a
garden.' The mystery of his hero's parentage, which
Fielding has long been juggling with, as if he were
writing another ' Œdipus the King,' is out; and there
is no longer an impediment to the marriage of Joseph
and Fanny. As the final title for his production
Fielding hit upon the term 'comic epic.' He had in
mind the lost 'Margites' of Homer, which bore, Aristotle says, the same relation to Attic comedy as the
'Iliad' bore to Attic tragedy.[1] The 'Margites' was a
dramatic epic, from which, according to Aristotle,

---

[1] Aristotle's 'Poetics,' iv. 9.

comedy was to detach itself. Fielding reversed the
process, investing comedy with epic proportions, and
as more suitable to modern society, writing in prose
instead of verse.

'Joseph Andrews' was followed by 'Jonathan Wild'
(1743), in which Fielding maintains the thesis that
force, fraud, and heartlessness — qualities which are
commonly regarded as the peculiar endowments of the
successful housebreaker and highwayman—are likewise characteristics of Alexander and Cæsar and of
great men in all ages, and particularly of eighteenth-
century England. It is more ideal in its motive than
was usual with Fielding. Its logical consequence was
Smollett's 'Count Fathom.'

'Tom Jones' was published in 1749. It stands for
the fulness of Fielding's art and manhood. Into it
Fielding compressed his richest observations on life
and his ripest thought; and expended in its composition 'some thousands of hours.' 'Tom Jones' is the
consummation of his earlier plan of transforming
comedy into the comic epic. Fielding still writes with
his eye upon Aristotle and the Greek drama. He
keeps from the reader the secret of Jones's parentage,
which he manages with greater artistic effect than
the similar secret in 'Joseph Andrews.' It becomes a
directing force on the course of events, and an element
of interest to the reader. The discovery, when it
comes, is not a fantastic surprise operated by the
machinery of gypsies and the exchange of children in
the cradle; the reader has been looking forward to it,
for he has been prepared for it. The scenes are still
constructed as in comedy. As we read on, it is as if
we were assisting at the representation of a score of

comedies, parallel and successive; some pathetic, some burlesque, others possessing the gay wit of Vanbrugh and Congreve — all of which, after a skilfully manipulated revolution of circumstances, are united in a brilliant conclusion. Instead of being burdened, as were the earlier epic romancers, with a number of narratives to be gathered up in the last chapters, Fielding in the main becomes his own story-teller throughout. Character is unfolded, and momentum is given to his plot by direct, not reported, conversations. All devices to account for his subject-matter, such as bundles of letters, fragmentary or rat-eaten manuscripts, found by chance, or given to the writer in keeping, are brushed aside as cheap and silly. Fielding throws off the mask of anonymity, steps out boldly, and asks us to accept his omniscience and omnipresence.

Before Fielding the localization of scene did not greatly trouble the story-teller or his reader. Arcadia would do. There were, however, some early attempts at a real background. Aphra Behn gave a smattering of local color to her 'Oroonoko.' The scenes of Pamela's struggles and marriage bliss are on her lord's estates in Bedfordshire and Lincolnshire. Vague as are these outlines, their comparative definiteness was one of the delights of Richardson's first novel, and literary pilgrims wandered about in search of the pond where Pamela meditated suicide. The adventures of Master Joseph Andrews and Mr. Abraham Adams took place in England, somewhere in the west, at inns unnamed. In 'Tom Jones,' Fielding more carefully considers the problem of geography, and in part works it out. He describes the country seat of Squire Allworthy as viewed from the terrace in early morning; the Gothic mansion and the 'ruined abbey grown over with ivy'; the lake at the foot of the hill from which issues the river, winding itself through woods and meadows until it empties into the sea. Over this wide prospect, unfolding it in detail after detail, rises the sun. One may easily follow Jones in his journey thence through Gloucester, Upton, Stratford, Dunstable, and St. Albans to Highgate, and thence by Gray's Inn Road to the Bull and Gate Inn in Holborn, and on to his lodgings in Bond Street. Fielding did rather more than give events a local habitation. Though he never professed any love for nature beyond a passion for the sea, never quite understanding Thomson, yet it is evident that he had been impressed and moved to rapture by the loveliness of the western downs. 'At Esher, at Stowe, at Wilton, at Estbury, and at Prior's Park,' he makes one of his characters say, 'days are too short for the ravished imagination.' It is, of course, too early for a minute observation of nature : that has come in its completeness only with the advance of science; but in his moon-lit hills, his parks and avenues of elms and beeches, and his clouds rolling up in 'variegated mansions,' Fielding, in a tentative way, indicated the place that nature might occupy in the novel of the future.

A characteristic of 'Joseph Andrews,' Fielding develops more carefully in 'Tom Jones,' and at more regular intervals, — those initial chapters, in which he chats of his art, his purpose, and his fame. These essays were passed over by the eighteenth-century French translators of Fielding (so far as I am acquainted with them), who could not appreciate the

art of Fielding any more than that of Shakespeare.
Some recent English novelists, too, who have learned
the technique of their art from the French, find it
against their literary conscience to indulge in the ex-
cursus; and, as Mr. Howells and Mr. James, they
publish in little books by themselves treatises on the
art of fiction, keeping silent on the pleasing question
of fame. But in Fielding's large conception of a
novel, these introductory chapters form a distinctive
part; they are the chorus of the drama interpreting
the meaning of the passing incidents, or they are
monologues and asides of the author turned player
when he wishes to take the audience into his confidence.

It was in these introductory chapters and other
digressions that Fielding found a place for that poetry
which the Euphuists tried to incorporate into fiction.
I have in mind that invocation prefixed to the thirteenth book of 'Tom Jones,' where Fielding runs so
delightfully from the serious to the gay and back
again from the gay to the serious; and the passage
in the second chapter of the third book — the high-
water mark of restrained eloquence — where he
alludes to his wife, then dead some years: —

Reader, perhaps thou hast seen the statue of the *Venus de
Medicis*. Perhaps, too, thou hast seen the gallery of beauties
at Hampton Court. Thou mayest remember each bright
Churchill of the galaxy, and all the toasts of the Kit-cat. Or,
if their reign was before thy times, at least thou hast seen their
daughters, the no less dazzling beauties of the present age;
whose names, should we here insert, we apprehend they would
fill the whole volume. Now, if thou hast seen all these, be not
afraid of the rude answer which Lord Rochester once gave to

a man who had seen many things. No. If thou hast seen all these without knowing what beauty is, thou hast no eyes; if without feeling its power, thou hast no heart. Yet is it possible, my friend, that thou mayest have seen all these without being able to form an exact idea of Sophia; for she did not exactly resemble any of them. She was most like the picture of Lady Ranelagh, and I have heard more still to the famous Duchess of Mazarine; but most of all she resembled one whose image never can depart from my breast. . . .

In deference to those who believe in the 'a-moral' in art, it would be agreeable to omit any special disquisition on the ethics of the novelist. This course is impossible. Dealing as it must with real men and women in the real relations of life, the novel of character could at no period have appeared as a new form of literature without its ethics; but coming into life as it did in the middle of the eighteenth century, it was inevitable that it should come laden with an obvious moral. The essay and the drama from which it drew so much had been moralized. On the other hand, the clergy had become derelict in their duty; hence the schism in the Church of England led by Wesley. Richardson stepped forward to give the people examples of right conduct and to add a moral code. Fielding followed him, first to ridicule him, with the license of Harlequin, and then to criticise him in sincerity, with 'all the wit and humor of which he was master.' In the moral teaching of Addison and Richardson the emphasis was placed upon mere conduct, and motives so far as they were appealed to were prudential. Do right, that you may prosper in this world and hope for felicity in the next. That is the general impression gained from their writings. As worked out in Richardson's first

novel, in which Pamela triumphant sits by the side
of her would-be betrayer, now her adored and adoring
husband, in a coach behind 'the dappled Flanders
mares,' the doctrine of moral expediency was pushed
to the ludicrous. Fielding appealed to higher motives
for right conduct, and in doing so never quite forgot
Richardson. In the dedication to 'Tom Jones,'
written after the novel was completed, he says, 'I
have shown that no acquisitions of guilt can com-
pensate the loss of that solid inward comfort of mind,
which is the sure companion of innocence and virtue;
nor can in the least balance the evil of that horror
and anxiety which, in their room, guilt introduces
into our bosoms.' Virtue, then, is its own reward in
the peace that ensues, and vice carries, with the con-
sequential disturbed conscience, its own punishment.

This is a complete repudiation of Richardson, if
not of Addison; the point of view has shifted from
the objective to the subjective, from doing to being,
and the shifting means war against formalism. In
withering irony Fielding illustrates his point in the
characters of Mr. Square and Mr. Thwackum; the one
tests every act by a vague formula of the Deists, 'the
unalterable rule of right and the eternal fitness of
things'; the other by the statutory mandates of religion, — and 'by religion he means the Christian
religion; and not only the Christian religion, but the
Protestant religion; and not only the Protestant religion, but the Church of England.' Both philosopher and theologian in their easy assurance have left
out of their reckoning 'the natural goodness of the
heart.' And to confound and to dismay them and all
other casuists, Fielding leads into their presence Mr.

Tom Jones, generous, chivalrous, and soft-hearted, but lamentably weak in some phases of his conduct, and asks, what will you do with him? This eighteenth-century gentleman, as Fielding himself well knew, can hardly be defended. Emotions and impulses cannot be relied upon as infallible guides in conduct; at times it is necessary to listen to a sterner and less pleasing voice, and to that voice Tom Jones was deaf. But we may surely mark Fielding's protest against the letter of the law, and point to the fact that with 'Tom Jones' the novel not only definitely assumes a new form, but a new ethics much more respectable than that founded upon utilitarianism and formulated in 'beautiful and edifying maxims.'

In 'Tom Jones' character and incident are brought into equilibrium. In 'Joseph Andrews' the main thing with Fielding was burlesque adventure; for its sake characters were sketched, and with the result that incident and character were often incongruous. In 1749 Fielding would not have thrown a Parson Adams among the swine or dipped him in a tub of water. 'Tom Jones' has its burlesque, — some of the finest examples in our language, — but as in that famous battle in the village churchyard it in no way militates against the conservation of character. To many scenes of the novel the imagination undoubtedly does not give its assent; such, for example, is the scene where Mr. Allworthy, suffering from a severe cold, imagines that he is going to die, and takes leave of his friends and servants in eloquent phrases remembered from the Stoics. The novelist has of course to adapt character to incident and incident to character, and though he be a Fielding, his success will not be uniform. In 'Tom Jones' Fielding for the most part concealed his art, and approached the highest ideal of a novel, in which the plot takes its coloring from the characters themselves, as if both plot and characters were of simultaneous birth in the imagination.

As a novel of character, 'Tom Jones' belongs to that class of novels which Walter Bagehot called ubiquitous, the aim of which is to present by a multitude of characters a complete picture of human life. Fielding begins his character building in Somersetshire with Squire Allworthy, Squire Western, Tom Jones, young Blifil, Sophia, a philosopher, a clergyman, a doctor, a housekeeper, and a gamekeeper. He starts Jones on a journey to London, introducing chance acquaintances by the way. In more hurried journeys Jones is followed by Sophia and Allworthy and Western. When Fielding gets them to London, he brings them into contrast with the more highly seasoned men and women of the town, as represented by Lord Fellamar and Lady Bellaston. The immense canvas, when filled, contains forty figures.

Now, in what respects are Fielding's characters nearer life than those in the fiction before him? And how far are they still unreal? Cervantes and Lesage had aimed at types rather than individuals; so, too, had Molière; so, too, to some extent had the Restoration dramatists, their immediate successors, and Steele and Addison. The characters of the English dramatists and essayists wear such placards as Vainlove, Fondlewife, Maskwell, Lady Touchwood, Lord Foppington, Ned Softly, Will Honeycomb. These figures are not all types; they are frequently

imaginary beings, who affect some humor or passion
to which they are supposed to be naturally inclined.
Here is Fielding's starting-point in character building.
All his characters are constructed on a further development of the art of the comic dramatist. He
would illustrate by means of a large number of men
and women taken from various spheres in life, the
manifestations of affectation as darkened by avarice,
self-interest, deceit, or heartlessness, and as softened
by justice, mercy, courtesy, or generosity. The danger
in working upon such a theory is that the outcome
will not be, as was intended, individuals, but after
all, types, or worse still, abstractions. Fielding's wide
and careful observation of real life was his great
corrective; and yet that Fielding quite succeeded in
his purpose is probably not true. Allworthy is generosity hardly moulded into a type; young Blifil is
black deceit hardly moulded into a type; and in the
character of Tom Jones himself, Fielding is laboring
a little too hard to maintain a psychological impos-
sibility; for goodness of heart and failure in execution
do not for long go hand in hand. There is also a
good deal in Fielding that was already conventional.
His Mrs. Towwouse, Lady Booby, and Mrs. Slipslop
belong to the comic drama rather than to the novel.
Trusting implicitly in Cervantes, Fielding seemed to
think there is some causal connection between nobility
and grotesque manners. No doubt every country has
its Don Quixotes; England had them in the eighteenth
century, in the elder Lyttelton and in Ralph Allen,
the postmaster at Bath. Still, in making exceptional
and Quixotic characters like these representative of
the better side of human nature, Fielding lent to his

portrait of eighteenth-century manners a want of sym-
metry and harmony. His best character is Squire
Western. Addison had sketched the Tory fox-hunter,
clothing him in the characteristics of the class,
'that he might give his readers an image of these
rural statesmen.' Squire Western has all the dis-
tinguishing marks of Addison's type, and beyond
this, he is individualized. He is a Somerset squire,
such as Fielding must have known, speaking a
Southern dialect; he is humanized by a love for his
daughter, 'whom next to his hounds and his horses
he esteems above all the world.' Of course, all his
traits are heightened for comic effect. One cannot
quite reach the actual by the path of ridicule. At
least, after 'Tom Jones' there remained for the novelist other points of view.

'Amelia,' Fielding's last novel, appeared in 1751,
and differs greatly in many ways from all the rest.
It was a movement toward the specific in art and
consequently toward realism. Fielding specializes
his satire, selecting as his point of attack the glorious
constitution of England. Many of the laws, made to
prevent crime, have their loopholes through which
the criminal escapes; others of them are unjust, and
entail suffering on the innocent. Furthermore, the
agents of the law are incompetent. The court presided over by Mr. Thrasher, who cannot read the
laws he must interpret and administer, is a scene of
open bribery and outrageous injustice. The house
of Mr. Bondman the bailiff is a place for fleecing the
wretched. Newgate, through the laxity of its discipline, instead of being a prison for the punishment
of crime or the reformation of the criminal, has been

turned into a place of diversion, riot, and sensuality.
Every administrator of the law has his price, which
is gauged according to the pocket of the malefactor.
Now Fielding feels the absurdity of all this, and
lights up these scenes with his most brilliant mock-
ery; but his satire has a new intensity.   It is not
precisely the Fielding who wrote 'Tom Jones' that
is speaking; it is Fielding the Bow street justice who
had delivered an impressive charge to the Westminster grand jury.   The younger Fielding had seen one
side of vice, its gayety and its flaunts; he now sees
the other side, its loathsomeness and its enervation.
As in 'Tom Jones,' he brings before the imagination
the masquerade, with its glaring lights and its rich and
fantastic costumes, but for a new purpose — to place
his finger on the libertinage beneath.   In Vauxhall
gardens, poor Amelia, enraptured 'by the delicious
sweetness of the place and the enchanting charms of
the music, fancies herself in those delicious mansions
we hope to enjoy hereafter,' only in a moment to be
disillusioned by the profanity and jests of a pair of
sparks who rudely address her.   In the severe realism
of scenes of this kind, in his denunciation of duels
and gaming, and in his dealing with all moral questions, Fielding has turned Puritan.

As a natural result of this new standpoint, the
characters are brought nearer to real life than in
'Tom Jones.' Sophia had been ushered upon the
stage in a cloud of eloquence and in a shower of
poetic fragments from Suckling and Dr. Donne.
Amelia is the plain, patient, forgiving housewife with
a visible scar on her nose. To his harlots and liber-
tines, Fielding now adds those revolting touches which

accompany the latter end of vice — obesity and disease and the disfigured face.

Indeed, the main situation in 'Amelia' is the favorite one of the modern realist. 'Joseph Andrews' and 'Tom Jones' had been brought to a close, after the analogy of romantic comedy, by a marriage. The last novel of Fielding's begins where they end, and only by way of retrospect are we told of the courtship and elopement of Booth and Amelia. It is the story of the hard lot of a woman of high breeding who has married for love a poor lieutenant. Owing to the husband's passion for gambling, and the wrongs of others, they are thrown upon London with a lieutenant's half-pay as their only income. Its scenes, described in stern and hard reality, are those of the miserable lodging-house, the sponging-house, the pawnshop, Newgate, and the homes of the disreputable London aristocracy. The most memorable are: 'Booth lying along on the floor, and his little things crawling and playing about him,' to be interrupted by the bailiffs; and Amelia in the kitchen and the children playing about her, as she is preparing the favorite dishes of a husband who will soon return to tell her that he cannot sup with her to-night. The wretched family sink lower and lower into poverty and squalor; the last guinea and the jewels and dresses of Amelia have gone to pay gambling debts, and Booth is confined to the bailiff's house, when they are rescued by the good Dr. Harrison, the *deus ex machinâ,* of the drama, and restored to their rightful fortune; and all who have wronged them are duly punished. Had Fielding worked out his situation to its logical conclusion; had he transported Booth to the West Indies;

had he turned Amelia with her children into the street,
or given her over as mistress to Colonel James — all
of which he suggests in the course of his story, — he
would have anticipated the relentless *débâcle* of naturalism. The infinite tenderness of Fielding, soon to
bid a most pathetic farewell to his children and then
to life, was mightier than the logic of art.

3. *The Novel versus the Drama*

With the publication of 'Clarissa Harlowe' and
'Tom Jones,' the novel has found its art and fit
subject-matter. They are, broadly speaking, realistic
novels, for their aim is to represent the outer and the
inner life somewhat as they are. The novel as Richardson left it was a sober dissection of the heart.
With Fielding, it was perhaps a no less serious effort,
though its purpose was clouded by extravagant wit
and humor. Richardson was reaching the inner life
through sentimentalism ; Fielding through our vices
and follies.   Because of their aim at the truth to
outer fact and appearance, 'Tom Jones' and 'Clarissa
Harlowe' are novels of manners. They are likewise
our first dramatic novels, for they show that the
novel, as well as the drama, can deal with the great
passions ; and in their direct presentation of conversation and in the management of plot, they are dramatic.
As dramatic novels, they are novels of character;
and as such they have in part, though not wholly,
distinct antecedents. Richardson is in the line of the
romances, the Arthurian cycle, 'Amadis de Gaula,'
'Clélie,' and 'Marianne'; Fielding is in the line of
the *fabliau*, the picaresque novel, and the burlesque

adventure. Both gathered into their conception of a novel elements from other sources. The character-sketch came to them fully developed from Addison and Steele. Fielding adopted the essayist's stand-point of general in distinction from personal satire. From the essayists, both Richardson and Fielding had to some extent ready constructed for them the scenes most suitable for their actions, the playhouse, the masquerade, and the squire's country seat. Both turned to the drama and its ancient critic for sugges-tions for plan, development, and dénouement of their plots. For comedy, Richardson turned to Steele's 'Conscious Lovers' — a moral disquisition arranged in dialogue; and for tragedy, apparently to Otway's 'Orphan.' Fielding turned to the light, gay, and burlesque comedy of Molière and Congreve. Ele-ments so varied each in the heat of his imagination welded into something quite new.

For doing this work in England, conditions were most favorable. We have never drawn between liter-ary forms the fixed lines of the ancients or of France since Racine. The drama of Shakespeare had some-thing of the ubiquity of the novel; it was founded upon prose-fiction and chronicle history. Its scenes were shifted from place to place; the period of its action might extend over the time necessary for infants to grow into youth ; and its *dramatis personœ* might crowd the stage to its full physical capacity : there councils were held, courts convened, mobs ad-dressed, and battles fought. Its plot might consist of two dramatic fables, each complete in itself, having points of contact here and there and finally blended in the fifth act; and full play was given to both sides of life, the tragic and the comic. As the democratic ideas of the Reformation more and more prevailed in English life in the seventeenth and eighteenth centuries, the drama came under their influence; and before Richardson wrote, it had become thoroughly bourgeois. What interested an age which drove a king into exile and whose fathers had beheaded another, was not the crash of a royal house, nor the passions of kings and princes, but the pathos of everyday life; and it demanded of the playwright the familiar *domestica facta*. Terror was banished from tragedy, and wit and humor from comedy, and their places were taken by long-drawn-out scenes of distress. As a consequence, the drama lost its rapid movement, and soon ceased to be at all. Dramatic representations continued, but where they were not melodramas or imitations of Restoration comedy, they were, in their slow development of plot, their analysis, and their moralizing, either essays in dramatic form, or already sentimental novels, rather than tragedies or comedies. The novelist was thus from one point of view but continuing a process that had already begun.

Though the English drama and novel have many characteristics in common, there are differences which mark the species. To the length of a play there are fixed limits. The audience expects that a dramatic action shall extend over not less than two and not more than three hours. To the novel there is practically no time limit; it may consist of one page or of a thousand pages. Unless the dramatist takes himself as a character, he can give his own views of the world and of life only by his choice of subject and the tone of his treatment; he cannot speak directly except in burlesque comedy. The novelist may stop and talk about his characters. Have not the excursions of Fielding their psychologic foundation in the glee he felt at his enfranchisement from the conventions of comedy? The environment of a dramatic action is restricted; the stage of one of the largest Elizabethan theatres was only forty-three feet wide and fifty-five feet deep. The novelist builds his own stage; it may be for only a small group of characters, as in a tale of Hawthorne's; it may be for above three hundred characters, as in 'Pickwick.' The dramatist can only suggest scenery; the novelist may hang his interior with the landscapes of Salvator Rosa, as did Scott. A detailed study in moral decay is well-nigh impossible in the drama; for we have an imaginative difficulty in circumscribing by the events of a short evening the utter break-up of character, which in real life is the work of a long period; and asides and monologues, however dexterously managed, can be only a partial substitute for the novelist's full disclosure of what is passing in head and heart.

These differences, however, are not fundamental, as they are often asserted to be. The limitations of the drama, genius, aided by great actors, has in a measure overcome. By creating an illusion in the imagination of the spectator, Shakespeare expands his stage to hold an action of epic magnitude; by his clear presentation of the significant moments in his hero's career, he makes it possible for his audience to supply details he himself is forced to suppress, and in a few lines he conjures up for them the splendor of an Italian night. Does there exist a fundamental distinction between the drama and the novel? On this

question, Goethe and Brunetière have speculated to
essentially the same conclusion, which is only in general true. Goethe says: 'In the novel it is chiefly
sentiments and events that are exhibited; in the
drama, it is characters and deeds.'[1] Note the antithesis of events and deeds (*Begebenheiten und Thaten*).
The hero of the serious drama, both among the Greeks
and the moderns, is, with few exceptions, a character
of tremendous energy of will. He has some purpose
to accomplish: he would avenge the death of a kins-
man, or he would usurp a throne, and we watch him
to see in what manner he will proceed. However
much he may delay (and there is probably method in
his delay), the time comes when he squarely meets
events, placing the issue upon the prowess of his arm.
The drama is thus a duel between the individual and
opposing forces, a challenge to the utterance, and the
freedom of the individual we must not question down
to and including the moment he succeeds or falls.
The novel came into existence when Europe, chastened
by its hard experience and its experimental philosophy, by Bacon, Hobbes, and Locke, was losing faith
in the ideal man who fashions his career as he wills,
when an audience (said Miss Sarah Fielding) sat un-
moved as Cato fell upon his sword, but wept to see
Dryden's Dorax and Sebastian embrace after their
quarrel. And what does this mean? That the standpoint from which life is viewed is no longer exactly
the same as it was in the glad Elizabethan age; man
is no longer the master of his destiny; what he is
and what he becomes is determined by his environ-

[1] 'Wilhelm Meisters Lehrjahre,' Carlyle's translation, bk. v.
ch. vii.

ment quite as much as by himself; pathos is in life itself, and, if in death, certainly not in the voluntary death of a Cato. The novel is an expression of the philosophic and less inspiring view. In the novel our attention is drawn to the force of events that constrain our activity. The hero of the novel (though we hardly have the right to call any character in the novel a hero) is not so active as the dramatic one. Hard circumstances hedge him in, and press about him as do the serpents about Laocoön. Upon his dependencies our attention is concentrated. He may be crushed as is Clarissa, or through a turn of events he may stand untrammelled once more as does Tom Jones; but in either case, he himself is not the main force that has had to do with his making or his unmaking; there are events which lie beyond his arm, and which have a law or mode of their own. There is, it is true, a similar network closing in upon the dramatic hero, but if he is freed, he frees himself; if he is overwhelmed, it is the result of a course of action he has deliberately chosen. This difference between the novel and the drama is not precisely fundamental; like all others, it is rather one of degree or of preponderating motive. The tragedies of Shakespeare, notably 'Hamlet,' vacillate between the idea of liberty and the idea of restraint. And George Eliot built her novels on crises very like dramatic moments. And yet our drama certainly fell into utter decay in the eighteenth century because no writer then living was able, or at least disposed, to reconstruct it in accord with the prevailing view of life; in which there was an element, largely unconscious, of vague determinism that only incidentally showed itself in the noble spiritual freedom of the Elizabethan age. And the novel then supplanted the drama because, in its large scope and style, it could easily analyze minutely the interplay of event and character.

4. *Tobias Smollett*

The first novels of Tobias Smollett appeared when Richardson and Fielding were doing their maturest work. 'Roderick Random' (1748) immediately follows 'Clarissa Harlowe,' and immediately precedes 'Tom Jones.' 'Peregrine Pickle' (1751) falls between 'Tom Jones' and 'Amelia.' 'The Adventures of Ferdinand, Count Fathom' was published in 1753. Smollett's other novels belong to a later period. 'The Adventures of Sir Launcelot Greaves' — a too patent imitation of 'Don Quixote' — was published in 1762, and 'Humphry Clinker' in 1771.

Smollett and Fielding professed the same source of inspiration — Spain. The Spanish picaresque stories of Aleman, Cervantes, Quevedo, and others, and the French offshoots of them by Sorel, Scarron, and Furetière had all found their way into English. Beginning with 'The Fraternity of Vagabonds' (1561) by John Awdeley, there was a long line of English picaresque sketches and stories extending down to Defoe. Fielding evidently read considerably in this fiction, and Smollett evidently read all at his command, whether Spanish, French, or English. More particularly, both Smollett and Fielding informed the reader that their models were Cervantes and Lesage. As a result, Fielding and Smollett have much in common; a novel, as they conceived of it, is a union of intrigue and adventure. But in the disposition of their material they were far apart. Fielding when at his best grouped and arranged incidents for dramatic effect, with his final chapter in view. Smollett, too, brought his stories to a close in the manner of 'Tom Jones,' with a marriage and a description of the charms of the bride; yet there was no logic in this; it was merely a mechanical device for stopping somewhere. Smollett's novels are strings of adventure and personal histories, and it is not quite clear to the reader why they might not be shuffled into any other succession than the one they have assumed. A literary form cannot exist without its art. If a fable may drift along at the pleasure of an author, with the episode thrust in at will, then anybody can write a novel. This inference was drawn by the contemporaries of Smollett. Between 1750 and 1770 the press was burdened with slipshod adventures, the writers of which did not possess Smollett's picturesqueness and immense strength of style. The novel thus put into the hands of the mob ceased to be a serious literary product; and, in consequence, its decline was rapid from what it was as left by Richardson and Fielding.

Fielding based his art as humorist and realist on the commonplace observation that we are not what we seem. His province as novelist was to remove the mask of affectation, that we may be seen as we really are. Except where his motive is purely literary, as in 'Jonathan Wild,' his principal characters are never 'sordid and vicious'; his Trulliber and Blifil come only by the way. Smollett, in his first novels, puts first 'the selfishness, envy, malice, and base indifference of mankind'; he does not strip his rogues, for they are stripped when introduced; he at once exposes to view 'those parts of life where the humors and passions are undisguised by affectation, ceremony, or education.' The least varnished scenes in our fiction are in 'Roderick Random': the flogging of Dr. Syntax, the impressment of Roderick, Dr. Macshane's review of the sick on the quarter-deck of the *Thunder*, and the duel between Roderick and Midshipman Crampley. It was the boast of Smollett that in drawing them 'nature is appealed to in every particular.' In 'Peregrine Pickle' and 'Count Fathom,' he is equally outspoken, but there his realism is somewhat artificial; he is writing to order for a public who find humor in the practical joke, or who would like to see refurbished those scenes in Richardson between Lord B—— and Pamela. In his ruffianism, and his savage analysis of motive, Smollett intensifies, enforces, and completes the reaction against Richardson.

Yet Smollett's realism is marked by the spot of decay. All his first novels have one characteristic of the fictions of Mrs. Manley and Mrs. Haywood, Tom Brown, and numerous other early eighteenth-century writers: he crowds his pages with well-known characters of his own time, usually for the purpose of fierce satire. He is a Swift without Swift's clear and wide vision. He ridicules Fielding for marrying his 'cook-maid'; Akenside — a respectable poet and scholar — is a mere 'index-hunter who holds the eel of science by the tail'; Garrick is 'a parasite and buffoon, whose hypocrisy is only equalled by his avarice'; Lyttelton is 'a dunce'; he insults Newcastle,

Bute, and Pitt, and sneers at his king, and the 'sweet princes of the royal blood.' In making his characters at will the mouthpiece of his venom, he takes no pains to preserve their consistency; and frequently, under the excitement of his ferocious hate, he forgets they are there, and speaks out in his own name. This kind of work, though done brilliantly and under the inspiration of robust indignation, does not form a novel. The logical outcome was his own 'History of an Atom' and Charles Johnstone's 'Adventures of a Guinea' — pamphlets and libels *in extenso*.

In the *débris* of the novel thus wrecked by Smollett, there are new scenes and characters. 'Roderick Random' is our first novel of the sea. Defoe and the romancers and the picaresque writers before him transferred imaginary adventure to an imaginary sea. It remained for Smollett to bring into the novel the real sea, a real ship, a real voyage, and the real English tars. As an example of Smollett's realism, Lieutenant Bowling may be contrasted with Crusoe: 'He was a strong built man, somewhat bandy-legged, with a neck like that of a bull, and a face which (you might easily perceive) had withstood the most obstinate assaults of the weather.' He has forgotten the language of landsmen and speaks only the 'seamen's phrase'; had the occasion occurred, he would have fought and died at his post with the cheerfulness of a Grenville. The English sailor lingers on in 'Peregrine Pickle' and 'Humphry Clinker.' In the former appears Commodore Trunnion, Smollett's most amusing seaman, who, retiring into the country with Lieutenant Hatchway and Tom Pipes, turns his house into a garrison; and, after nursing his whims and superstitions for a period of years, dies in a hiccough and a groan. Smollett's land characters are as novel as his seamen; his Scotchmen, his Irishmen, his Welshmen, and his Jews, — drawn at full length, as Lieutenant Lishmahago, or characterized by a happy phrase, as the Scotch schoolmaster who advertises to teach Englishmen the correct pronunciation of the English language. They are caricature types, at once professional and national. As national types they are the first in English fiction.

The author of 'Humphry Clinker' is also the exponent of a new kind of humor. Written while Smollett was dying at Leghorn, the novel is milder in tone than the rest; fierce satire has disappeared. Though thrown together like his other novels, it is most brilliant in conception. Matthew Bramble, a bachelor well on in years, the master of Brambleton Hall in Monmouthshire, is a sufferer from the gout and many imaginary diseases. At the advice of his physician, Dr. Lewis, he takes a circular tour through England and Scotland for his health, visiting Bath, London, Scarborough, Edinburgh, Glasgow, and the Western Highlands. He is accompanied by his shrewish sister Tabitha Bramble, her dog Chowder, her maid Winifred Jenkins, and his niece and nephew, Miss Lydia Melford and Mr. Jeremiah Melford. Smollett's object is to excite continuous laughter by farcical situations. The novel thus announces the broad comedy of Dickens, so different from the pure comedy of Fielding, and best characterized by *funny*, a word then just coming into use.

Smollett, however, is never merely funny. In this one instance he tells his story by means of letters from the various characters to their various friends, in which the same scenes are described as viewed by a hypochondriac, a man of the world, a sentimental young woman, an aged spinster seeking a husband, and a waiting-maid who has never before crossed the Severn.   Lydia thus writes of Ranelagh to her friend Laetitia : —

Ranelagh looks like the enchanted palace of a genie, adorned with the most exquisite performances of painting, carving, and gilding, enlightened with a thousand golden lamps that emulate the noonday sun ; crowded with the great, the rich, the gay, the happy, and the fair ; glittering with cloth of gold and silver, lace, embroidery, and precious stones.   While these exulting sons and daughters of felicity tread this round of pleasure, or regale in different parties and separate lodges, with fine imperial tea and other delicious refreshments, their ears are entertained with the most ravishing delights of music, both instrumental and vocal.

Then Matthew Bramble gives his impression of Ranelagh in a letter to Dr. Lewis : —

What are the amusements at Ranelagh ?   One half of the company are following one another in an eternal circle ; like so many blind asses in an olive-mill, where they can neither discourse, distinguish, nor be distinguished ; while the other half are drinking hot water, under the denomination of tea, till nine or ten o'clock at night, to keep them awake for the rest of the evening.   As for the orchestra, the vocal music especially, it is well for the performers that they cannot be heard distinctly.

This is comedy become philosophic; it is comedy which arises (to use a popular current phrase) from profound insight into the relativity of knowledge.

Finally, Smollett's novels look toward the new romance which was soon to displace the novel of sentiment and ridicule. Smollett's imagination delighted in terror. A tragic gloom colors many a scene on board the *Thunder*, especially that one where Roderick, chained to the deck on a dark night, lies exposed to the furious broadside of a French man-of-war. It pervades 'Count Fathom,' his most romantic novel; and perhaps above all his scenes of horror, rises the midnight the count passes in the robbers' cave. Here are the shadows, the poniard, the bleeding corpse, the cold sweat, and the trance machinery which usher in Gothic romance.

5. *Laurence Sterne*

The claims of the Rev. Laurence Sterne to be classed among the novelists rest upon 'The Life and Opinions of Tristram Shandy, Gent.,' in nine duodecimo volumes (1759–67), and 'A Sentimental Journey through France and Italy,' in two duodecimo volumes (1768). Both productions are incomplete.

This York prebendary, when in full middle life, pulled off his wig, and assumed the cap and bells once worn by that 'fellow of infinite jest' who presided over the revels at the court of Hamlet, king of Denmark. Of the practical jokes of which he is the father, one of the most exquisite is, that thirty years after the publication of 'Tristram Shandy,' it was gravely announced by Dr. John Ferriar, in his learned 'Illustrations of Sterne' that 'poor Yorick' had stolen his most eloquent passages, his droll turns of expression, his whims and his fancies, from the Schoolmen, from Rabelais and French jest-books, and especially from Bishop Hall and 'Anatomy of Melancholy'

Burton. By far too much has been made of these 'thefts' by Scott and succeeding biographers of Sterne. They were in part known to Voltaire and Lessing, who had too fine a sense of the ridiculous to insist upon them. When we give ourselves into the keeping of the king's jester, we do well to be on the alert.

Sterne, like all writers, had his antecedents; and some of them were very remote from his time. He has furnished the reader of 'Tristram Shandy' with a very full list of them, in which are his 'dear Rabelais and dearer Cervantes.' He found in old English and French humorists a body of stories, jests, and witticisms, — learned, heavy, quaint, and salacious, — and he helped himself. He might, like honest Burton, 'have given every man his own,' but it was his whim not to do so. The contribution of the 'Anatomy' to 'Shandy,' in respect to suggestion and actual material, is immense. The influence of Cervantes on Sterne was all pervading; when a friend criticised him for describing too minutely Slop's fall in 'Shandy,' Sterne appealed, not to nature, not to the laws of the imagination, but to Cervantes. Rabelais led him to seek wit in questionable sources. He also drew freely upon a group of Queen Anne wits, of which Swift was the centre. For the general plan of 'Tristram Shandy,' he was surely indebted to the 'Memoirs of Martinus Scriblerus,' written mostly by Dr. John Arbuthnot, and first published with Pope's prose works, in 1741. 'Martinus Scriblerus' is a satire in the Cervantic manner on 'the abuses of human learning.' Its out-of-the-way medical knowledge, its account of the birth of Scriblerus, its disquisitions on playthings and education — all have their more Quix-

otic counterpart in the first volumes of 'Shandy.' The
purpose of Sterne, however, is not satire, except perhaps in the delineation of Dr. Slop; he is trying to
see how much sport he can get out of good-natured
men who have lost their wits by their learning.

The formlessness of Smollett becomes with Sterne
an affectation. The title, 'The Life and Opinions of
Tristram Shandy, Gent.,' is a misnomer. Tristram is
not born until near the end of the third volume, and
he is not put into breeches until the sixth. Sterne
deserts his characters in the most ridiculous situations,
— Mrs. Shandy with ear placed against the keyhole,
Walter and Toby conversing on the stairway, — and
runs off into digression after digression, which are
called 'the sunshine, the life, and the soul of reading.' He tampers with his pagination, and abounds
in dashes, asterisks, index-hands, and 'and-so-forths';
he leaves entire chapters for the imagination of the
reader to construct, and then unexpectedly returns
to these blanks, filling them in himself; he writes
a sentence and calls it a chapter; or begins a chapter,
breaks off suddenly, and starts in anew; and of one
of his volumes he plots the curve, showing twistings,
retrogressions, and plungings. Nothing was left for
Sterne's imitators but to write their words upside
down. Undoubtedly there is method in this madness. Sterne was not a careless or hasty writer;
he selected and presented his material with infinite
pains. 'I have burnt,' he writes ambiguously in one
of his letters, 'more wit than I have published.' But
it was a sad day for English fiction when a writer of
genius came to look upon the novel as the repository
for the crotchets of a lifetime. This is the more to

be lamented when we reflect that Sterne, unlike Smollett, could tell a story in a straightforward manner
when he chose to do so. Had the time he wasted in
dazzling his friends with literary fireworks been devoted to a logical presentation of the wealth of his experiences, fancies, and feelings, he might have written
one of the most perfect pieces of compositions in the
English language. As it is, the novel in his hands,
considered from the standpoint of structure, reverted
to what it was when left by the wits of the Renaissance.

There is, however, in Sterne a great though not a
full compensation for his eccentricities of form. In
passages now immortal, as that one in which the recording angel drops a tear upon an oath of Uncle
Toby's, he strove to write prose that should possess
the precision, the melody, and the sensuousness of the
highest poetic expression. The proverb, 'God tempers
the wind to the shorn lamb,' belongs in its present
form to Sterne; clergymen have taken it for a text
to their sermons, and then searched the Scriptures
for it in vain. In indicating delicate shades of feeling, he refined upon Marivaux and Fielding. And in
the course of his work he created great and extraordinary characters.

Fielding, Smollett, and Sterne, all had the reputation in their time of taking their leading characters
from actual experience. Fielding selected, and, except in 'Amelia,' made men and women conform to
a theory of the ludicrous. Smollett drenched his
rogues and seamen in a bath of indignation, brutality, and revenge. Sterne was more an idealist than
either. Characters which had a real basis in his boy-

hood observations in English and Irish barracks, in his
association with droll and not over-fastidious Yorkshire wits, and in his French travels, he lifted into 'the
clear climate of fantasy.' Hypocrisy, vanity, affectation, and ruling passions—the material which Fielding
and Smollett worked—he subtilized into the strangest
whims; as, for example, the hobby that our whole
success in life depends upon the name with which
we happen to be christened. These faint shadows
of real life, though they do speak, converse with us
quite as much through attitude, gesture, and movement. Trim is discoursing upon life and death. 'Are
we not here now, continued the Corporal (striking the
end of his stick perpendicularly upon the floor, so as
to give an idea of health and stability)—and are
we not—(dropping his hat upon the ground) gone!
in a moment!—'Twas infinitely striking! Susannah
burst into a flood of tears.' Passages might be selected to show that Sterne was capable of descending to the antics of a jester or to the pantomime of
a Parisian music hall; but at his best, he displayed
in the study of gesture a fine and high art. He enlarged for the novelist the sphere of character-building, by bringing over into fiction the pose and the
attitude of the sculptor and the painter, combined
with a graceful and harmonious movement, which he
justly likened to the transitions of music.

Sterne's characters belong to that Shakespearean
brotherhood of fools which Macaulay must have had
in mind when he sketched Boswell. Mrs. Shandy on
the famous 'bed of justice,' echoing her husband's
observations on Tristram's need of breeches, is that
delightfully stupid Justice Shallow who, standing by

Westminster Abbey, gave his assent to the absurd remarks of Falstaff and Pistol, with ' It doth' and ' 'Tis so indeed.' Dr. Slop is of the dull and blundering class. Trim is the pragmatic fool, haunted at times by a deep philosophy. Walter Shandy is the learned fool, whose poor brain, involved in a labyrinth of *a priori* reasoning, is now and then visited by gleams of intelligence. Listen to him on his favorite hypothesis: ' How many CÆSARS and POMPEYS, he would say, by mere inspiration of the names, have been rendered worthy of them? And how many, he would add, are there, who might have done exceeding well in the world had not their characters and spirits been totally depressed and NICODEMUSED into nothing!' Uncle Toby is the innocent gentleman who knows nothing of the real world; who sits in his sentry-box, pipe in hand, looking into Widow Wadman's left eye for ' moat or chaff or speck,' wholly unaware that it is ' one lambent, delicious fire,' shooting into his own. And in their kindness of heart, all Sterne's characters are cousins to that Yorick whose lips Hamlet ' kissed how oft.' Walter Shandy, though sometimes assuming a subacid humor, never does so without a prick of conscience. Uncle Toby's heart goes out in sympathy for all in misfortune and distress. Aged and infirm as he is, he would walk through darkness and storm to console a dying soldier. Sterne writes:

My Uncle Toby had scarce a heart to retaliate upon a fly. — Go — says he, one day at dinner, to an over-grown one which had buzzed about his nose, and tormented him cruelly all dinner-time, — and which, after infinite attempts, he had caught at last, as it flew by him. I'll not hurt thee, says my Uncle Toby, rising from his chair, and going across the room with the fly in his hand, — I'll not hurt a hair of thy head : — Go, — says he, lifting up the sash, and opening his hand as he spoke to let it escape ; — go, poor devil, get thee gone, why should I hurt thee ? — This world surely is wide enough to hold both thee and me.

Before Sterne, there was in our literature no incident like this. To characterize the soft state of the feelings and the imagination that could originate it, Sterne himself was apparently the first to use the epithet sentimental[1]; and by a curious coincidence he so employed it in the very year Richardson published 'Pamela.' Viewed largely, Richardson is a sentimentalist by virtue of the fact that he dwells upon the sin and shame of a world given over to the debauchee. Rousseau, when he sits down by Lake Geneva, and watches his tears as they drip into the water, is asking the spectator to sympathize with the wrongs — real or imaginary — which he has endured. Sterne never takes a lyrical view of life. He listens to the tale of human misery only because it gives him 'sweet and pleasurable nerve vibrations.' In his sentiment is always involved the ludicrous. He moves into ripple our feelings by the starling which ought to be set free, by the fly, the hair of whose head ought not to be injured, and by the donkey which ought to be chewing a macaroon instead of an artichoke. When he seeks to awaken pleasure in a real distress, then he seems ignoble, until we reflect that author and work are an immense hoax. The absurdity lurking in special scenes of the 'Sentimental Journey' is elusive; but it is there. It is a kind of humor that evokes only the gentlest emotions of

_____
[1] Dictionary of National Biography, liv., 201.

pity, to be followed by the smile. It enfranchises the heart, purging it of melancholy, and giving zest to the mere bagatelles of existence. When Sterne's influence began to be felt throughout Europe, in translations and imitations — zigzag journeys here and there — it did more than all else to free literature from the depression of the serious sentimentalism of Richardson, Rousseau, and their school.[1]

6. *The Minor Novelists: Sarah Fielding, Samuel Johnson, Oliver Goldsmith*

The first great period in the development of the English novel, which begins with 'Pamela' (1740), closes with the death of Sterne, or more precisely, with the publication of 'Humphry Clinker' (1771). The novels of this period which have become a recognized part of our literature, whether they deal in minute incident as in Richardson and Sterne, or in farce, intrigue, and adventure as in Smollett and Fielding, have one characteristic in common: their subject is the heart. Moreover, underlying them, as their *raison d'être*, is an ethical motive. Richardson makes the novel a medium for Biblical teaching as it is understood by a Protestant precisian; Fielding pins his faith on human nature; Smollett cries for justice to the oppressed; Sterne spiritualizes sensation, addressing 'Dear Sensibility' as the Divinity whom he adores. Surrounding this group of novelists are several writers of similar aims, who, for the excellence of their work, or for other reasons, deserve special mention.

[1] Goethe: 'Sprüche in Prosa,' No. 489; and Letter to Zelter, 5 October, 1830.

'David Simple' (1744), by Sarah Fielding, was occasioned by the success of 'Pamela.' It was approved by Richardson — Miss Fielding was one of his adopted daughters, — and it was justly commended and prepared for the press, with some ironical thrusts of his own, by her brother, Henry Fielding. In form it is a modification of the picaresque type. David, a self-conscious and vapid young man, takes lodgings in different parts of London, ostensibly in search of a true friend, whom he eventually finds in the fair and sweet Camilla. The story abounds in shrewd observations on different phases of London life, in imperfectly welded character sketches, and in episodes, which, though often unconnected with the main plot, are allied to it in spirit. Richardson sang of chastity; Fielding sang of patience; 'David Simple' is an exaltation of friendship. The episode of Dumont and Stainville is as noble and tender as the mediæval story of Palamon and Arcite. Its place in English fiction is as a little companion piece to 'Pamela' and 'Amelia.'

'Rasselas, Prince of Abyssinia' (1759), by Dr. Samuel Johnson, is a logical outcome of the novel of Richardson. If a story may be written for the purpose of reducing Christian ethics to special maxims of conduct, it may likewise be written as a warning to those 'who listen with credulity to the whispers of fancy, and pursue with eagerness the phantoms of hope.' The 'Prince of Abyssinia' contains in little space Johnson's reflections at a moment when, saddened by the death of his mother and the poor returns from his literary work, he found life hardly worth living. In it Johnson compressed his 'Ramblers' and the 'Vanity of Human Wishes,' and in language which, though sometimes artificially antithetical, for the greater part runs on in sweet and plaintive melody. The various conditions and ideals of life pass by him in review, and he pronounces an adverse judgment on them all. The prince and princess who escaped from the happy Abyssinian valley, hoping to find in the wide world some occupation worthy of hand or brain, return to the ennui of their youthful Eden, there to prepare for eternity. The novel of Richardson has thus been turned to the purpose of an eloquent funeral sermon.

'The Vicar of Wakefield' (1766) is, of all eighteenth-century novels, the one that many readers would the least willingly lose. Some years before Oliver Goldsmith wrote his charming narrative, the subject-matter available to the story-teller had become pretty well understood. There was the sentimental young lady, the villain, and the abduction; that was, in the professional and commercial view, Richardson's contribution to the novel. There was the intrigue, the adventure, the singular character, and the kind-hearted gentleman; that was Fielding's contribution. There were English seamen and scenes at sea; that was Smollett's contribution. There must be some sermonizing, some ridicule of prevailing vices and affectations, or an attack upon those who make or administer the laws of the realm. The novelist might put his story into a series of letters, as did Frances Sheridan, mother of Richard Brinsley; or he might adopt the loose epic. The publisher had settled upon the size of the volume. That it should be a duodecimo was an item in the definition of the novel; one volume would do, two volumes were better, three or four volumes would be accepted.

Goldsmith took his material from the common storehouse and transfused it with his own spirit. He works into his story a weighty essay on the penal code and prison discipline, anticipating public opinion by a full half-century; he delivers an oration on liberty and patriotism, declaring that he would die for his king; he preaches a sermon on hope for the wretched, pervaded with the spirit of the Sermon on the Mount. He has his sweet young women with romantic names, his graceful villain, his magnanimous country gentleman, and his eccentric country parson. He beautifies, softens, and tones down; the villain has some good in him and must finally be forgiven; the abduction is a summer storm which passes, leaving no incurable suffering in its course. Less self-conscious than Pamela, less brilliant than Fielding's Sophia, Goldsmith's Olivia and Sophia — butterflies though they be, bedecking themselves with 'rufflings, and pinkings, and patchings' — are the nearest approach to real country girls that had yet appeared in the novel. Less learned and less extraordinary than Parson Adams, Dr. Primrose, too, comes nearer to the real country vicar. He is subjected to little farce; his Quixotism is less artificial than that of Parson Adams; he is touched by madness only on the question of second marriage among the clergy; his notions of his duty are always clear, and he has the ability and the courage to act as he thinks. In thus taking off the harsh edges of eccentricity, instead of further roughening them, Goldsmith's method is the reverse of Sterne's. Sterne was lifting the novel into the hazy atmosphere of sentimental humor; Goldsmith was bringing it down to the village fireside.

Goldsmith, however, was always a poet. In 'The Vicar,' he is singing of the same 'Dear lovely bowers of innocence and ease' which he was to sing of in 'The Deserted Village.' He cannot for long keep his attention on things as they are. He falls into reverie, and sees all through a regretful longing. In spite of himself, he breaks out in the midst of his story into verse. Contrasted with Fielding, he has turned the novel into a prose poem, as Johnson had turned the novel of Richardson into a sermon. Moreover, from another point of view, 'The Vicar' ought to be read in contrast to Lodge's 'Rosalind.' Here is the golden age once more, not however in Arcadia, but somewhere in England; here is the imagination idealizing real, not conventional scenes. 'The Vicar of Wakefield' as a generative force has been felt throughout Europe. Recollections from it furnished a dramatic setting to the Frederike episode in Goethe's 'Dichtung und Wahrheit.' It is the literary parent of Auerbach's village tales, George Sand's 'Mare au Diable,' Björnson's 'Synnöve Solbakken,' a far-off Icelandic story, 'Lad and Lass' ('Piltur og Stulka'), by Jón Thóroddsen, and a legion of similar idyls in which reality shades off into poetry.

As a humorist, Goldsmith set himself squarely against his contemporaries, and, with what little gall there was in him, expressly against Sterne. He never twitches at our nerves with the sentimental scene, but relieves his deepest pathos with a kindly irony. To him there is no humor in the dash, the asterisk, the wink, and the riddle; his sentences always have their logic and their rhythm. He despises ribaldry, and implies, with a grain of truth, that Sterne is only a second Tom D'Urfey, one of the most profane of Restoration wits. The professional humorists of his day had a conventional sentence which they put into their prefaces. Though slightly variable in form, this is its type: 'Nothing is said or implied in the following pages that can shock the nicest ear, or kindle a blush on the face of innocence itself.' What others spoke in jest, he did in earnest.

The finest thing about Goldsmith is his sane philosophy of life. Goldsmith had experienced the hard rubs of fortune as well as Johnson, but with different feelings. With robust resignation Johnson submitted to the inevitable, but only after bitterly complaining. Goldsmith cleared away despair, taking as the text of his story, *Sperate, miseri, cavete, felices.* By a different route he reached the same effects that Sterne was producing by his paganism. In adversity, Dr. Primrose hopes and works for a better turn of fortune, enduring in the meantime without fret. This is not the questionable optimism of a Leibnitz; it is that reasonable philosophy 'which,' says Goethe, in recording his debt to Goldsmith, 'in the end leads us back from all the mistaken paths of life.'[1]

[1] Letter to Zelter, 25 December, 1829.

CHAPTER III

FROM 'HUMPHRY CLINKER' TO 'WAVERLEY'

1. *The Imitators*

EXCEPTING Jane Austen's, the novels published between 'Humphry Clinker' (1771) and 'Waverley' (1814) were written mostly for the amusement or the instruction of the day, and, having served their purpose, they deservedly lie gathering dust in our large libraries. Undoubtedly a few of them, for their art, their humor, or their keen perception, will withstand, as they have done so far, the winnow of time; others may live with the reading public as literary curiosities; still others possess very great historical interest, and consequently have a life assured them among the students of our literature. In form, though not in content, all the fiction of this period is in immediate descent from our first school of novelists. Down to 1790, the novel of letters and that of direct narration were in nearly equal vogue; after that date the novel of letters lost ground. There were curious imitators of Fielding who divided their novels into books with introductory chapters, writing, they said, epics on which, like Fielding, they spent thousands of hours. Of all these imitations, by far the best is 'Henry' (1795), by Richard Cumberland the dramatist. In this novel Cumberland adjusted 'Tom Jones' to the

manners of the end of the century, and in initial
chapters he discoursed, with the rich observations of
a long literary career, on the present and the past
state of learning, remarking, by the way, that in his
youth he frequented the home of his 'facetious'
master.

The sentiment and gesture of Sterne were diffused
everywhere; the correspondence of lovers were 'sentimental repasts'; and letters of business were punctu-
ated with the dash and the star. Most of Sterne's
imitators, as Richard Griffith, author of 'The Koran'
(1770), are inexpressibly dull. 'The Man of Feeling'
(1771), by Henry Mackenzie, written in a style alternating between the whims of Sterne and a winning
plaintiveness, enjoys the distinction of being the most
sentimental of all English novels. One scene of it,
in which the frail hero dies from the shock he receives
when a Scotch maiden of pensive face and mild hazel
eyes acknowledges that she can return his love for her,
deserves to be remembered : 'He seized her hand —
a languid color reddened his cheek — a smile bright-
ened faintly in his eye. As he gazed on her, it grew
dim, it fixed, it closed — He sighed and fell back on
the seat — Miss Walton screamed at the sight — His
aunt and the servants rushed into the room — They
found them lying motionless together. — His physician
happened to call at that instant. Every art was tried
to recover them — With Miss Walton they succeeded
— But Harley was gone for ever.'

Notwithstanding so much imitative work, the latter
half of the eighteenth century was the seedtime of
the nineteenth-century novel. The sentimental novel,
expanding and gathering to itself politics and ethics,

passed into the purely didactic novel, whose only
reason for being was as a medium for promulgating
theories of government, conduct, and education. The
novel of manners, mostly in the hands of women, was
refined into a detailed and subtle novel of social satire;
of which the perfect type is 'Pride and Prejudice.'
As a reaction against the novel of manners, was developed a new romance, which in its most popular
form had its beginning with Smollett. This movement culminated in the romantic tales of Scott and
Cooper.

2. *The Novel of Purpose*

Ever since the Reformation, the theories of moralists and philosophers had filtered into popular literature, and in several notable instances had done service
to fiction. 'Utopia,' 'Euphues,' 'Oroonoko,' and all of
Richardson's novels have their didactic aspects. In
the years preceding the French Revolution, the speculations of Hooker, Hobbes, and Locke, on government,
society, and education — developed, distorted, and
emotionalized — were given over to the masses by
men and women who wrote, not to convince, but to
persuade and to arouse. This work began in France
with the Encyclopædists, Rousseau, Holbach, and
others; it was completed by a group of philosophers
known as perfectibilians, among whom was Condorcet.
William Godwin and Mary Wollstonecraft were the
English perfectibilians, amateur philosophers, who,
instead of looking backward, as Rousseau had done,
for the earthly paradise, looked forward: the one to
the golden age of anarchy; the other to the social

emancipation of women. Minor writers, many of whom wrote treatises, pamphlets, and letters, on conduct, education, and government, resorted to the novel for the purpose of popularizing current ideas. This didactic view of fiction upon which Richardson had set the seal of his authority was encouraged in England by the success of Rousseau. In his 'Nouvelle Héloïse' (1761) he represented by a concrete picture the state of nature, in which the elemental passions ruled supreme, and then he contrasted this state with the conventions of contemporary society. His intense emotionalism and the very great beauty of his descriptions of external nature held in a sort of solution his discourses on rank *vs.* merit, masculine *vs.* feminine perfection, real *vs.* apparent honor, etc. In 'Émile' (1762) he tried to conceal an entrancing idyl in an educational programme. The didactic fictions which appeared during the half-century following 'Émile' fall, in a general way, under the two classes, pedagogic and revolutionary. The inspiration of the former was a dissatisfaction with the prevailing method of education; the inspiration of the latter was dissatisfaction with the existing social order. Both classes had a common source of inspiration in a desire of reaching what is in accord with nature.

The first of the English pedagogic romances was written by Henry Brooke, whose 'Fool of Quality' appeared in parts during the years 1766–70. It is a book that one can hardly speak of unreservedly without falling into antitheses which would seem untrue. Its main object was to describe in detail the education of a Christian gentleman. The hero visits all in poverty and distress, in prisons and in hospitals, relieving them out of exhaustless funds supplied by his uncle. One of its distinctive features is the stress laid upon physical training, the most absurd examples being cited of the hero's strength and agility. It would be impossible to imagine a novel more wretchedly put together. On the other hand, it contains passages of magnificent rhetoric, incidents and tales of deep pathos, and inspiring ideals of Christian manhood.

An interesting variation in the pedagogic story is marked by Thomas Day's 'Sandford and Merton' (1783–89). Though it contains an elaborate scheme for parents to follow in the education of their children, it was equally a book to be read by the children themselves. By means of stories and Socratic conversations, the young are taught to see the worth of astronomy, geography, zoölogy, botany, ethnology, political economy, and the cardinal virtues; and to appreciate duly the sweet temper of the negro and the savage grandeur of the American Indian. Some characteristics of a new woman appeared in 'Sandford and Merton.' Rousseau's ideal, as depicted in Sophie educated expressly for Émile, was thoroughly assimilated to the conditions of English life in the flamboyant 'Sermons to Young Women' (1765) by Dr. James Fordyce, a Presbyterian minister of London; and she was made attractive in fiction by Frances Burney and Maria Edgeworth. Serious objections, however, were urged against her by the advanced women of the century. She was over passive, soft, and delicate; she dissembled too much; her airs were too enticing, and her foot made too pretty. The attributing to her of what were called peculiarly sexual virtues which

differentiated her from man, was especially distasteful.
Why a girl should not receive the same education as
a boy was not quite clear. Thomas Day was among
the first to protest against the delicacy of Rousseau's
heroine. His young woman looks first to her health.
'She rises at candle light in winter, plunges into a
cold bath, rides a dozen miles upon a trotting horse or
walks as many even with the hazard of being splashed
or soiling her clothes.' She becomes acquainted with
the best authors in the English language, and learns
French to read it but not to speak it, that she may
not be corrupted by barbers and dancing-masters.
She is instructed in the established laws of nature,
and to a small degree in geometry; and finally she is
an expert in the duties of the household. Offshoots
of this type of fiction were the purely juvenile stories
of Maria Edgeworth, such as 'Frank' and 'Rosamond,' which among children took the place of the
fairy tales which Rousseau had so harshly condemned.

Toward the close of the century there was general
criticism among educationists of boarding schools,
which did not adopt the new educational programme.
It was argued that they rendered young women weak,
vain, indolent, and sly; and in place of them national-
ized day schools were advocated, where boys and girls
should receive the same training. Among novels
written against boarding schools, the only one now
remembered is Elizabeth Inchbald's 'A Simple Story'
(1791). Though marred by the author's anxiety to
attribute to the influence of early education the gradual moral decay of her heroine, it contains the
strongest situation that had yet appeared in the
English novel — the conflict between religious preju-

dice and love, such as we have on a grander scale in Charles Reade's 'Cloister and the Hearth.'

The revolutionists were a group of London novelists whose work fell mostly in the last decade of the eighteenth century. The group consisted of Thomas Holcroft, William Godwin, Elizabeth Inchbald, and Amelia Opie (who afterward broke away from the coterie and joined the Society of Friends). Charlotte Smith was of them in part; and Robert Bage, a Tamworth paper manufacturer, who had posed in literature as a second Sterne, taught in his later novels the same doctrines as the London set. Charlotte Smith may be regarded as speaking for her associates as well as for herself, when she says, 'There is a chance that those who will read nothing if they do not read novels, may collect from them some few ideas, that are not either fallacious or absurd, to add to the very scanty stock which their insipidity of life has afforded them.' The ideas that were neither fallacious nor absurd were the ideas of the 'Social Contract,' the 'System of Nature,' and the 'Rights of Man,' — Rousseau, Holbach, and Paine.

The most radical opinions of current philosophy were most boldly expressed, within the limits of the novel, by Holcroft in 'Anna St. Ives' (1792): 'Everything in which governments interfere is spoiled.' 'You and your footman are equal.' 'You maintain that what you possess is your own. I affirm that it is the property of him who wants it most.' 'Marriage is the concern of the individuals who consent to this mutual association, and they ought not to be prevented from beginning, suspending, or terminating it as they please.' 'Promises are nonentities; they mean nothing, stand for nothing, and nothing can claim.' After these and similar perspicuous compliments to civilization, Holcroft drew, in the fifth of the six duodecimo volumes of which his novel is composed, an enthusiastic picture of the perfect state toward which mankind had been set moving. The people of the earth will form one great family living in brotherly love. All the absurd distinctions of rank will be abolished. Selfishness is to be no more as a motive to conduct, and universal benevolence will take its place. There will be no more personal property; hence the detestable word 'bargain' will become utterly unintelligible. It is true there may be some sort of agreement between the sexes, but it will be nothing like the modern marriage compact. Priests, princes, legislators, justices, and jailers will find their occupation gone. Man will win back the patriarch's length of life, and may gain the secret of immortality. Manual labor, in which all will engage, will be reduced to a minimum, and thus men will be able to 'expend their whole powers in tracing moral and physical cause and effect; which, being infinite in their series, will afford employment of the most rational and delightful kind.'

Not all the novelists of his school agreed with Holcroft on all points; and none of the rest presented in the pages of one novel the whole revolutionary programme. Marriage and the relation of the sexes was the popular subject. Godwin in his 'Political Justice' asserted that 'the institution of marriage is a system of fraud,' but in his novels he was more conservative. For example, much pains is taken in his 'St. Leon' (1799) to show that a man may possess

special affection for wife and children without inter-
fering with a benevolent and passionately just attitude toward his neighbors. In 'Barham Downs'
(1788) Bage argues for the purity of a woman who
has been betrayed by a young lord. Charlotte Smith's
'Desmond' (1792) has as its interesting situation the
generous and well-regulated passion of a young man for
a married woman. The husband becomes dissipated,
meddles with cold iron, and the widow, after twelve
months' mourning, marries her platonic Werther. In
Mrs. Opie's 'Adeline Mowbray' (1804) — the incidents
of which are a rendering of certain passages in the
career of Mary Wollstonecraft — the heroine, who very
early in life comes to the conclusion that the only
marriage worthy of the name is one 'founded on rational grounds and cemented by rational ties,' falls
a victim to her theory. Mrs. Opie apologizes for her
opinion that so long as men are inconstant and neglect
their children, 'marriage is a wise and ought to be a
sacred institution.'

Neither did Holcroft's contemporaries see their way
clear to bringing into the novel his prophetic vision of
the philosopher's paradise in which men were to find
the supreme pleasure in following up the thread of
causal relations. They were content to point to some
place and people on the earth that might poetically
and approximately stand for their ideal of the perfect state. In Bage's 'Barham Downs' the ideal was
the *pays de Vaud,* and the rocks of *Meillerie,* where
lived and died Julie Wolmar, 'the most virtuous of
her sex.' In Godwin's 'Fleetwood' (1805) the life of
simplicity and quiet voluptuousness was found in the
valley of Urseren at the foot of St. Gotthard, which,

as Scott observed, he covered with 'a wood of tall
and venerable trees.' In Bage's 'Hermsprong' (1796)
and Charlotte Smith's 'Old Manor House' (1793), the
earthly paradise was placed in the forests of North
America among the aborigines, who, 'possessing none
of the *tœdium vitœ* of the Europeans, dance, play, and
weary of this, bask in the sun and sing.' Of all existing governments, it was agreed that the Federal
Constitution of the United States was the best; for,
whatever might be its shortcomings, it was without
question a social contract.

The scheme on which the revolutionary novel was
constructed was that which the propagandist with
difficulty avoids — strong and exaggerated contrast,
and development on parallel lines. A tyrant or villain was selected from the upper class, who, hedged
about by law and custom, wreaks a motiveless hatred
on the sensitive and cultured hero, who, though born
free, is not born to wealth and a title. The gentleman after a career of crime may or may not come to
a disgraceful end. That was optional. The hero,
after years of drudgery and abject labor, after perhaps being compelled to play the violin or to write
poetry to keep from starving, either is crushed, or by
a revolution of fortune gains comparative ease. The
best examples of this distinctively 'victim-of-society'
story are Godwin's 'Caleb Williams' (1794) and Elizabeth Inchbald's 'Nature and Art' (1796). Another
procedure of the novelist was to place in the plot
a young negro, or an English boy born and bred in
the West Indies, and to let him comment on English
customs in the light of nature. The child of nature
can never be brought to comprehend the content of

such words as poverty and property; and, however much scolded, insists upon calling compliments lies, and battles massacres.

The leading characters necessary to work the machinery of this kind of novel have been suggested by the course of our narrative. The African whose idealization began with Mrs. Aphra Behn became a 'tawny boy,' gentle and faithful. The romanced Indian, the pattern of honor and courage, employed as a foil to the duplicity and the cowardice of the English aristocracy, was a new creation. There was always present the philosopher, who, disregarding the conventions of society, took as his guide, even in selecting a wife, the principles of justice and universal benevolence. He was an evolution, under the influence of the new philosophy, of Fielding's Mr. Square, who conducted himself according to 'the unalterable rule of right and the eternal fitness of things.' How far removed the ethics of the revolutionist was from Fielding is seen by their attitude toward essentially the same gentleman. In 'Tom Jones' he was a villain; in Bage's 'Hermsprong' he was the hero.

The revolutionists left behind them no great novel. The best they produced were 'Caleb Williams' and 'St. Leon,' which Hazlitt, led astray by his sympathy with some of Godwin's opinions, pronounced 'two of the most splendid and impressive works of the imagination' that had appeared in his time. As romances, Godwin's stories, with their secret trunks and inhuman monsters, possess the same imaginative qualities as the contemporary Gothic romance, which we are presently to describe. 'St. Leon' has long been forgotten; 'Caleb Williams' alone has survived.

Nevertheless the work of Godwin and his friends is historically important. They took the novel as it came to them — the sentimental romance, the story of adventure, the Gothic romance — and incorporated into it the social treatise. When they had done this in fictions that were for a period readable, they had created the didactic novel. What they were unable to do was to embody their ideas in high and enduring art. That was done for them by Shelley in the 'Revolt of Islam' and 'Prometheus Unbound.'

3. *The Light Transcript of Contemporary Manners*

It would be difficult to lay one's finger on any novel current near the close of the eighteenth century in which the author does not somewhere enlighten the reader as to what the story is intended to teach. Instruction, however, was not commonly put uppermost in the novels we are about to place in a group by themselves; they were not written to overturn the English Constitution or to bring about a general reformation of society, but 'to mark the manners of the time.' There is ample evidence in the prefaces and critical digressions of these novels that Richardson and Fielding were regarded as antiquated. It was not questioned that a Tom Jones existed in 1750, but he was not to be found in 1790. The English gentleman of the higher type now resisted rather than yielded to temptation. Likewise the Lovelaces had become selfish and listless 'danglers' about places of amusement, too indolent to take in hand an abduction. Women, treated with cynical indifference, lost their passiveness, became 'rattles,' sometimes took the initiative in love-making, and expressed their surprise in exclamations no longer in good form. Farcical eccentricities were wearing down into lighter humors. Manners were not so coarse as in the previous generation or two. 'Pamela' and 'Clarissa,' which had once been eulogized from the pulpit, the novelists themselves now denounced as immoral.

'Evelina' (1778) is the novel in which we move from the old to the new manners. Miss Frances Burney leads us into the assembly or London places of amusement, the opera, the playhouse, Vauxhall, Ranelagh, and the Pantheon, among the beings she no doubt had observed there : the Miss Branghtons, who give themselves out as being two years younger than they are; their brother, who insists on establishing their true age; Mr. Smith with his 'smart airs' and 'quality looks,' who mistakes a figure of Neptune for a general; the dissipated Lord Merton, who has announced that he is going to reform; Mr. Lovel, who stands half an hour before the glass on a morning, meditating what he shall put on; and Lady Louisa, who, entering the drawing-room at Mrs. Beaumont's assembly, 'flings herself upon a sofa, protesting, in a most affected voice, and speaking so softly she can hardly be heard, that she is fatigued to death.'

The shadows of smart people who flit by us in 'Evelina' assume fixed postures and more definite outlines in 'Cecilia' (1782). We are taken into the same haunts of fashion, and all is described in minute detail. Characters which in 'Evelina' were representative of mere humors are now moulded into types : the 'insensible' Mr. Meadows, who lounges and yawns about the drawing-room, assuming a look of absence and a weariness of the music, the dance, the conversation, and the faces he has seen a hundred times; the 'supercilious' Miss Leeson, who, when addressed by any one that does not belong to her peculiar coterie, stares, and replies, 'Indeed I know nothing of the matter'; the 'voluble' Miss Larolles, who dances five hours in a 'monstrous crowd,' is 'monstrously fatigued,' and goes home with feet all blisters, 'excessively delighted.'

'Cecilia' is the best caricature we have of English society just before the French Revolution. Before the appearance of Miss Burney, the novel of manners had been cultivated almost exclusively by men. The absurdities of society had been viewed from the standpoint of the man of the world, the preacher, the recluse, and the rogue. Richardson alone had gained the reputation of interpreting the feminine mind with any degree of success. The outlook is now completely reversed. The world is presented in fiction as it appears to a woman. Man falls from the pedestal he has erected for himself. Young ladies are the centres around which young men gyrate. The question ever kept before us concerning the character of a man is, Does he promise well as a husband? Feminine dress is described in painstaking minutiae, and sensations are recorded which were never dreamed of by men. Moreover, the novel had been written not only by men, but for men. Frances Burney created for it a wholesome moral atmosphere.

Miss Burney was an inspiring example to many other women, among whom was Maria Edgeworth This agreeable writer gave the society novel its vogue in 'Belinda' (1801) and 'Fashionable Tales' (1809–12), comprising 'Ennui,' 'The Dun,' 'Manœuvring,' 'Almeria,' 'The Absentee,' 'Vivian,' 'Madame de Fleury,' and 'Emilie de Coulanges.' Barring 'Ennui' and 'The Absentee,' which have to do mostly with Ireland, these novels are an exposure of the extravagance, nonsense, and frivolity of fashionable London society, which, though not positively immoral, is thoroughly 'rantipole.' Harum-scarum manners is the theme; the frolics of women who despise their dissipated and gambling husbands, flirt with their cousins and chance acquaintances, fight duels, and go about in masque or disguised as men. These fine ladies are reclaimed in the last chapters, or with the display of corded trunks piled up in the great hall they take a farewell of their husbands forever. Into this fashionable life Miss Edgeworth puts a young heiress, who, if she has been properly educated at home, receives no harm from her season in town, reconciles a husband and wife, and marries a man who knows his place. But if that early education has been faulty, she soon degenerates into a 'dasher' or 'title-hunter.' The Edgeworth morality was always sane and healthy; false sentiment and sophistry were always detected and exposed to the dry light of truth. *Here* is a mansion where there is no love nor esteem; *there* is a cottage where all the pains of life are forgotten in its innocent pleasures. Look upon this picture and upon that, and then choose for yourself. Such was the Edgeworth plea for the simple affections against artificial manners.

'Ennui' and 'The Absentee,' whose scenes are partly in England and partly in Ireland, are constructed on the plan of the since popular international novel. For writing this kind of fiction Miss Edgeworth was admirably equipped. She had passed her girlhood in England, and when at the age of sixteen she went to Ireland to live, she looked upon Irish manners with the wonder of a London boarding-school girl. After settling in Edgeworthtown, in the heart of Ireland, she attained in her view of England the Irish standpoint. In 'Ennui,' along with dissertations on 'the causes, curses, and cures' of a prevailing malady, and on the best method of ameliorating the condition of the Irish peasantry, there were necessarily sketches of Irish life as it was. In 'The Absentee' all special pleading is forgotten by author and reader in two brilliant groups of contemporary portraits. There are the London scenes in which Lady Clonbrony tries to purchase a foothold in society by the Oriental splendor of her 'gala,' and by the present of dried Irish salmon to Lady St. James, and struggles pathetically to rid herself of her Hibernian accent by adopting pure cockney. Then there are the moving scenes on the abandoned Irish estate, where the tenants are living in rags and mud, racked by the heartless agent. In this effective contrast of manners, Miss Edgeworth is historically midway between Smollett and Henry James.

The popularizer of the society novel, the creator of the international novel, Miss Edgeworth, as the author of 'Castle Rackrent' (1800), has other and greater claims to attention. The Irishman as he appeared in London had been for a long time an incidental character in fiction. 'Castle Rackrent' is a story of the Irishman in his castle. It was written by one who saw all the absurdities of the Irishman's character, relished the picturesque exaggeration of his speech, and felt pity for his distress. From it flowed all those Irish stories which for the next fifty years flooded England. Moreover, it was the most specialized portrait of manners that fiction had produced. The English novel at this time, though in individual instances it had shown a disposition to do so, had not freed itself from traditional characters. Sir Charles Grandisons, for example, were as thick as the mock kings in mediæval battles. 'Castle Rackrent' was a revelation of what could be done by direct and careful observation. Its characters were all new. Nobody had ever heard of Sir Patrick, the inventor of raspberry whiskey, who 'had his house, from one year's end to another, as full of company as ever it could hold and fuller'; of the litigious Sir Murtagh, who, 'out of forty-nine suits which he had, never lost one but seventeen'; of Sir Kit, who, though 'he hit the toothpick out of his adversary's finger and thumb,' was himself mortally wounded; of Sir Condy, the last of the Rackrents, who, with a breathless gulp, quaffed off the huge ancestral horn filled to the brim, and, turning black in the face, 'dropped like one shot.' No philosophy of humor was expounded, but there was humor ranging from farce to subtle suggestion, and it came without apparent premeditation.

4. *The Gothic Romance*

Just as the novel of sentiment and humor, when social and educational theories were brought to bear upon it, passed through a series of changes, resulting in the delineation of national characteristics, so the same novel, under other influences, was turned into romance. The two movements were exactly contemporaneous. It was shown that the novel of Richardson and Fielding has writ upon it certain characteristics of mediæval and early modern fiction. A common incident of the old romancers, both English and Continental, was a young woman rescued from a miscreant or a satyr by a brave and courteous knight. Richardson relieved the incident of its feudal or pastoral setting, of its enchantment and witchcraft, and made it the backbone of all his novels. The miscreant or the satyr became a Lovelace; the knight, a Grandison; and the princess, a Miss Byron. Likewise Fielding shore the picaresque novel of its farcical villany; and at length the Spanish rogue was transformed into Tom Jones, a typical English gentleman. To be real, to be sane, to restrain the imagination, was equally the aim of Richardson and Fielding, who were in perfect accord with Augustan canons of criticism. But in the second quarter of the eighteenth century, there were signs of dissatisfaction with the poetry and criticism of Pope; and this marks the faint beginnings of the so-called romantic movement, which eventually revolutionized literature. For the form of the novel, this literary revolution meant that the epistolary and dramatic analogies employed by Richardson and Fielding were to be displaced by the epic narrative; for the content of the novel, it meant the abandonment of analysis and ridicule, and a return to magic, mystery, and chivalry.

These changes were initiated by Smollett. With the exception of 'Humphry Clinker,' his novels are all loose epics. Realism he carried to that point where by its enormities it becomes romance. And certain passages in 'Count Fathom' show a revived interest in superstition as unmistakably as does the poetry of Collins and Gray. Renaldo, who has been informed that his Monimia is dead and buried, visits her reputed tomb in a church lying in a sequestered field. It is a night of 'uncommon darkness.' As he enters and walks up 'the dreary aisle,' the clock strikes twelve and the owl screeches from the ruined battlements. He turns his 'blood-shot eyes' to his attendants, beckons them to withdraw, and falls prostrate on the cold grave, where he remains in the gloom till morning. He repeats his midnight pilgrimage, and becomes entranced. He is startled by solemn notes from the organ touched by 'an invisible hand,' and the sudden and simultaneous illumination of nave, transept, and choir. Looking into vacancy, he sees the 'figure of a woman arrayed in white,' who, approaching with easy step, cries Renaldo! in a voice very like Monimia's. He is speechless with terror; 'his hair stands upright,' and 'a cold vapor thrills through every nerve.' That phantom is really Monimia, who has feigned death to get clear of the villain of the story and to contrive an interview with her lover. Here is a note that our literature lost with the last of the Elizabethans. Superstition, it is true, was not absent from the Queen Anne writers. But there is a marked contrast between their treatment of it and Smollett's. Defoe, Addison, and Pope described coldly and minutely the devil, the ghost, and the sylph, as if they were tangible realities; Smollett awakened wonder at a mystery, which, however, he finally accounted for. The trick of first exciting fear and then letting it suddenly tumble flat became the usual procedure of Gothic romance for the next half-century.

The publication of 'Longsword, Earl of Salisbury, an Historical Romance' (1762), attributed to the Rev. Thomas Leland of Dublin, must have delighted the romanticists. Not since the death of Defoe had there appeared in English (so far as I know) an original historical novel. There is, furthermore, no similarity between the 'Memoirs of a Cavalier' and 'Longsword.' The former is a story of adventure with the Civil Wars as a background, related with the detail of an authentic historical document. The latter is a reproduction of feudal scenes such as we have in Shakespeare's historical plays; and the object of its author was not to impose upon the credulity of the reader, but to entertain him with a *splendida fabula*. Nearly all the elements of Scott's historical romances lie in 'Longsword': the tournament, the bravery and courtesy of knighthood, baronial crimes and jealousies, and the romantic thread of virtuous and constant love. Unfortunately the romance lacks historical perspective; consequently its great scenes — as the Earl denouncing Hubert de Burgh in the presence of King Henry the Third — lose the force due to their conception.

A new impetus was given to romance by Horace Walpole, who built near Twickenham a whimsical Gothic structure, known as Strawberry Hill. His 'Castle of Otranto' was published in 1764. The events of the romance, though they are assigned to Italy and to the twelfth or the thirteenth century, have no definite historical background; all is built up in the imagination. A castle with a black tower, long dark stairways, airy chambers where doors slam and screech on rusty hinges, trap doors, subterranean caverns leading to a great church — this is the scene of the mediæval tragedy. Within the castle Walpole places the tyrant Manfred, a patient and long-suffering wife, domestics, two romantic girls of exceeding beauty, and 'a lovely young prince, with large black eyes, a smooth white forehead, and manly curling locks like jet.' A great, gloomy, upper chamber is haunted by a giant in armor, who in shaking himself stupefies the domestics with terror. The troubled portrait of Manfred's grandfather 'utters a deep sigh, heaves its breast, quits its pannel, descends on the floor with a grave and melancholy air,' and beckons his wretched grandson to follow. The romance is the embodiment of a dilettant's nightmare, as he sleeps and writes by chimney pieces modelled from the tombs of Westminster and Canterbury. Smollett, it was said, gave to the romance its method of dealing with the superstitious. Walpole gave it its machinery, its characters, its castle, and its Gothic name.

Walpole implied in his preface to the second edition of the 'Castle of Otranto' that he had aimed to find a middle way between the extravagance of mediæval romance and the matter-of-fact novel. Miss Clara Reeve thought he had not accomplished his purpose; and she accordingly set out to correct him by writing the 'Champion of Virtue' (1777), afterward called the 'Old English Baron.' The result was a clever story, in which contemporary life and manners were placed in a mediæval setting. Two things are perhaps to be principally noted in this romance. It contains both Gothic and historical incidents, as if Miss Reeve were blending 'Longsword' and the 'Castle of Otranto' into one romance; and the scene of the supernatural visitations becomes what it was almost invariably to be in succeeding Gothic writers, not the entire castle, but a wing of it.

Still another direction was given to romantic fiction by William Beckford, who, having grander whims than Walpole and the wherewithal to gratify them, built an immense mansion in Wiltshire, called Fonthill Abbey, in whose mysterious halls, galleries, and tower, he endeavored to realize his dreams of Oriental luxury and magnificence. 'Vathek, an Arabian Tale,' written in French, and published at Lausanne and Paris in 1787, was translated from the French manuscript by Samuel Henly, an English scholar and schoolmaster, and published, without Beckford's consent, in London in 1786. A fresh interest had been excited in the marvels and superstitions of the East by Antoine Galland's French translation of the 'Arabian Nights' (1704-17). Anthony Hamilton and Voltaire had adapted these fictions to a light and facetious satire on contemporary French society. In his sarcasm, Beckford carried on this humorous treatment of Eastern fable. The kicking of 'the stranger' through the apartments, down the steps, through the courts of the Caliph's palace, and then through the streets of Samarah, is a piece of extravagance as delightful as anything in the romances of Voltaire. In his love of grotesque horror, Beckford is brought into line with Walpole. His Caliph, in league with the Intelligences of Darkness, commits to admiration every form of crime simply because he has nothing else to do. His bloated Giaour, 'with ebony forehead and huge red eyes,' drinks the aristocratic blood of fifty beautiful youths, and still his thirst is not slaked. The tale closes with a cleverly devised punishment for the damned. In the magnificent Hall of Eblis, strewn with gold dust and saffron, amid censers burning ambergris and aloes, they walk a weary round for eternity; their faces corrugated with agony, and their hands pressing upon hearts enveloped in flames.

Thus we see the new romance was of three varieties shading into one another: the historical, the Gothic, and the Oriental. If in 1786 it was uncertain which of them would become the most sought-for novel of the circulating library, the question was soon settled by the success of Mrs. Ann Radcliffe, who, in the redundancy of her style, her passion for music and wild scenery, and her ability to awaken wonder and awe, is the most complete expression of romanticism in English fiction before Scott. During the years 1789–97 she published five romances, in the following order: 'The Castles of Athlin and Dunbayne,' 'A Sicilian Romance,' 'The Romance of the Forest,' 'The Mysteries of Udolpho,' 'The Italian.' The order of their publication indicates their relative literary merit.

These romances always have their castle, usually in ruins, which is located in the Highlands of Scotland, in southern France, in Italy, or in Sicily. In the haunted wing of the castle, Mrs. Radcliffe shuts up o'nights her heroine, who passes her time in various occupations. If the night is clear, Emily throws open

the casement, and lets the moonlight stream into her
room; and as she sits and thinks of her distant lover
from whom she is cruelly separated, she hears from
a distance the soft tones of a lute; she goes to bed,
sleeping soundly and dreaming of the quiet scenes of
her early home. If there is outside thunder, lightning, and rain, she reconnoitres her room, and finds
in an old chest a dusty manuscript. She sits down
by a table and begins reading; as the ink is paled by
age, she has much difficulty in making out the words;
but she learns enough to be aware or to suspect that
a horrible crime was once committed in this very
chamber. At this moment her candle burns blue and
goes out; she is left in darkness, and she screams.
On another night, if it is very dark, if winds rock the
battlements, and, blowing through casement and crev-
ice, shake the tapestries, she discovers a door leading
to her room, before strangely unnoticed; in fright and
dishevelled hair she tugs at it, but it will not open, for
it is bolted on the outside. Exhausted, she goes to
bed, and a little after midnight she hears the bolt
gently pushed back and the door gently opened. The
moon is now out, and the shadow of a man moves
along the wall, who, with uplifted dagger, approaches
the bed of his victim, feigning to be asleep. As he
looks upon the sweet and beautiful face before him,
his corrugated features relax, and he retires in haste.
In 'The Italian,' Mrs. Radcliffe drew upon less
artificial sources of fear; the crimes of banditti and
monks and the rack of the Inquisition — a word
which she was able to invest with the dread of the
mediæval Demogorgon. In scenes descriptive of the
pomp and devotion of the Roman Church, such as

the novice taking the veil, and the nun dying before the high altar, her only equal is Chateaubriand.

Mrs. Radcliffe wrote for the story, and not for the characters, which are all types, and soon became conventional. There is always the young lover, a gentleman of high birth, usually in some sort of disguise, who, without seeing the face of the heroine, may fall in love with her 'distinguished air of delicacy and grace' or 'the sweetness and fine expression of her voice.' The only variation in the heroine is that she may be either dark or fair. The beautiful creature is confined in a castle or a convent because she refuses to marry some one whom she hates. She finally has her own way and marries her lover. The tyrant is always the same man under different names; add to him a little softness, and he becomes the Byronic hero.

Mrs. Radcliffe was praised in her own time for her ability to describe places she had never visited. She had seen mountains, castles, and abbeys, but not those of southern Europe. Her descriptive epithets were accordingly general, suitable to the type, and not to the individual. 'Terrific' or dreamy scenes assumed clear outlines in her imagination, and she was able to transfer the image of them to the reader. She saw into the art of description far enough to maintain without incongruity a point of view. Perhaps she was at her best in noting the changing aspects of forest, castle, and sea, at the approach of evening twilight.

There followed Mrs. Radcliffe a large number of Gothic writers, most of whom were young men and young women. Matthew Gregory Lewis, a talented gentleman of the Werther-Jerusalem type, published

'The Monk' in 1795, and was ever afterward known as 'Monk' Lewis. He employed magic and necromancy as the machinery of meretricious scenes, which were intended to be humorous; he descended into the vaults of the dead, where nuns were buried alive, and he described in detail all that he saw there. William Godwin's 'Caleb Williams' (1794) and 'St. Leon' (1799) are Gothic tales, as well as didactic novels. The former is the first detective story, and the latter is a revelation of Rosicrucian mysteries. Charles Brockden Brown, the father of American fiction, was also of the Radcliffe school. The hero of his first romance, 'Wieland, or the Transformed' (1798), haunted by voices he does not understand (which are finally explained as coming from a ventriloquist), runs mad, and murders his wife and children. 'Edgar Huntley' (1799–1801) is a detective story, and a much better one than 'Caleb Williams.' A man having no enemies is shot dead under an elm, on a 'dark and tempestuous night.' How shall the murder be accounted for? A clew is discovered which leads to a laborer, who committed the deed while walking in his sleep. The freshest parts of this romance are those descriptive of life on the frontier, the caverns of the Alleghanies, Indian massacres, and a contest with a panther. 'Arthur Mervyn' (1799–1800) is likewise a romance of crime, having for its Gothic incident a case of suspended animation, and as a realistic background the ravages of yellow fever in Philadelphia in 1793. The poet Shelley wrote two romances, 'Zastrozzi' (1810) and 'St. Irvyne, or the Rosicrucian' (1811), which are a sort of union of Radcliffe and Godwin. His heroine plunges the dagger into her heart, and falls 'weltering in purple gore'; his hero, enveloped in a flash of lightning, expires 'blackened in terrible convulsions.' Mrs. Mary Shelley's 'Frankenstein' (1818) is at once the best written and the most ghastly production of Gothic art. The sixteenth-century romancers, for example Spenser, created the semblance of human beings by necromancy; Mrs. Shelley created a monster on pseudo-scientific principles.

The Gothic romance was a reversion to material which the realists had cast aside. But it is to misconceive the course of literary evolution to suppose that the restoration of an old fashion or an old form is ever complete. Just as Richardson and Fielding show unmistakably whence they came, so the Gothic romance continued to the end to bear marks of the realistic novel whence it immediately proceeded. Mrs. Radcliffe conveyed the tyrant, the disobedient child, and the detested lover from Harlowe Place to a castle, and in lingering over monastic crimes, she was on a morbid search for new sensations as much as was Sterne in the 'Sentimental Journey.' Richardson strove to awaken pity for innocence in distress. The romancer was his complement; with pity he would unite terror. Though he could make the hair stand on end for several hundred pages, the result was not true tragedy; for there were no psychological reasons for his ghosts and sleep-walkings; and his takings-off were so motiveless and bloody as to be humorous. The Gothic romance was not, as its authors supposed, a reproduction of 'Hamlet' and 'Macbeth,' but rather of the melodrama from which Shakespearean tragedy arose, and into which it de-

generated. Moreover, it never attained, in its transformations and revelations, to the beauty of Spenser's
magic, which it endeavored to imitate.

And yet the Gothic romancer helped to make
the English novel what it is to-day. He rightly insisted that literature is not merely utilitarian; that
there is outside the real world, to use a phrase of
Bishop Hurd's, 'a world of fine fabling.' In his
attention to his plot he lost sight of his characters,
which reverted to types and abstractions; but he was
making possible a 'Jane Eyre' in which high romance
should lend its aid to the sternest realism. Though
he never went very far into mediævalism, he pointed
out the path to Scott; Strawberry Hill, Fonthill
Abbey, and Abbotsford are successive manifestations of the same spirit. The lineal descendants of
the Gothic romance are the tales of terror and wonder
by Irving, Poe, and Hawthorne. The romance of
crime such as was written by Bulwer and Dickens
is a realistic treatment of Gothic melodrama. Godwin
and Charles Brockden Brown were the first to explore
the mazes of the detective story; and the latter
began the transformation of the Radcliffe romance
into the Indian tales of Cooper. Mrs. Radcliffe,
possessing a real passion for deep woods, mountains,
storm, and sea, — those aspects of nature which
impressed Byron, — was able to add a new interest
to fiction. Her influence, either directly or through
Scott, has been felt on every variety of the nineteenth-century novel, whether romantic, psychological,
or naturalistic. She made the landscape one of the
conventions of fiction.

5. *The Historical Romance*

As has been indicated already, the Gothic revival
was a revival of interest not only in ghosts but also in
history. The historical romance of the kind written
by Barclay and Calprenède became nearly extinct
in the eighteenth century. Occasionally something
like it appeared in England; such, for example, are
the secret histories of Mrs. Manley and Mrs. Haywood.
Between them and ' Longsword ' (1762), a faint interest in history was probably kept up in England by
the Abbé Prévost's historical tales. They would naturally appeal to an Englishman, for their scenes were
familiar to him. His ' Doyen de Killerine,' published
in 1735 and translated into English in 1752, has as
an historical background Ireland in the time of James
the Second; and the hero of his ' Histoire de M. Cléveland ' (1732–39) is a natural son of Oliver Cromwell.
Our romancers must have known of Prévost's work,
and as late as 1789 there is an allusion by a reviewer
to Calprenède's ' Cléopâtre ' and ' Cassandre,' which we
may infer from another allusion by Scott were in well-
appointed circulating libraries. The line of connection is from internal evidence undeniable; along it
were passed ' dignity of sentiment,' ' elegance of dic-
tion,' the hero of uncertain parentage, and the critical
position that romance may recombine historical facts,
add to them, and make whom it please contemporaries. Still, though there is this line of descent,
too much may be easily made of it, for the old history lost itself in the libel. Our romancers, coming
in the wake of a new enthusiasm for Shakespeare,
had in mind his historical plays, from which they

derived fresh material and suggestion. They modified significantly the seventeenth-century historical formula, for they rarely employed the historical allegory.

'Longsword' with its spirited chivalry stands in isolation. Nothing very like it appeared during the following twenty years. But its influence was at once apparent in Gothic romance, where it led to historical details as a background to the castle and the ghost in armor. The year when the new historical novel began to have the air of a distinct species is 1783, when Miss Sophia Lee published the first volume of the 'Recess,' to be followed in 1786 by two more volumes. It is a tale of the time of Queen Elizabeth, into which are brought most of the court worthies. Its heroine, who is a daughter of Mary Queen of Scots and the Duke of Norfolk, is of course as preposterous a creation as Prévost's son to Cromwell. The part of most sustained interest is that which unfolds the character of the Earl of Leicester, who is banished and recalled by his queen, intrigues with Lady Essex, and removes his wife by contriving that she eat by mistake a dish of poisoned carp, which she has expressly prepared for him.

From the 'Recess' there is a steady flow of historical romances down to Scott. Most of them, deriving their facts from the Elizabethan historical drama, have to do with the contentions between the houses of York and Lancaster. But they are not confined to this period; they spread out over English history back to William of Normandy and forward to the execution of Charles the First. Their authors had no very fixed method of procedure. The 'Recess' is essentially a sentimental novel, in which historical

characters weep, sigh, and swoon; and it is one of
many similar pathetic tales. Other romances are
Smollett adventures, in which the actors are well-
known gentlemen in history. A good example of
this type is 'The Adventures of John of Gaunt' (1790),
by James White. John of Gaunt, the Duke of
Gloucester, and the Black Prince visit Chaucer at
Woodstock. On the way there, they meet Owen
Glendower, who joins them. Chaucer entertains them
at breakfast, reads to them from his unpublished
'House of Fame,' and receives calmly the Black
Prince's observation that 'in some parts of the divert-
ing and instructive poem, the lines are incorrect as
to metre.' They all together set out for 'a gorgeous
tournament to be solemnized at the royal castle of
Carnarvon,' and on the way are allured to a den of
robbers by wine, confections, and songs of beautiful
damsels. They escape and reach Wales. Of the same
kind are two more fictions by White: 'Earl Strongbow' (1789), and 'The Adventures of Richard Cœur
de Lion' (1791). Other romancers paid more attention to the facts of history. Clara Reeve in her
'Roger de Clarendon' (1793) gave at the end of her
preface a list of the authors she had consulted, among
whom are Froissart, Holinshed, and Smollett. She
sketched the characters of the great men of the second Richard's reign, taking as her model Plutarch;
and her purpose was to show the young that the men
who had helped to make England what it is, were not
as represented by the revolutionary novelists.

The romances of Jane Porter were a great improvement over any imaginative treatment of history that
had yet appeared. The first of the four volumes of

'Thaddeus of Warsaw' (1803) is almost wholly historical, having as subject those heartrending events that
gather around the partition of Poland in 1793, and
as hero Kosciusko under another name. The Polish
battle scenes are introductory to a picture of the
Polish refugees roaming about in London, in poverty
and distress. The romance is spoiled in its last volumes by Wertherized domestic scenes; and its plot is
amateurish and impossible. For writing 'The Scottish Chiefs' (1809) Jane Porter was better equipped.
She had lived in Edinburgh, was familiar with the
Wallace and Bruce traditions, supplemented her
knowledge by reading the fine old Scotch poem, the
'Bruce,' by John Barbour; and — what no other romancer had ever thought of doing — she visited the
places she had planned to describe. She had assimilated, too, the spirit of chivalry in the 'Arcadia'
and the 'Faery Queen.' There is no melodrama
in romantic fiction that holds the attention more
closely than the capture of Dumbarton Castle, or the
scene in the council hall at Stirling, when Wallace
pushes his way through the angry and treacherous
chiefs.

A very curious experiment in historical fiction was
made by the antiquarian Joseph Strutt in 'Queenhoo-
Hall.' Left incomplete by its author, it was hastily
completed by Sir Walter Scott, and published in 1808.
Of it, Strutt wrote in his preface : 'The chief purpose
of the work is to make it the medium of conveying
much useful instruction, imperceptibly, to the minds
of such readers as are disgusted at the dryness usually
concomitant with the labours of the antiquary, and
present to them a lively and pleasing representation

of the manners and amusements of our forefathers, under the form most likely to attract their notice. The scene of the piece is laid in England, and the time (in which the events are supposed to take place) is in the reign of Henry the Sixth.' In describing May games, tavern scenes, and mediæval 'spectacles,' Strutt brought to bear on his work what was then regarded as profound antiquarian and linguistic knowledge — with never a gleam of imagination. The importance of such a publication in 1808, is that it stated a definite programme for the historical novelist — an exact reproduction of the past. Jane Porter sent to school to Joseph Strutt would have been a rival to Sir Walter Scott.

6. *Jane Austen — the Critic of Romance and of Manners*

The last half of the eighteenth century was an era of immense expansion. Men found their hearts and sobbed like children; they formed for themselves new ideals of conduct, and vast and visionary schemes for their social amelioration. Their sympathies were enlarged; they described the impressions that the sights and sounds of nature made upon them in words trembling with enthusiasm and passion; their imaginations enfranchised, they were carried away from the world around them into a romantic past or into a romantic future. The novel, which from Richardson downward had been a faithful record of this dilation of heart and imagination, became in the closing years of the eighteenth century the literature of crime, insanity, and the nightmare. Romanticism had drunk

immoderately of new emotions, and needed sharp cas-
tigation from good sense.

Jane Austen was the daughter of a humble clergyman living at Steventon, a little village among the
chalk hills of South England. There and in neighboring places she passed her life. Her novels were published during the years 1811–18, in the following
order : 'Sense and Sensibility,' 'Pride and Prejudice,'
'Mansfield Park,' 'Emma,' 'Northanger Abbey,' and
'Persuasion.' The last two appeared together and
posthumously. Dates of publication are misleading
as to the composition of three of them. 'Pride and
Prejudice' was written in 1796–97; 'Sense and Sensibility' in 1797–98; and 'Northanger Abbey' in 1798.
Furthermore, there is a discrepancy between the dates
of actual composition and conception. 'Sense and
Sensibility' is the completion of an early sketch ante-
dating 'Pride and Prejudice'; 'Northanger Abbey'
is a return to the spirit of burlesque tales written and
destroyed before 'Sense and Sensibility' was begun.
While the philosophers were teaching that a man
should enlighten his generation without pay, and in
the meantime were publishing expensive editions
of their novels, Jane Austen quietly went on with
her work, making no great effort to get a publisher,
and, when a publisher was got, contenting herself
with meagre remuneration and never permitting her
name to appear on a title-page. She is one of the
sincerest examples in our literature of art for art's
sake.

'Northanger Abbey' is primarily a comic version
of the Gothic romance, and is thus to be classed with
the great burlesques, 'Don Quixote' and 'Joseph

Andrews.' The heroine, Catherine Morland, has nothing heroic about her. At ten, she 'had a thin, awkward figure, a sallow skin without color, dark, lank hair, and strong features.' 'She never could learn or understand anything before she was taught, and sometimes not even then.' At fifteen, as is nature's way, appearances mended, and she grew quite a good-looking girl. When her imagination had become sufficiently excited by the 'dreadful situations and horrid scenes' of romance, she received an invitation to pass some time at Northanger Abbey in Gloucester-shire. The Abbey was very disappointing, for it was a luxurious and thoroughly modernized gentleman's house, containing no gloomy chambers and no subterranean passage leading to a chapel two miles away. The first night at the Abbey, however, was stormy; there were high winds and pelting rain, and distant doors slammed. Left alone in a cheerful and comfortable room, Catherine went through all the pleasing frights of the 'Mysteries of Udolpho.'

In 'Sense and Sensibility,' Jane Austen, in more subdued irony, ridiculed the sentimentalists. She took as the leading characters in her story two sisters who stand respectively for sense and sensibility: Elinor suppresses her feelings and acts sanely; Marianne rejoices in misery, seeks it, renews it, and creates it. Marianne's favorite maxim is that a second attachment is a crime. After being jilted by a villain, who carries off with him, instead of her dear self, a lock of her hair, and after some dangerous experiments in hysterics, which end in fever, she is cured of her sentimentalism, and marries a man twenty years her senior, who has likewise suffered from a former passion, and wears a flannel waistcoat as a protection against the English climate.

In 'Northanger Abbey' and 'Sense and Sensibility,' Jane Austen gave her view of what a novel should not be. She sheared away epic digressions, commonplace moralizing, hysterical sentiment, the lovely weather of romance, and the prattle of young ladies to their confidantes about their beaux and sprigged muslin robes. In these very novels, but more directly in those conceived later, she took the same critical attitude toward the manners of her times.

For her material Jane Austen never went outside her experience; and accordingly nearly all her scenes are in South England. Her characters are taken mostly from the aristocracy and upper middle class of the English village and its vicinity. Incidentally there are accounts of the season at Bath with its fast set, and of the humble sailor life at Portsmouth and Lyme. She always has her young gentlemen with good incomes, who are seeking or ought to be seeking wives; and young women not very well provided for, whom matchmaking mothers and aunts are trying to marry off; and they themselves are glad to go. There are country clergymen, who in the course of the story get wives, unless, like Dr. Grant, they have them already; and he gets, instead, a stall in Westminster, and dies of apoplexy 'brought on by three great institutionary dinners in one week.' There are gentlemanly villains, who induce beautiful girls to elope with them; and their friends for family reasons pass by the incident, and provide for them liberally. The men seem to have no occupation, not even the clergy; they attend balls, dine out, take part in private theatricals, talk about their horses, go up to London, and move about from estate to estate. The young women read romances, collect and transcribe riddles, thumb the harp or pianoforte, play whist five evenings in the week, drink tea, and eat buttered bread and baked apples; make garments for the poor, cut out stomachers for aunts, knit garters for grandmothers, take a little horseback riding for exercise, pick strawberries, visit the estates of their future husbands, and work transparencies for their windows, 'where Tintern Abbey holds its station between a cave in Italy and a moonlight lake in Cumberland.' All is pure comedy. 'Let other pens,' Jane Austen wrote, 'dwell on guilt and misery' — a rule to which she almost invariably held. The most prominent exception is a portrait of the slovenly Price family, done in the stern manner of the poet Crabbe.

Beneath the whims and nonsense that bubble to the surface of her novels, there is an undercurrent of common sense and respectable thinking. So consummate an artist as Jane Austen certainly did not make her characters a mere mouthpiece for herself, and yet in the selection and in the treatment of her material she spoke plainly her opinions and ideals. Young women had better marry husbands who can support them. Gentlemen suffering from ennui may find a very useful occupation in looking after their tenants. Her ideal of manhood was the heroism of the sea. In her most careful character-building, she considered, and gave due weight to, the bearing of early education, environment, wealth, and poverty; and on the subject of heredity, she went somewhat beyond current humors and ruling passions. A guiding principle of hers was that the lighter conduct of men and women results from their being dupes of misconception. 'One takes up a notion and lets it run away with him,' as when the Rev. William Collins imagines that his fair cousin Elizabeth will jump at an opportunity of becoming his wife. 'One believes herself in the secret of everybody's feelings, and with unpardonable arrogance proposes to arrange everybody's destiny;' such are the irrepressible matchmakers, and the inexperienced Emma, who at length sees the almost tragic consequences of 'the blunders of head and heart.' Herein, in the detailed application to life of Bacon's Idols of the Cave and the Market Place, lies in a large measure the humor of Jane Austen. The reader, being in the secret, looks on at the mistaken and mistaking actors, seeing men and women, variously obtuse, moving in shadows and half-lights. This is a delicate psychological humor akin to the higher comedy of Shakespeare.

No novelist since Fielding had been a master of structure. Fielding constructed the novel after the analogy of the ancient drama. 'Pride and Prejudice' has not only the humor of Shakespearean comedy, but also its technique. Elizabeth first meets Darcy at a village ball. She at once becomes prejudiced against him on account of the general *hauteur* of his bearing toward the village girls, and especially on account of a remark of his to his friend Bingley, which she overhears — a remark to the effect that, though she is tolerable, she is not handsome enough to tempt him to dance with her. Jane Austen now displays very great skill in handling events to the deepening of Elizabeth's prejudice, and to the awakening of Darcy's love, in spite of his pride. When prejudice and proud love have reached the proper degree of intensity, she brings Elizabeth and Darcy together at the Hunsford Parsonage; there is an arrogant and insulting proposal of marriage and an indignant refusal. From this scene on to the end of her story, Jane Austen is at her very best. By easy gradations, through a process of disillusioning, Elizabeth's prejudice vanishes, and with its gradual vanishing goes on the almost pitiable humiliation of Darcy. The marriage of Elizabeth and Darcy is not merely a possible solution of the plot; it is as inevitable as the conclusion of a properly constructed syllogism or geometrical demonstration. For a parallel to workmanship of this high order, one can look only to Shakespeare, to such a comedy as 'Much Ado about Nothing.'

Of 'Pride and Prejudice' the author left behind her a playful criticism, which in part runs thus: 'The work is rather too light and bright and sparkling; it wants shade, it wants to be stretched out here and there with a long chapter of sense, if it could be had, if not, of solemn specious nonsense, about something unconnected with the story, an essay on writing, a critique on Walter Scott, or the history of Buonaparte.' These questionable faults she undertook to correct in her last three novels. She went deeper. The transition from 'Pride and Prejudice' to 'Mansfield Park' and 'Emma' is somewhat more pronounced than the transition from 'Much Ado about Nothing' to 'Twelfth Night.' In 'Persuasion' she took as her central idea 'the uncertainty of all human events and calculations.' Her characters were now inclined to come perilously near moralizing; but this was never

excessive nor commonplace. Her sincere delight in
the loveliness of the world about her, which she had
kept to herself, because the language of the picturesque was 'worn and hackneyed,' she now gave some
freedom of expression to, — especially to her love of
the unclouded night and the sea. She placed in
shadow many subordinate incidents and characters;
some event of past years, briefly narrated, and some
one living in London or in the North, briefly described,
make themselves felt on the village comedy as it is
acting. In this way, she made the story of Fanny
Price appear but as a part of the wider life of her
time.

Jane Austen's novels have their momentum mostly
in conversation, with which is combined narration in
little patches. Description, too, does not stand by
itself for more than a few sentences, but is knit
into the narrative. Letters are frequently employed,
usually serving the same purpose as the monologue
or the soliloquy of the stage. This dilated drama
moves forward slowly, but it always moves, for the
reason that so little is introduced for its own sake.
After a breakfast-table conversation, a visit, a walk,
or an excursion, and by means of them, the characters
are shifted about, new light is thrown upon them, and
a step has been taken toward the final issue.

The style of Jane Austen cannot be separated from
herself or her method. It is the natural easy flowing
garment of her mind, delighting in inconsistencies
and infinite detail. It is so peculiarly her own that
one cannot trace in it with any degree of certainty
the course of her reading. There is in it no Dr.
Johnson nor much Madame d'Arblay, both of whom

she read and admired greatly. The only presences that can be detected there are Cowper the letter-writer, and Crabbe the village poet, of whom she once said she could fancy herself the wife, were she ever to marry. Her close scrutiny of a word before she used it, or at least let it stand, is illustrated by several little remarks in the course of her stories, as, for example, the observations on 'nice' in 'Northanger Abbey': the day is nice, the walk is nice, young ladies are very nice, 'Udolpho' is the nicest book in the world, and the word itself is so nice that it does for everything. In the arrangement of words in the sentence for the unexpected turn, she attained to great skill; and she had an ear for the æsthetic values of a pleasing rhythm and cadence. When in 'Persuasion' (apparently the only instance of the kind) she became perplexed over the proper dénouement of her story, her 'felicity in the flow of words' nevertheless remained with her. There, in the tenth chapter, among the last sentences she ever wrote, occurs this one: 'The sweet scenes of autumn were for a while put by, unless some tender sonnet, fraught with the apt analogy of the declining year, with declining happiness, and the images of youth, and hope, and spring, all gone together, blessed her memory.'

Now when we come to bring together in a few sentences Jane Austen's contribution to fiction, it is quite clear what must be said. She was a realist. She gave anew to the novel an art and a style, which it once had had, particularly in Fielding, but which it had since lost. Fielding was master of two styles, the burlesque and the rich eloquence of the great orators and moralists; he was at will Cervantic and

Demosthenic. Jane Austen's style is the language of everyday life — even with a tinge of its slang — to which she has added an element of beauty. In the manipulation of characters and events, she left much less to chance than did Fielding. The series of events by which Fielding gets Partridge from Somerset to the London playhouse, to frighten him with the ghost in 'Hamlet,' and to pay a compliment to Garrick, is very extraordinary, and it was so intended. Jane Austen brings together her village folk and their visitors, at the dinner-party and the ball, as naturally as they would meet in real life. There is never any question needing explanation why a certain young lady or a certain young gentleman happens to be present. It is not to be supposed that there ever occurred a ball just like that one in 'Mansfield Park,' or a strawberry party just like that one described in 'Emma.' Jane Austen, like all country girls, was fond of dancing, and she not unlikely picked strawberries; but it would be to misinterpret her art to infer that in these scenes she is merely transcribing actual experience. What she is doing is building up scenes in her imagination, taking details from various occasions. Furthermore, we are not to suppose that there ever existed a woman quite so silly as Mrs. Bennet, or a country clergyman obtuse in precisely the same way as Mr. Collins; or a rattle exactly like Jack Thorpe, who hurries Catherine into his gig 'that the tumble may soon be over,' and refuses to take his sister out riding 'because she has such thick ankles.' Fanny Price is no specialized portrait, a friend of the author's put into 'Mansfield Park' as a compliment, but a country girl whose conduct is in perfect accord with her antecedents and surroundings. The matter of observation, in passing through Jane Austen's imagination, was never violently disturbed; the particular bias it received was from a delicate and delightful irony; there was precisely that selection and recombination and heightening of incident and character that distinguish the comedy of manners from real life.

CHAPTER IV

Nineteenth-century Romance

1. *Sir Walter Scott and the Historical Novel*

The realistic tendencies in fiction which were culminating in the refined comedy of Jane Austen, were in part arrested by Sir Walter Scott. The novel he wrote is of composite character. In it is the story of adventure, the realistic sketch of manners, and the saner elements of the Gothic romance; and these varieties of the novel, blended, are placed in an historical background.

The first of Scott's novels was published in 1814; the last, in 1831. The series, when brought to a close by failing health and then death, consisted of more than thirty novels and stories. To his contemporaries he appeared 'to toss them off in careless profusion'; and they looked in vain, as they well might in recent literary history, for a phenomenon equally marvellous. The popularity of the 'Scotch novels' was so great, that the contemporary critic apologized for reviewing at all works that were everywhere bought, borrowed, and stolen. For reasons that cannot be well appreciated now, Scott did not publicly acknowledge himself as their author until 1827, and then it was done dramatically; but from the very beginning it was generally understood that they proceeded from Abbotsford. In November, 1814, Jeffrey wrote of 'Waverley' in the *Edinburgh Review:* 'If it be the work of an author hitherto unknown, Mr. Scott would do well to look to his laurels.'

Jane Austen, it was said, wrote comedies analogous to Shakespeare's. Scott endeavored to mould the loose romantic epic to the form of the historical drama. Whether, as in 'Waverley,' he merely gave the story of adventure a dramatic ending, or, as in 'The Bride of Lammermoor,' he was dramatic throughout, his romances have in every instance double plots. There are the deeds of the aristocracy; and there is the commonalty, among whom, as in Shakespeare's histories, appear comic characters. In catenating the events of these plots and in uniting them into one, Scott was not so eminently successful as Jane Austen; for his work was extempore. Of her 'cropping and lopping' he never thought, but sent off to the Ballantynes his pages as fast as he wrote them, while he imagined he heard the press 'thumping, clattering, and banging.' In consequence his style has not that subtle adjustment of words and phrases found in the great masters of English prose.

But the mechanism of his plots and his sentence structure he almost concealed in the picturesque descriptions of romantic poetry. With the publication of 'Waverley,' 'local color,' at which the romancers had made wild attempts, — Ann Radcliffe and Jane Porter with most success, — definitely becomes a part of romantic fiction. 'Waverley' is really an unrhymed 'Lady of the Lake.' Its scenes are in the open air, in the Highlands or on their verge. Edward Waverley first meets Rose Bradwardine of 'paley gold' hair in the garden of Tully-Veolan, amid fruit trees, flowers, and evergreens. Into the solitudes of a Highland glen, Flora Mac-Ivor of wild dark eyes lures Waverley, and there sings to him of the sleeping sons of the Gael, tuning her harp to the murmur of a distant waterfall, the sighing of the evening breeze, and the rustle of leaves. In the same glen she tells him why she cannot marry him. The Highlanders march to the battle-field of Preston, in the fading starlight of morning, 'plunging into a heavy ocean of fog which rolls its white waves over the whole plain and the sea by which it is bounded.' The sun appears above the horizon; 'the vapors rise like a curtain and show two armies in the act of closing.' Then comes the fierce yell and the butchery. In his prefaces and in his notes, Scott warns the tourist against supposing that he copies landscapes, old manor-houses, and castles, directly from nature; but he is equally careful to say that real scenes with which he is familiar have afforded him leading outlines. His descriptions, interpreted in the language of criticism, are a wavering between the real and the ideal. The ideal mood prevails disagreeably when, as has been observed by Professor George Saintsbury, he lets, in the seventh chapter of 'The Antiquary,' 'the huge disk' of a setting sun sink into the ocean off the east coast of Scotland; it prevails beautifully in his Renaissance gardens and in his Ossianic glens and battle-fields. Realism is in the ascendant when he describes a scene from Salisbury Crags, a Scotch village, or a peasant's cottage.

Upon the drama of adventure with its bright background Scott threw the shadows of superstition, fanaticism, and crime. The romancers just before him seem to have known nothing of gypsies, bandits, and ruffians, and so they went in search of them into Spain, Italy, and Switzerland. Their demon was an imaginary being of gigantic stature, imported from the East; their ghost was a skeleton wrapped in decaying cerecloth, who had broken from his coffin. Scott knew of manor-houses where the ghost of the founder regularly made his appearance in chambers appropriated to his use, and in presentable dress. In youth and in manhood he associated with a peasantry who believed that supernatural beings were around them, on the heath and among the hills, sent to warn, counsel, and aid them; and their conduct was guided by that belief. Scott so represents them, and thus reaches the very heart of superstition. He takes you into a Highland cave and shows you what a real bandit is: 'not a stern, gigantic, ferocious figure,' but a man 'thin in person and low in stature, with light sandy-colored hair and small pale features.' He takes you down into Galloway, and shows you the real freebooter, the real ruffian, superstitious, cruel, impudent, and careless in manner. In more ideal characters, such as literature had not seen since Shakespeare's witches, he epitomizes the wildest superstitions of the North — in Meg Merrilies, Madge Wildfire, and Norna of the Fitful Head. And in 'Old Mortality,' where his imagination assumes a terrible gloom, he combines the hatred, malignancy, and superstitious insanity of fanaticism in Habakkuk Mucklewrath, the Cameronian preacher of extenuated feature, and eyes, 'gray, wild and wandering.'

Superstition is not always employed by Scott for

darkening effects. It is employed humorously in 'Woodstock,' and with fine psychology in 'The Bride of Lammermoor.' Frequently it is a tenuous literary covering; as the spectre that appears to Fergus Mac-Ivor on a slip of moonshine, through his prison window, on the night before his execution, and smiles, and fades away; and particularly the vision of Lovel as he sleeps in the Green Chamber hung with tapestry representing a sixteenth-century hunting scene. The huntsmen with their greyhounds, stags, and boars move about in the arras, and one leaves his station and stands by the bedside of the slumberer. In scenes like these is the very spirit of mediæval dream poetry, of 'Blanche the Duchess' and the 'Romance of the Rose.'

As to how far Scott's men and women are true to life, critics were at variance in his own time and have been so ever since. In graceful eulogy, Scott often repeated that the success of Miss Edgeworth's Irish stories was the main incentive to the publication of 'Waverley.' What Miss Edgeworth had done for Ireland, he would do for Scotland; he would bring before the public Scotch men and women speaking the Scotch dialect amid Scotch scenes. Because of this realistic aspect of his work, 'Waverley' on its first appearance was discussed by Jeffrey not so much as a romance, as 'a Scotch Castle Rackrent.' 'Waverley' and its immediate successors were filled with Scotch scenes, in the Edgeworth manner of light transcription, — drinking bouts of Scotch lairds and barristers, hunting and fishing excursions, shooting matches, the stagnant village and its vulgar rabble, the inn, the blacksmith's shop, the schoolhouse, and the peasant's cottage. And as a part of these scenes are some of Scott's best characters: Paulus Pleydell, Edie Ochiltree, Dandie Dinmont, David Deans and his daughter Jeanie.

Scott's lairds, as the Baron of Bradwardine and Jonathan Oldbuck, with their musty learning and antiquarian knowledge, are largely traditional; they are eighteenth-century humorists who have settled in Scotland. Scott's artistic treatment of eccentricity, however, is more realistic than Fielding's or Sterne's, for he shows how naturally the whimsical Scotch gentleman grows out of his surroundings. The same skill, too, he displays in his insane women of heightened stature; he is very careful to make clear how Scotch life produces a Norna, a Meg Merrilies, and a Madge Wildfire. So real are they to a Scotchman that he will insist he has seen and known these very uncanny creatures. It is noticeable that Scott's heroes and heroines — the characters that are married off or die in concluding chapters — are wholly literary. Edward Waverley and Rose Bradwardine are types rarely absent from Scott's novels. Like the hero and heroine of Teutonic mythology, they fall in love and marry, because the man is manly in form or deed, and the woman is fair. Fergus Mac-Ivor and his sister Flora are likewise poetic creations, Scott's ideal of the Celt, and probably the true ideal. Fergus is ambitious, passionate, and superstitious, and with gay heart dies for the cause that he has fought for. Flora, independent and beautiful, will choose her own husband. Waverley may go down into England, return with an army, fall at her feet; then she may think him worthy of her affection. She is of the

race of the fairy mistresses of Celtic legend who
compel their lovers to come to them in long voyages
over lake and sea. Two of Scott's finely poetical
heroines dwell apart from the rest, for they excite
the deeper emotions as well as the æsthetic sense.
They are Lucy Ashton, who spills the blood of her
detested husband over the bridal chamber, and Jeanie
Deans, the peasant girl of St. Leonard's Crags, who
goes on foot to London through perils and dangers
that she may plead with the queen for a sister's life.

Thus Scott was a realist when dealing with lowly
life; but his prevailing mood was romantic with the
historical bias, as became his descent, education, and
early surroundings. He was descended from a Border chieftain who made raids into Cumberland; he
passed his youth in view of Edinburgh Castle and
the Eildon Hills, and for a period of years made
excursions along the Borders and into the Highlands,
conversing with old men and old women who could
tell him what happened fifty years before. He began
in his childhood to lay away in his memory the wild
legends of his country, and when older he 'devoured'
the mass of romantic literature that had been collecting for a half-century, — new editions of the old
romances and ballads, and imitations of them written
by the moderns. Toward him all the lines of the
romantic revival converge. None of his novels were
written to represent the state of manners contemporaneous with publication; they all dipped into the
past. Nearest to contemporary portraits were 'St.
Ronan's Well' and 'The Antiquary,' which have as
subject Scotch and English society around the year
1800. From that date Scott traversed, with some

lacunæ, English and Scotch history back to the time of William Rufus. The largest number of his romances have to do with the reigns of the first three Georges; his most distinctively historical novels have to do with the reigns of Elizabeth, the first James of England, and the Protectorate of Cromwell; his histories in which there is the most romance have to do with the Crusades, the age of chivalry, and the struggles of the Stuart Pretenders to recover the throne of England. Taken all together, they form the most splendid series of historical scenes that fiction has yet produced.

Of course no rigid historical test should be applied to the Waverley novels, though in individual instances, as 'The Fortunes of Nigel,' they would stand the ordeal. They are primarily not history, but literature. As Shakespeare was the first to write an historical play that continued to attract theatre-goers, it was quite natural that Scott should take him as his master. Shakespeare read in Holinshed that Prince Henry 'slue lord Persie called Sir Henry Hotspurre,' and letting his imagination play on this bald statement, he worked up that impressive single combat scene between Hotspur and Prince Hal, with all its high poetry and rich detail from the age of chivalry. That is the literary and romantic treatment of history. Scott stands on an old battle-field, knowing some details of the battle that once took place there, and he constructs in his imagination the whole scene; he places the armies, dresses up the combatants in appropriate dialect and costume, arranges his moon, stars, and fog, and then lets the fight begin. He visits an old kirkyard where the Covenanters have long slept neglected; he raises them to life, and tells one just how they looked, what fantastic clothes they wore, and what strange and insane things they did, — how, that they might not murder their victim on the Sabbath, they would set the clock *forward*, because 'the sun went *back* on the dial ten degrees for intimating the recovery of holy Hezekiah.' He sees an old Norman castle in ruins, and knows just how it appeared when Robin Hood and his merry men stormed it, and who were in it. He reads an old ballad on Cumnor Hall, a few pages in an antiquarian, a contemporary account of the revels at Kenilworth, and Shakespeare's 'Antony and Cleopatra,' and he has the facts and machinery of a great historical tragedy.

Shakespeare believed himself justified in tampering with history for dramatic ends. He compressed events, changed their order, and introduced into his histories events which never occurred at all, and for which there was no authority in the chroniclers. Scott did the same thing; and when criticised by Dr. Jonas Dryasdust for doing so, he referred him to Shakespeare, and sent Miss Dryasdust a brand-new pair of spectacles. Scott, however, was not so skilled in manipulating history as was Shakespeare. Shakespeare — to give the substance of Coleridge's masterly defence of him — grouped and arranged his 'stars in the sky' to the issue of a higher unity than that of chronological sequence. Scott was undoubtedly justified in making the murder of Amy Robsart contemporary with Leicester's princely reception of Elizabeth at Kenilworth in 1575, though it occurred fifteen years before. It was really necessary to do this, in order to combine in one picture the gayety, the display, and the crimes of the Elizabethan age. But when, in this same romance, he makes the schoolboy Shakespeare, then only eleven years old, the author of 'Venus and Adonis,' and a few years later, in 'Woodstock,' implies that the dramatist died somewhere around 1590, before he had written one great play, our sense of historical propriety receives a shock. Probably every one of Scott's novels contains similar deviations from history, some of which were made purposely, and others no doubt from carelessness or ignorance. These slips, though so glaring as mistakes in heraldry, armor, and geography, he never corrected for his critics, but coolly called their attention to others which they had not observed.

The main interest in Scott's historical novels is often not historical, and the historical interest is at least always divided with a purely fictitious interest. In 'Waverley' the hero and heroine are not historical; and the same is true of 'Old Mortality,' 'Ivanhoe,' 'The Fortunes of Nigel,' and 'The Abbot.' 'Kenilworth' is different only in appearance. Amy Robsart bears an historical name, but she is really the typical tragic heroine, and Leicester is the conventional villain with some facts taken from the Earl of Leicester's life for an historical semblance. The attention is thus distracted from Elizabeth, Mary, James, Cromwell, and the young Stuart Pretenders. In adopting this method of dealing with history — which was in part Shakespeare's also — Scott was able to give within the vaguely defined boundaries of fact and legend a very free play to his imagination.

From Scott nearly all the successful historical novelists since his time have learned their craft. This is not tantamount to saying that his management of history is definitive. It is only one of the successful

ways in the evolution of a form. The modern historical romance, as has been seen, was the creation of John
Barclay. As he wrote it, it was allegorical, and yet
fully satisfactory to the seventeenth century, when
one of the conventions of literature was to hold
before life a thin veil. Defoe manufactured history;
that, too, was for a time pleasing. The romanticists,
later in the eighteenth century, put well-known historical characters through the adventures of the Smollett novel. Scott and a small company of novelists
before him constructed an historical background
sprinkled with a few historical characters, and placed
in the foreground imaginary figures. This union of
fact and fiction has prevailed, with some exceptions to
be noted, throughout the nineteenth century. It may
not be the fixed type of the historical novel. There
yet remains to be written a novel in which historical
characters shall be brought to the front and kept
there.

And finally, the real power of Scott's novels, that
which makes them of perennial interest, is not merely
their romance, their accumulation of historical facts,
their Scotch dialect, and smattering of obsolete words
— their local coloring. All these are accessories,
which as time goes on will be pleasing to one age and
displeasing to another. Beneath all is human nature,
which is practically the same in all times. Men love,
and men hate, they are faithful to their promises and
they are treacherous, they are sometimes wise and
sometimes foolish; they always have been and always
will be thus, and Scott in a comprehensive outlook
over long stretches of Scotch and English history
has so represented them. The novel he wrote is

essentially, as Fielding's, a human epic, but placed back, as he chose, a few years or many centuries.

Yet in the matter of formal ethics, Scott completely broke away from Fielding. Even the Gothic romancer had his moral. 'I am, I own,' wrote Scott, 'no great believer in the moral utility to be derived from fictitious compositions.'[1] He never preached. Possessing a healthy, buoyant spirit, he let it permeate his work, and with that he was satisfied.

2. *Scott's Legacy*

Sir Walter Scott is the greatest force that has yet appeared in English fiction. He had the pleasure of seeing, some years before he ceased writing, rivals enter the field against him from Scotland, England, and the United States, and some of them with the professed intention of vanquishing him on his own ground. Even an appreciable fraction of what they wrote can be learned only by looking over lists of publications in contemporary periodicals. A count of the romances mainly or partially historical announced in *Blackwood's Magazine* for 1825, as just published or about to be published, runs above twenty-five. Among them are: 'Rameses, an Egyptian Tale, with Historical Notes of the Era of the Pharaohs'; 'New Landlord's Tales; or Jedediah in the South'; 'Anselmo; a Tale of Italy, illustrative of Roman and Neapolitan Life from 1789 to 1809'; 'Thomas Fitzgerald, the Lord of Offaley, and Lord Deputy of Ireland, a Romance of the Sixteenth Century'; 'Lionel Lincoln'; 'London in the Olden Time; or Tales in-

[1] Introduction to 'Fortunes of Nigel.'

tended to illustrate some of the Localities, and Manners and Superstitions of its Inhabitants from the Twelfth to the Sixteenth Century'; 'A Peep at The Pilgrims, 1636'; 'The Abduction; or The Adventures of Major Sarney; a Story of the Time of Charles II.'; 'Ned Clinton; or, the Commissary; comprising Adventures and Events during the Peninsular War, with Curious and Original Anecdotes of Military and other Remarkable Characters'; 'The Adventurers; or Scenes in Ireland in the Days of Elizabeth'; 'Lochandhu, a Tale of the Eighteenth Century'; 'The Last of the Lairds'; 'The Refugee; a Romance, by Captain Murgatroyd'; 'William Douglas, or the Scotch Exiles'; 'Eustace Fitz-Richard; a Tale of the Barons' Wars, by the author of "The Bandit Chief"'; 'The Twenty-ninth of May; or Joyous Doings at the Restoration, by Ephraim Hardcastle'; 'Sephora, a Hebrew Tale,' which promises to contain 'a minute description of Palestine, and of the manners and customs of the ancient Israelites.' Of these seventeen romances, only two have escaped oblivion—one by Cooper and one by Galt. A list for any other of the last six years of Scott's life (1824–32) would not greatly vary in number from this; its novelty would consist in the indications of different scenes and different historical periods.

Scott also—to use his own phrase—'set the chimes a-ringing' in France, Germany, and Italy. Under the title of 'Walladmor,' a Waverley novel was forged for the Leipzig Fair in 1824. The author of this mystification was Wilhelm Häring, who lived to write many similar histories, and to be honored as the German Sir Walter Scott. About 1830, a Silesian boy, by name Gustav Freytag, was reading Scott's novels, one after the other, 'with ever increasing delight.' Forty years later he began 'The Ancestors' ('Die Ahnen'), a collection of historical and military tales connected by the thread of heredity. The work of Georg Ebers is everywhere known. To these three writers might be easily added a score more, who, like Scott, constructed a national and patriotic epic. In 1824, Alessandro Manzoni published the first instalments of 'The Betrothed' ('I Promessi Sposi'), a masterly introspective novel with an historical setting. This was the beginning of Scott in Italy. As far back as Calprenède, France had the historical novel, which lingered on through the eighteenth century. In 1826 it was revived in the poetic and antiquarian manner of Scott, by Alfred de Vigny in 'Cinq-Mars.' De Vigny was followed by Prosper Mérimée with 'La Chronique du règne de Charles IX.' (1829). Then came Victor Hugo's 'Notre-Dame de Paris' (1830–31); and then the enormous output of the elder Dumas and his collaborators.

The immense vogue of Scott is undoubtedly to be explained in part by the mood of Europe in the first quarter of the century. Scott and the romancers accompanying him are a reflection of the militarism of the period and of an aristocratic revolt from the levelism of the French Revolution. Still the success of Scott is not mainly to be thus accounted for. He hit upon a kind of novel elastic enough to contain about everything in fiction which pleases; and he thereby appealed to various orders of mind. For the romantic he had his gorgeous scenes; for lovers of mystery he had secrets to be disclosed in the third volume, and sliding panels and trap-doors for the entrances and exits of ghosts; for lovers of wild adventure he had caves, prisons, crypts, bandits, and hairbreadth escapes; for those who turn to the novel for a description of manners he furnished probably as accurate transcripts of real life as are to be found in the professed realists.

It was with this species of novel, so easy to imitate, that the second romantic revival of English fiction opened, as the first had opened with the Gothic tale of terror. In spite of a very strong reaction against romance in Scott's own time, which led to the rehabilitation of other forms of fiction, romance and a fantastic treatment of real life continued their sway down to about 1850, when Thackeray and others took a stand for realism. The story of this legacy of Scott to English fiction we will now proceed to tell in outline. Mere blundering imitators we shall pass by or touch upon lightly, and dwell upon those writers who modified and, in some respects, improved upon Scott's own model, or turned romantic fiction into new directions.

Among the successors to Scott first in the field was Mrs. Anna Eliza Bray. Beginning her romancing in 1825, she gained a public three years later by 'The Protestant,' the subject of which is the persecution of the Protestants under Queen Mary Tudor. Though purely historical in intent, the romance had the appearance of a flaming brand, thrown by the high church party into the angry debate over Catholic emancipation. After various experiments, Mrs. Bray, in 1830, 'struck out a new path in the field of romance,' and for a time was kept from wandering out of that path by the excellent advice of Robert Southey, 'her friend and idol.' Her subject now became the scenes, the antiquities, the traditions, and the family histories of Devon and Cornwall. This series of 'The Romances of the West' comprises 'Fitz of Fitzford,' 'Warleigh,' 'Courtenay of Walreddon,' 'Trelawny of Trelawne,' 'Henry de Pomeroy,' 'Hartland Forest,' and 'Roseteague.' These romances, popular for a quarter of a century and still worth reading, are representative of a tendency thus early toward specialization. If Devon may have its historian, so may Lancashire.

Horace Smith also practised the historical novel. His 'Brambletye House' (1826) is a good example of the working of the time-spirit; for the first of its three volumes covers the same period as Scott's 'Woodstock,' and was published in the same year. It was followed by 'The Tor Hill,' 'Reuben Apsley,' 'Oliver Cromwell,' 'Arthur Arundel, or a tale of the English Revolution of 1688,' and some others. No one would ever dream that they emanated from the brain that helped produce the 'Rejected Addresses,' which are among the cleverest burlesques in our language. Smith's lightness, wit, and humor seem to have evaporated as soon as he touched the novel, and to have left as a residuum only the dullest prose. But in 'Brambletye House,' once regarded as his most successful effort, he made passably vivid the vagabond condition of the cavaliers during the supremacy of Cromwell. He drew good sketches of Milton and Marvel, of Charles the Second, Rochester, Nell Gwyn, and Lady Castlemain. The most generous judgment that can be passed upon his work as a whole is, that he endeavored to arrive at the truth of history.

From the productivity of Scott it was inferred that a writer's talent should be measured by the literary output. His imitators let it be known how many pages they wrote daily, in how many weeks they put together their volumes, and how many novels they could keep going simultaneously. Between 1825 and 1850, G. P. R. James wrote fully a hundred novels and tales; some long, some short, most of them historical, and the first of them — 'Richelieu,' written in 1825, published in 1829 — famous for Thackeray's burlesque of it. Whether he chose as his scene England, France, Italy, or Germany, all his historical romances were constructed according to one formula. They commonly opened with two horsemen riding in the midst of grand or beautiful scenery, or with an invocation to them before they were introduced. On rare occasions the horsemen were omitted, and for them were substituted two mysterious travellers at an inn, conversing in subdued tones over their cups. There were always lovely heroines whose figures harmonized with the landscape, and soft and sweet moralizings. All this was but preliminary to being brought face to face with great historical characters — a Philip, a Louis, Henry the Eighth, or Cardinal Wolsey — described minutely and conscientiously.

Contemporary with James was William Harrison Ainsworth, whose popularity began with 'Rookwood' (1834), and lasted for full twenty years. Throughout this period he sought the aid of the most gifted illustrators, among whom was Cruikshank. The main effort of Ainsworth was directed to the rehearsal of historical cruelties and crimes, which he treated, not for the purpose of tragedy, but for picturesque or

comic effect. Executions, which Scott threw the veil
over, he thrust into the full light of day, analyzing
the sensations of the condemned as he lays his head
on the block and the executioner raises the gleaming
axe. His style was purposely flippant: for example,
his highwayman looks forward with resignation to
the time when he shall 'be put to bed with a mattock,
and tucked up with a spade.' 'Rookwood' is a cross
between the Gothic romance and the Newgate Calen-
dar. Details in the taste of 'Frankenstein' are made
endurable, by being brought into juxtaposition with
the old English squirarchy and the brilliant feats of
Dick Turpin and his associates on the road. Dick's
ride on 'Black Bess' from London to York, with
bridle reins in his teeth and a pistol in each hand,
is a spirited piece of descriptive narration, which has
become a classic in rogue literature. The romance
is placarded with the date 1737, and is throughout
English in its setting. A less Gothic and less imaginative reproduction of criminal life is 'Jack Sheppard' (1839).

In his more regularly constructed histories, Ainsworth is a link between French and English romance.
Hugo's 'Notre-Dame de Paris' is a romance of an
order very different from any of Scott's; it is further
from reality, it is more highly charged with poetry,
fantasy, and passion. Its action centres about Notre-
Dame, to which — its bells, its arches, and its towers
— Hugo lends a personality, so that the magnificent
cathedral pulsates with a sort of galvanized life. A
romance like this invites imitation; for it is so elastic
that the introduction is made easy of many chapters
and even whole sections on the history of the struc-

ture, on the dark deeds committed within its walls, and on the comparative merits of Greek and Gothic art. Ainsworth's best-known histories are English reflections of 'Notre-Dame de Paris.' Such are 'The Tower of London' (1840), 'Old Saint Pauls' (1841), and 'Windsor Castle' (1843); the main plots of which have to do with the career of Lady Jane Grey, the great plague and the great fire of London, and Henry the Eighth's bloody experiences with his wives. When Ainsworth left his house-breakers, prison-breakers, and gentlemen of the road for the illustration of Gothic buildings, it was but for the portrayal of crime on a grander scale and in more picturesque surroundings. In their final analysis, all his historical romances are melodramas. Ainsworth had a wide following among contributors to popular periodicals, such as *Bentley's Miscellany, Ainsworth's Magazine, The London Journal, The New Monthly Magazine,* and *Reynolds's Miscellany.*

Bulwer-Lytton produced five historical romances: 'Devereux' (1829), 'The Last Days of Pompeii' (1834), 'Rienzi' (1835), 'The Last of the Barons' (1843), and 'Harold' (1848). To these is to be added the incomplete 'Pausanias,' published posthumously in 1876. With the exception of 'Devereux' and 'The Last of the Barons,' their subjects are evident from the titles; of these two, the former is a philosophical romance of the eighteenth century, and in the latter, the last baron is the mighty Earl of Warwick, the kingmaker, who put Edward the Fourth on the throne only to depose him, and who was at length defeated by Edward and slain in the battle of Barnet (1471). Scott's model was Shakespeare; Bulwer's, Æschylus and Sophocles. Bulwer was inclined to take as the climax of his story some great turning-point in history, as the clash of new and old ideas; and he approached his objective point by the road of a long epic narration, compiled from huge commonplace books, into which he had transcribed from the historians what he thought might be of use to him. Countless details which Scott would have cast aside, Bulwer put bodily into his narrative. The result was more history, less imagination, and a slower movement.

It will be remembered that the usual method of the historical romancers anterior to Scott was to select a group of historical characters, and to invent for them a series of adventures. What they really did was to write a Smollett novel, manipulated by characters bearing historical names. Scott brought together historical characters and events, and characters and events wholly fictitious. 'The Last Days of Pompeii' was a successful novelty. Bulwer climbed Mt. Vesuvius, studied Italian antiquities, observed Italian manners, and had behind all a wide reading in Latin literature and Greek philosophy. He realized in his imagination Pompeii and its decadent life just before the eruption of Vesuvius, and then, not having any historical characters with contemporary biographies as a guide, he created imaginary characters such as he thought were in harmony with the period. Others — and one of them was Lockhart — had attempted the classic novel and had failed. Probably no historical romance has had more readers than 'The Last Days of Pompeii.'

Though it was not in perfectly good taste for Bulwer to speak, as he did, of the art of his predecessors (meaning Scott) as 'Picturesque' and of his own, in

contrast to theirs, as 'Intellectual,' yet there is truth
in the remark; and this brings us to a second original
element in Bulwer. In 'The Last of the Barons,' he
looked at history from the standpoint of the philosopher and the psychologist. The broils of Edward's
reign it was his business not only to portray but to
interpret. He thoroughly discussed the social forces
that rendered inevitable the rise of the middle classes
and the fall of Warwick; he probed for the motives
that actuated the intrigues at court and Warwick in
the final stand he took against his king. This, Bulwer's masterpiece in historical fiction, is a *Kultur-
geschichte*.

Charles Kingsley also had very great tact in selecting dramatic crises for the climax of his romances.
'Hypatia' (1853) still remains the sublimest subject
that historical fiction has appropriated to its use —
the death struggle between Greek and Christian civilization in the fifth century. Well might Kingsley say
when at work on 'Hypatia,' 'If I fail in it, I may as
well give up writing.' Before Kingsley, historical fiction had been written either to please, or to instruct
in historical fact. Kingsley had other aims to which
he did not scruple to sacrifice. He was out of patience
with a tendency in the thought of his time to exalt
Greek letters and philosophy, at the expense of Chris-
tianity and the art and literature that have come in
its train. This paganism, which had been expressed
with deep lyrical longing in Schiller's 'Die Götter
Griechenlands,' he set out to counteract. A second
purpose is unmistakably conveyed in his sub-title to
'Hypatia': 'New Foes with an Old Face.' Kingsley
was bitterly anti-Roman, and wished to arrest the move-

ment toward Rome that Newman had given the Church of England. These ulterior aims lent to 'Hypatia' a modern tone, making out of it a novel of aggressive purpose. But they stood in the way of real history. What purports to be historical fact in 'Hypatia' Leslie Stephen [1] has pronounced a bubble that bursts on the most delicate touch; the Church of Rome as therein represented is not the church of the fifth century, and the Goths are mythical. Certainly no one should quarrel with a romancer for misrepresenting history, provided his purpose is not ethical, and that he states frankly that he is not writing history. Scott, for example, was quick to acknowledge that 'Ivanhoe' was Froissart modernized. But Kingsley asserted that, even where he was not writing authentic history, he was true to the life, the manners, and the spirit of the fifth century. Whatever may have been their immediate effect, Kingsley's hysterics against Romanism are now gay comedy, giving a pleasing relish to 'Hypatia.' When Kingsley denounced the ancient church, he also weakened faith in the church he adored. Such is the irony of purpose. 'Hypatia,' like Schiller's poem, is a beautiful lament over the passing of the gods.

Thackeray, as a boy, read his 'dear Walter Scott'; in mature life, he burlesqued him, and then wrote 'Henry Esmond' (1852) and 'The Virginians' (1857–59). Thackeray stripped the muse of history of her mask and cothurnus, and requested her to lay aside the voice and manners of the stage. She may, if she likes, rehearse the doings of royalty and generals, but she must also tell of 'burning farms, wasted fields,

[1] 'Hours in a Library,' third series, London, 1879.

shrieking women, slaughtered sons and fathers, and drunken soldiery.' Thackeray denied her, too, all her usual adornments. There are in 'Esmond' no wanderings by the way into architecture, antiquities, sunrises, sunsets, fair prospects, and 'dearly beloved readers.' The men and women of the eighteenth century appear in his pages in their habit as they lived, whether the characters be historical, as Steele, Addison, Marlborough, and Wolfe; or whether they be purely fictitious, as Esmond, Beatrix, and the Castlewoods. It had been the aim of all the historical romancers to suggest the past by sprinkling their pages with obsolete words — *trow, weet, shoon, yclept, emprise,* etc. The attempts at a more accurate reproduction of old style than by taking these words from Spenser had not met with public favor, owing chiefly to the fact that the periods selected were in the Middle Ages, when the English language was in appearance quite different from what it is to-day. Since the age of Queen Anne our speech has undergone no important changes in grammar or in spelling. But the style of that period has a peculiar classic flavor, easily felt, with difficulty expressed, and with greater difficulty imitated, as every one knows who has been so bold as to try his hand at a *Spectator* paper. Thackeray caught precisely its spirit; he did not write like Addison or Steele or Bolingbroke, but as one of their friends and companions.

Just as in Ainsworth appeared Scott indirectly through Hugo, so in 'Esmond' may be observed Scott through Dumas. Dumas wrote history much as Defoe would have done, had Defoe followed the romantic revival instead of coming before it. Dumas made

history a background for imaginary adventure and
sword-play, originating a species of novel which the
French aptly call *le roman de cape et d'épée*. ' Esmond '
differs from the D'Artagnan romances in that it is
more faithful to the spirit of fact; otherwise it is
analogous. Two incidents of this novel, somewhat
in the manner of Dumas, criticism has long reckoned
among the very greatest in romance, for they are
strokes of genius. The one takes place at the dinner-
table of Prince Eugene in Lille, where, besides the
English officers, are present the ' Prince of Savoy,
the Electoral Prince of Hanover, and the envoys of
Prussia and Denmark.' General Webb, who has just
read the *London Gazette*, in which the Duke of Marlborough has not given him the deserved credit for the
victory of Wynendael, rises, draws his sword, thrusts
it through the *Gazette*, and, bending forward to his
superior officer, says with the utmost courtesy: ' Per-
mit me to hand it to your Grace.' The other incident
occurs in an upper chamber at Castlewood, when
Colonel Esmond and Frank Castlewood break their
swords in the presence of the Stuart Pretender, thus
denying him, and the colonel gives him the satisfac-
tion of a gentleman: —

' Eh bien, Vicomte,' says the young Prince, who was a boy,
and a French boy, ' il ne nous reste qu'une chose à faire ; ' he
placed his sword upon the table, and the fingers of his two
hands upon his breast : —' We have one more thing to do,' says
he ; ' you do not divine it ? ' He stretched out his arms : —
' *Embrassons nous !* '

3. *The Romance of War*

The romance of war as a deviation from the ordinary historical novel made its appearance in the second quarter of the nineteenth century, when the imagination began to clothe the events which led up to Waterloo in the high colors of a romance, of which the heroes were Napoleon and Wellington. It is the historical novel as the soldier writes it, or one who has come into contact with some phase of military life; its characters are privates and minor officers, with now and then a glimpse at a general; and its scenes are in the barrack and the camp, and on the battle-field. The flow of military autobiographies and fictions is very noticeable in 1825, when appeared the anonymous 'Ned Clinton,' and G. R. Gleig's 'Subaltern' (*Blackwood's Magazine*), both of which deal with Wellington in Spain. The stream was fed by W. H. Maxwell, Charles Lever, and James Grant; the first was an Irishman; the second, born in Dublin, was Irish on the maternal side; and the last was a Scotchman. Not aspiring to a regularly constructed novel, Maxwell wrote tales more or less connected and usually autobiographic in appearance. It was his way to begin with pictures of the wild life in the extreme west of Ireland, where he passed many years, enjoying a church living without the burden of a congregation; to bring on the scene an English regiment stationed at Connemara for the purpose of dislodging illicit distillers of 'dew' among the mountains, and then to go over to the Continent with his Englishmen and Irishmen, to Spain and to Waterloo. Representative of his work are ' Stories of Waterloo '

(1834) and 'The Bivouac, or Stories of the Peninsular War' (1837). Lever was a friend of Maxwell, and from him he took his cue of writing sketches rather than novels. The points of departure were greater length and greater stress on the humorous anecdote. There was no limit to the funny stories and hoaxes Lever was able to reel off at will in 'Harry Lorrequer,' 'Charles O'Malley,' and 'Tom Burke of Ours.'

Grant wrote with more attention to structure. The first of his novels, 'The Romance of War, or the Highlanders in Spain' (1845), opens with scenes of love-making in Perthshire; the hero serves as ensign in the ninety-second regiment, or Gordon Highlanders, during the Peninsular campaign and later at Waterloo; and, after a career of bravery, duelling, and flirtation, he returns to Scotland, marries Alice, and is 'the happiest of men.' By the way are detailed accounts of Spanish manners, and some good sketches of typical Spanish character. The battle scenes are attempts to narrate what really happened; the fiction is in the love-romance and the personal affairs and experiences of the hero when off duty. 'The Romance of War' was the best work of its kind that had yet been written; in it the military novel got a distinct form, and on its scaffolding Grant constructed fifty other popular histories.

4. *James Fenimore Cooper, and the Romance of the Forest and the Sea*

When the romantic wave reached the United States, the possibility of an American historical novel was discussed to the conclusion that America had no history before the Revolution, and that the events of that struggle were too recent for treatment. Still, there were some essays at history. In 1792, the Rev. Jeremy Belknap published an American tale entitled 'The Foresters,' in which is given an allegorical account of the colonial settlements. Mr. Bull is represented as dividing a vast forest among his fourteen servants, John Cod-line, Peter Bull-frog, etc., who are always quarrelling with their neighbors on the north and on the south — Mr. Lewis and Mr. Strut. Equally curious is 'The Asylum; or Alonzo and Melissa' (1811), by Isaac Mitchell. It belongs to the class of half-Gothic and half-historical tales that were then appearing in England, and its title would indicate a specific connection with Sophia Lee's 'Recess.' It has a castle, situated in western Connecticut, in which the heroine is locked up to be frightened by dark shadows, strange footsteps and whisperings, and balls of fire rolling through the halls. It describes in flamboyant language colonial manners just before the Revolution, and a sea fight between the British and the Americans, in which, after 'the decks were piled with carnage and the scuppers spouted blood,' the British struck their colors and their frigate was gloriously sunk. The historical character we see most of is Dr. Franklin, giving the good advice of 'Poor Richard' to the hero, who is a graduate of Yale college. Washington Irving, who in 'Knickerbocker's History of New York' (1809) worked the vein opened by Belknap, left two thoroughly American pieces, 'Rip Van Winkle' and 'The Legend of Sleepy Hollow.' Cooper's 'Spy' (1821), which at once attained a world-wide fame, and has kept it, is written on the plan of Defoe's 'Memoirs of a Cavalier.' It is a romance

of the Revolution, with meagre historical foundation. At genuinely historical work, requiring the
examination of historical documents, Cooper was,
so far as posterity is concerned, an utter failure.
'Lionel Lincoln,' with its graphic and accurate description of the battle of Bunker Hill, is no longer read.
Hawthorne did some perfect work in the historical
sketch, as in 'The Gray Champion' and 'Endicott and
the Red Cross.' More than this he did not attempt.

Though the writers in the United States thus accomplished very little in history, in pure romance
they, however, not only did respectable work, but in
some ways excelled their British cousins. Some years
before the Revolution, settlers in Virginia and the
Carolinas broke through the passes of the Blue Ridge
into Kentucky and Tennessee. This westward movement, impeded by the outbreak of the Revolution,
reappeared after the peace of 1783, in emigration from
New England to western New York and Ohio. Another
check came with the war of 1812. At its close the
children of the first wave of emigration pushed farther
on, spreading along the river valleys of the limitless
West. This frontier life early found its way into
American literature, as in Charles Brockden Brown.
Its romance was immortalized by James Fenimore
Cooper, in 'The Leather-Stocking Tales,' comprising
'The Pioneers' (1823), 'The Last of the Mohicans'
(1826), 'The Prairie' (1827), 'The Pathfinder' (1840),
and 'The Deerslayer' (1841). Cooper passed his
youth in the border village of Cooperstown, on Otsego Lake, by the source of the Susquehanna. 'The
Pioneers' is a reminiscence of his boyhood, and must
be taken as a realistic picture of what he had seen.

In the other Leather-Stocking stories, the scene changes
to Glens Falls, the great prairies of the middle West,
Lake Ontario, and back to Otsego Lake.   They all
bear some date, but in reality they have no very
precise historical background.   It is sufficient to place
them somewhere in the eighteenth century.   Except
'The Pioneers,' they are all, in Cooper's phrase, pure
legends.

Cooper was a poet.   How tame is Mrs. Radcliffe's
or Charlotte Smith's romancing of the forests, when
compared with that of the man who had lived in them.
The aspects of the North American forests that most
impressed Cooper were their boundlessness and their
mystery.   He noted their changes, their ever varying
tints in light and shade, the rich and glorious coloring
of an ocean of leaves in an autumn sunset, their
sinister darkness as the storm-cloud hovers over them,
the moaning of mighty branches, the crash of some
falling giant and the reverberation through the wilder-
ness, and the mountain in flames.   What he hated
was the woodman's axe.   Of these boundless, mysterious, living forests, Cooper created two captivating
inhabitants, Chingachgook and Nathaniel Bumppo,
otherwise known, from his long deerskin leggings, as
Leather-Stocking.   They are constructed on a plan
which, though the romancer had often tried it, had
never been very successful, that of uniting in one person the characteristics of two races.   Chingachgook is
an Indian who in his intercourse with the English settlers acquires some of the best qualities of his new associates, and preserves at the same time the endurance,
fortitude, and scalp-loving instincts of the savage
state.   Leather-Stocking Cooper followed in detail after

detail from youth to old age. In 'The Deerslayer' he appears as a mere boy. Here he shoots his first Indian, and with Chingachgook enters upon his first war-path; he is first tempted by a scarlet woman, and triumphs, telling her that his only sweetheart is in the soft rain, the blue heavens, and the sweet springs where he slakes his thirst. In 'The Last of the Mohicans' he is in the prime of youth, and, because of his sure shot, is known as Hawkeye. He is subtle in dealing with his enemies, skilful in discovering and following up the trail, and alert for all the sounds of the woods. In 'The Pathfinder,' still a young man, he is in love with Mabel Dunham, the most lovable of Cooper's heroines, who is given to Jasper as a more fitting match. In 'The Pioneers' he appears as an old man above seventy; shouldering his gun and calling his dog, he bids farewell to his friends and turns his face toward the Great Lakes. In 'The Prairie' he is invested with great dignity and tenderness. Here he is introduced as a trapper in the region of the upper Missouri, driven thence by the advance of civilization. Though he is over eighty years old, his limbs stiff and his strength failing, he is still a good shot. Finally death comes. Standing erect with his face toward the setting sun, he responds in clear voice to the summons from cloud and sky. Leather-Stocking, possessing all the virtues and none of the vices of two races, is thus the counterpart of Chingachgook. He is brave, truthful, honorable, clean in his life, of a noble piety, and a lover of the forest and the chase. In his highest idealization he never passes the bounds of what the imagination grants as possible. Moreover, he is the most complete

portrait in fiction. Since Cooper's time the novel of
frontier life has kept pace with the progress of civilization westward. Sketches more realistic than his have
been written by Bret Harte and Owen Wister; the
Indian likewise has been poetized by others. But no
writer, though there have been many experiments, of
which may be cited John Galt's 'Lawrie Todd' and
Gustave Aimard's 'Last of the Incas,' has ever thrown
Cooper's magic veil over the American forests and
lakes.

Between Smollett's 'Roderick Random' (1748) and
Scott's 'Pirate' (1822), there appeared no tale of the
sea. It is true there were in this interval many
stories of adventure that were represented as taking
place in part on the ocean, but they made no pretence
to portraying the life of the sea in those respects
wherein it differs from life on land. The rude and
uncouth seaman and his impoverished family in an
English port town, Jane Austen described in the perfection of her art, but she knew better than to venture on an unknown ocean. Moreover, a man who
picks up 'The Pirate' expecting a sea story will be
disappointed. It is a romanced account of the manners and superstitions of the Scotch and the Norse
inhabitants of the Shetlands. The sea runs up into
moonlit bays; it lashes the cliffs in storm; a vessel
is wrecked, and one man rescued; a whale is left by
the tide within the bar, and gets away from the land-
men who try to capture him; a brig is boarded by
pirates, and a sea fight is viewed through a spy-glass.
These scenes are all in the story that relate to the
sea.

As a direct challenge to the seamanship of Scott,

Cooper wrote 'The Pilot' (1824). For this work he was excellently prepared, for he had served as midshipman in the American navy. His aim was to show just how a ship is managed in combat, and in storm off a dangerous coast; and that he did in scenes as thrilling as those in his Indian romances. The one great character of the story is the coxswain Long Tom Coffin, who was born on the sea, and cared for no land except a little mud-flat on which to grow vegetables. All the brutality and coarseness of seamen Cooper kept well in the background. In distinction from 'Roderick Random,' 'The Pilot' is the romance of the ocean.

Of the numerous imitations of Cooper the best were 'Tom Cringle's Log' and 'The Cruise of the Midge,' by Michael Scott. Eugène Sue, who had served as surgeon in the French navy, began his literary career with five sea tales produced in rapid succession, and several of his countrymen followed him. Germany also soon had Coopers as well as Sir Walter Scotts. The older form of sea adventure, as written by Smollett, was revived by Frederick Marryat, who had been a naval officer during the Napoleonic wars. 'Peter Simple' (1834), which has been the most popular of his stories, though hard pushed by 'Mr. Midshipman Easy' (1836), is a fair specimen of his work. It is pervaded with the spirit of fun for which there was no place in Cooper's romances, and is interspersed with yarns of the Baron Munchausen order. Marryat's freshest scenes are his pictures of life in the West Indies, as the negro ball to which only the *élite* are invited. His most amusing characters are Captain Kearney

and the boatswain Chucks. The former, who can
never tell the truth, dies with a lie on his lips, and
leaves directions for his epitaph, which is to begin
thus: 'Here *lies* Captain Kearney.' The latter, half
gentleman and half blackguard, betrays his double
character in his speech when giving his orders to his
subordinates, a rhetorical device partaking almost of
inspiration.

Charles Kingsley placed the sea tale in an historical setting.   Westward Ho!' (1855) is in some
respects similar to Thackeray's work in 'Esmond.'
Kingsley sought to clothe his narrative in Elizabethan prose.   He affected long parenthetical sentences; used the second person singular of the verb
in direct address, and sometimes dared to clip off the
d's of the past participles of weak verbs.   The great-
ness of the romance is because of its reproduction
of the buccaneer spirit of the Elizabethan age.   Most
graphic is Kingsley's account of the stir and bustle
when a captain is getting ready to embark for the
west.   Sir Humphrey Gilbert is about to set sail from
Plymouth; he has two hundred and sixty men, ship-
wrights, masons, carpenters, and mineral men who
know gold when they see it, and can refine it too.
There is a goodly store, too, of musical instruments
and morris-dancers and hobby-horses, to allure and
charm the savages.   Queen Elizabeth sends down
her greeting to Sir Humphrey just before he weighs
anchor, bidding him 'great good hap and safety,' and
requesting that he send up to London his portrait just
painted by a Plymouth artist.   Sir Walter Raleigh
bears the message from her Majesty, accompanies
the fleet on the first day's sail, and would like

to go farther, but does not dare, for he has the per-emptory command of his queen to return with the portrait at once. Of the Elizabethan worthies Kings-ley makes live once more, Sir Richard Grenville is the most carefully studied; he is the high-minded and heroic captain of Raleigh's 'Revenge': —

Men said that he was proud, but he could not look around him without having something to be proud of; that he was stern and harsh to his sailors, but it was only when he saw in them any taint of cowardice or falsehood; that he was subject, at moments, to such fearful fits of rage, that he had been seen to snatch the glasses from the table, grind them to pieces in his teeth, and swallow them, but that was only when his indignation had been aroused by some tale of cruelty or oppression.

5. *The Renovation of Gothic Romance*

The Gothic romance, the superstitious elements of which had been incorporated for minor effects into 'Waverley,' continued to exist, taking the form of the tale of terror, the detective story, and the fantasy, just as it had done before Scott. From Mrs. Radcliffe down to 1850, the novelists were exceedingly few who did not on occasion excite their readers by the strange and the marvellous, or frighten them by some sort of supernatural or bloody performance. Leigh Hunt wrote in 1819: 'A man who does not contribute his quota of grim story nowadays, seems hardly free of the republic of letters.' Shelley produced two 'terrific' pieces, and then gave over the occupation to his wife. The inability to rival Mrs. Mary Shelley was one of the woes of Lord Byron. No better evidence is there of the hold Gothic machinery had on the imagination than the fact that it was resorted to as an embellishment of the political treatise. The majestic ghost of Sir Thomas More called upon Robert Southey at Keswick, and through the watches of the night held long conversations with him on the present state of society.[1] What the tale of horror needed before it could be fully effective was a thorough overhauling and a redecoration. It was too long, and it had not found its art.

The work of renovation began with Charles Robert Maturin, in his time a well-known Irish clergyman and *littérateur*. The tale in which he displayed his finer imaginative power is 'Melmoth the Wanderer' (1820). He eliminated from the Radcliffe romance the 'sentimental miss who luxuriates in the rich and weeping softness of a watery landscape,' and depended on fear as his sole motive. In many scenes, resembling the punishments in the lower circles of Dante's 'Inferno,' he reached, if not terror, the borderland where horror becomes terror. Such is the incarceration of a young monk among serpents, whose 'cold and bloating' forms crawl over him, and the starvation and madness of lovers in a subterranean prison. But the incoherency and extreme length of the romance have long since overwhelmed it; one of the last references to it being Thackeray's, who compared Goethe's eye to Melmoth's.

Four years after the publication of 'Melmoth,' the presence of German romance is distinctly visible in English romantic fiction. It had indeed made its appearance previously. 'Monk' Lewis and Charles Brockden Brown had appropriated German material, and the German romanticists had exerted an influence

---

[1] 'Colloquies on Society,' 1829.

on Scott. The Germans were the first to see how futile are three or four volumes of horror piled upon horror, strangulations, and shrieking statues. Ludwig Tieck and Ernst Hoffmann cut their fantasies down to the brief tale, of from fifty to a hundred pages; and Washington Irving imported the German tale, with a further cutting, into England and America. But except in this novelty of form, Irving's 'Tales of a Traveller' (1824) are in no way remarkable. Irving was too much of a common-sense realist to deal with superstition. His moving portraits, phantom faces, and dancing furniture were in intention comic, and always carried an obvious explanation. On the other hand, his Addisonian taste shielded him from all grossness.

Bulwer-Lytton humanized Gothic art and evoked its poetry. In the 'Pilgrims of the Rhine' (1834), he brought on the scene the swarms of English fairies that had been sleeping in the flowers and under the leaves ever since Shakespeare and Drayton had dreamed of them. They go on a visit to the fairies of Rhineland, and there in 'cool caverns,' talk, banter, woo, and marry. In 'Zanoni' (1842) Bulwer went deep into the mysteries of the Rosicrucians. According to their theory earth and air are filled with supernatural beings which preside over the destinies of man and nature. Those initiated into the Rosicrucian brotherhood are able to penetrate the veil that separates crude phenomena from this spiritual world, and to win from the insight the secret of eternal youth. But to preserve the clear vision and the freshness of youth, the initiated must keep his heart free from mortal passions. The process of initiation is somewhat obscure, but the candidate must come into the presence of an exacting demon and swear a 'horrible oath,' the exact purport of which is kept secret from the reader. The older romancers — Godwin, Shelley, and then Maturin — made free use of Rosicrucian doctrines, laying particular stress upon the demon. Bulwer has very little to say about this malignant gentleman, being more interested in the Rosicrucian himself, who, in this instance something like five thousand years old, becomes acquainted with a beautiful opera singer, marries her, loses his phenomena-piercing vision, and falls a victim to the Reign of Terror. 'Zanoni' has been much read by theosophists, who see in it a foreshadowing of their doctrine of reincarnation.

Bulwer-Lytton was in aspiration a philosopher fashioning Gothic material to modern purposes; Edgar Allan Poe has been called a born Goth. Whatever he touched was at once imbued with Gothic beauty, Gothic blood, and Gothic fear. Eastern and Renaissance luxuriousness he painted with the startling brilliancy of Beckford, and concealed within it the sting of poison and death. He writes a sea-tale, to depict not so much the manners of the sea, as the horrors of mutiny, starvation, and cannibalism. He writes a tale of adventure in the realistic style of Defoe, and the adventure is a descent into the Maelström. He describes a search for hidden treasure, and the guide is a madman. He constructs a finer detective story than was in the power of Godwin, Brown, or Hoffmann, but is satisfied only when he has made graphic those details of the crime which they passed over. He does not stop with the burial of the dead; he places you at midnight in a room where you hear the first faint movements of the cataleptic in the copper vault beneath, then the rending asunder of the coffin, the grating of massive doors; and then the emaciated figure of Lady Madeline stands before you in her shroud spotted with the blood of her struggles. The real power of the physically horrible, hints of which there were in Maturin, was never revealed until Poe revealed it. Three of his tales are the perfection of Gothic art. All romances of the terror of death are dull grays before the coloring of ' The Masque of the Red Death' (*Graham's Magazine*, 1842); the mood of utter desolation has been nowhere else so completely expressed as in ' The Fall of the House of Usher' (1840), nor of forlornness as in ' Ligeia' (1840).

Within the circumscribed limits of the short story, Poe was a consummate artist when he chose to be. It was a dictum of his, in accord with a very common practice of Hoffmann and Irving, that no story should be too long to be read at one sitting. Moreover, he conveyed the impression that it was his custom to begin with the dénouement, and to work backward just as the Chinese write their books. Whether or not he proceeded in just this way, there can be no doubt that, before writing a sentence of his finest tales, he knew when and how he was to end. None of the nineteenth-century novelists after Jane Austen, and none of Poe's contemporaries except Hawthorne, wrought with so great care. His masterpiece in structure is ' The Fall of the House of Usher.' It contains not the slightest distracting detail; the house, its ill-fated occupants, the dreary landscape, the chill autumn days, are all in unison, and the narrative, in perfect harmony with the theme, moves on in a solemn and magnificent march to the close, when the cracked walls burst asunder, and in a moment lie buried beneath the stagnant tarn.

Nothing is more remarkable about Poe than his ability to interest permanently without an appeal to the moral nature. Of all his tales, not more than five lay any pretence whatever to this appeal, and even in these instances the attention is won by his melodrama or superb imagination. Surely no one looks to Poe for a probing of the conscience or for moral guidance. The very greatest writers have never thus laid hold of the supernatural or the supermortal in and for itself, but as a forcible means of representing excited or diseased states of the imagination, and their narrative, without being openly didactic, carries with it a moral inference. Corroborative of this statement, at once come to mind the royal ghost that haunted the palace of Elsinore, the blood-sprinkled hand of Lady Macbeth, and 'The Rime of the Ancient Mariner.' To this fact Leigh Hunt called the attention of Gothic romancers, and in these words: 'A ghost story, to be a good one, should unite as much as possible objects such as they are in life with a preternatural spirit. And to be a perfect one, — at least, to add to the other utility of excitement a moral utility.'

To illustrate his criticism, he wrote, 'A Tale for a Chimney Corner,' which possesses the ethical and realistic qualities he insisted upon, but none of the excitement. It has, however, an importance in the history of Gothic romance, in that it quietly ushers in the ideal of Hawthorne. Nearly all the Gothic machinery of Walpole, Mrs. Radcliffe, and Godwin is to be found in this Puritan : high winds, slamming doors, moonlight and starlight, magic and witchcraft, mysterious portraits, transformations, malignant beings, the elixir of life, the skeleton, the funeral, and the corpse in its shroud. To these sources of excitement were added, as time went on, mesmerism and clairvoyance. The novelty of Hawthorne's work is in his treatment. Like Shakespeare, he offers only a partial explanation of his unusual phenomena or none at all. Most unconventional is his use of witchcraft, as was pointed out by Poe, in 'The Hollow of Three Hills,' where to the imagination of the woman of sin, as she lays her head upon the witch's knees beneath the magic cloak, distant scenes of sorrow for which she is responsible are conveyed, not by viewing them in a magic mirror, but by the subtle sense of sound. And almost equally novel is the use made of the fountain of youth in 'Dr. Heidegger's Experiment.' The persecuting demon of romance, when he appears in Hawthorne's pages under the name of Roger Chillingworth, or the Spectre of the Catacomb, is a personification of the mistakes, misfortunes, and sins of our past life, which will not out of our imagination. The transformations — Pearl from a capricious, elfish being into a sober woman, and Donatello from a thoughtless, voluptuous animal into a man who feels the sad weight of humanity — have their analogies in real life. The supernatural world was with Hawthorne but the inner world of the conscience.

The ethical import of his narrative is always conveyed by means of a fanciful symbolism. The embroidered 𝔄 that is hung about Hester Prynne's neck, the red stigma over Arthur Dimmesdale's heart, and Pearl in scarlet dress, are obviously symbolical. The black veil with which a Puritan minister conceals his face is the shadow of a dark deed. Donatello's hair-tipped ears are suggestions of his animalism. More-over, Hawthorne was inclined to interpret figuratively events, nature, and art. Little Pearl runs from her mother and cannot be coaxed to return; that is typical of a moral gulf separating them. The sunless wood in which Hester stands alone images a moral solitude. Light streaming through the painted windows of a Gothic church is a foretaste of the 'glories of the better world.' As Hawthorne views a half-finished bust, and sees the human face struggling to get out of the marble, he remarks: 'As this bust in the block of marble, so does our individual fate exist in the limestone of time.' It has been said that Poe was a myth maker; Hawthorne likewise built up his own myths, and then he allegorized them like Bacon, turn-ing them into apologues. Even the allegorical inter-pretation sometimes given to 'The Marble Faun' is not to be ridiculed, for the allegory is there. What-ever may have been the origin of language, it has now become, in its common use, a direct representation of things, ideas, and feelings. Hawthorne did not always so treat it, but rather conceived of it as a system of hieroglyphics; a secret he does not call a secret, 'it is a wild, venomous thing' imprisoned in the heart. This is the way of Spenser.

The story of Hawthorne is only half told when we say he refined Gothic art and fashioned it to high ethical purposes. As in the case of Poe, one of his great charms is his workmanship in structure and style. In the technique of the short tale, Poe was at least his equal; in the longer tale, where Poe left many loose ends, Hawthorne succeeded twice — in 'The Scarlet Letter' (1850) and 'The House of the Seven Gables' (1851). Poe modelled his style on Defoe and De Quincey, now suggesting the one and now the other. Hawthorne by laborious practice acquired a more individual style; the good taste of Addison and Irving are visible in it, and the brooding and dreamy fancy of Tieck, disguised however in the fusion.

In literary history the precise time order of events is not always the precise logical order. The long vista of the purely Gothic romance, at whose entrance stands the blood-stained castle of Otranto, is closed by a storm and passion beaten house on the Yorkshire moors. The motive of Emily Brontë's 'Wuthering Heights' (1847) is vengeance. Relieved of all impertinences of time and place, the situation is this: A man sits down and reflects: I was born in shame; men have denied me education; and they have taken from me the woman I loved, on the ground that I am unworthy of her. I am not responsible for being what I am; I did not preside over my birth; the demon within me that I tried to suppress, others loosed from his bands. The vengeance that the Almighty has allowed to sleep I myself will wake and wreak upon those who have wronged me, and upon their children. After years of appalling success in meting out the punishment of a Jehovah, one obstacle stands in the way to the consummation of the entire scheme of revenge. Face to face with defeat, the will loses none of its tension; the defier of gods and men starves

himself into delirium and death; his eyes that will
not close still glare in exultation, and his lip is curled
in a sneer, displaying sharp white teeth beneath. He
is placed in the ground near the woman the side of
whose coffin he had long ago in his mad grief torn
away, that he might lie the closer to her. Beyond
the madness and terror of 'Wuthering Heights,'
romantic fiction has never gone. Its spiritual counterpart in real life is Emily Brontë, who preserved
her inexorable will far into the day on which she
died.

CHAPTER V

THE REALISTIC REACTION

1. *The Minor Humorists and the Author of 'Pickwick.'*

THOUGH Scott dominated the world of fiction so long as he lived and was a directing influence for nearly two decades after his death, yet even during the greatest popularity of Waverley, there were novelists of other aims. Their subject was not primarily history and superstition, but contemporary manners, or the manners of their youth. They were not, according to present canons, realists, for they commonly recombined the matter of real life for instruction, farce, or satire; and yet their efforts made for realism. To begin with, their product was not of the first grade, but in course of time Dickens came, who built his great romances on their tacitly assumed artistic principles.

All along his career Scott was accompanied by Scotch novelists who depicted the humorous side of Scotch life without the historical setting or with only patches of it. Among them were Susan Ferrier, John Galt, and Dr. David Macbeth Moir. Miss Ferrier was a friend of Scott's, and one whom in his latter days he liked to entertain at Abbotsford, as she was 'full of humor and exceedingly ready at repartee.' Her three novels, 'Marriage' (1818), 'The Inheritance' (1824), and 'Destiny' (1831), conceived

168

in the spirit of broad comedy, have now the appearance of complementing, in the way of humor, Scott's romances of Scotland. Historical rarely and only in episodes, Miss Ferrier held herself closely to contemporary society. Her ideal of a novel seems to have been Miss Edgeworth's 'Absentee,' for her scenes alternate between London and the Western Highlands. The heroine of her first novel (and the main situations in her other two are similar) is a spoilt, languishing English girl of fashionable society, who is transported with a trio of pet dogs, 'the sweetest cherubs,' to a Highland castle, and compelled to live there for a time with a Scotch husband and his strange sisters and aunts. One exquisite piece of caricature Miss Ferrier added to fiction; that of the woman who is always quoting the opinions of an absent friend; in 'The Inheritance' she appears, — the cool, staring, and talkative Miss Pratt, who tells you what her nephew Anthony Whyte says, what Anthony Whyte does, and what Anthony Whyte likes. That Anthony Whyte is one of the redundancies of Miss Pratt's imagination.

John Galt was a more prolific writer. The first novel he published, 'The Ayrshire Legatees' (*Blackwood's*, 1820), put together on the plan of 'Humphry Clinker,' consists of a bundle of letters from an Ayrshire clergyman and his family to friends at home. Its humor arises from a Scotchman's comments on London sights and amusements. 'The Annals of the Parish' (1821) is the novel of Galt's most written about by his contemporaries; and it is surely one of his most characteristic and original productions. It is a chronicle history of an Ayrshire village minister,

Mr. Micah Balwhidder, a kind-hearted and Quixotic Scotch Dr. Primrose. Charming is the quiet humor of Balwhidder, as he records the events of his long reign, sketching the characters of his three wives, and telling of his perplexities, and the disturbances that came to his parish with smuggling and its consequent tea-drinking, with the American war, and with the invasion of utilitarianism, rationalism, the meeting-house, and the spinning-jenny. The thread of gold running through 'The Annals' is the story of the industry and the heroism of Mrs. Malcolm, 'the widow of a Clyde shipmaster, that was lost at sea with his vessel.' Her daughters she lived to see well married, and her sons well placed. Only one grief came to her in her resigned old age, — the loss of a son who died gallantly fighting the French on the sea. 'Her morning was raw, and a sore blight fell upon her fortunes, but the sun looked out on her midday, and her evening closed loun and warm, and the stars of the firmament, that are the eyes of Heaven, beamed, as it were, with gladness when she lay down to sleep the sleep of rest.' Equally delightful is 'The Provost' (*Blackwood's Magazine,* 1822), a companion-piece to 'The Annals.' These chronicles their author regarded as 'treatises on the history of society in the West of Scotland during the reign of George the Third.' More conventional in form is 'The Entail' (1823), a history of three generations of Scotch lairds. Here Galt went into more minute and picturesque detail on Scotch customs, and more deeply than elsewhere into the harder side of Scotch character. Though Galt is not of the great masters of fiction, he laid bare the heart of Scotland as only Burns had done. Dr. Moir

was a friend and collaborator of Galt's. The outcome
of the literary friendship was 'The Autobiography of
Mansie Wauch' (1828); which is an account of the life
and adventures of an industrious and simple-minded
tailor of Dalkeith. The humor of the piece is of that
convivial kind to which the contemporary 'Noctes
Ambrosianæ' owed their very great popularity. Its
truest and simplest pathos is in a sketch of Mansie's
apprentice, who comes out of 'the howes of the Lammermoor hills,' and, yearning for the blithe scenes and
'kent faces' he has left behind, pines away in the village
shop, and at length dies broken-hearted on the way to
his 'ain hame.' Galt and Moir were the pioneers in
what since the advent of Mr. J. M. Barrie and Mr.
John Watson has been called kailyard fiction, though
the happy epithet conveys a measure of depreciation
to which every sane critic must demur.

Older types of the novel of humor still persisted.
The subdued comedy of Jane Austen was for a long
time the least influential. Scott himself imitated her
in 'St. Ronan's Well'; Mary Mitford had in mind her
'delicious novels' when she composed the sympathetic
sketches entitled 'Our Village' (1824–32), and traces
of Jane Austen are in Harriet Martineau's 'Five Years
of Youth, or Sense and Sentiment' (1831). 'Northanger Abbey' was one of a group of anti-romances, of
which another clever specimen was E. S. Barrett's
'Adventures of Cherubina' (1813). Thomas Love Peacock, in 'Nightmare Abbey' (1818), and 'Crotchet
Castle' (1831), extended burlesque to all forms of
contemporary romance, whether in verse or prose,
taking as a text, 'The Devil has come among us.'
The Oriental tale became again one of the fashions;

but reverted to what it was before Beckford. In it as now written, a Gil Blas was put through a series of laughable adventures in the East; or, somewhat after the manner of Goldsmith's 'Citizen of the World,' the Persian ambassador with his retinue invaded England. The funniest of the Oriental tales were James Morier's 'Hajji Baba of Ispahan' (1823) and 'Hajji Baba in England' (1828). Maria Edgeworth lived till 1849, and continued to publish; her 'Ormond' (1817) being nearly as good an Irish tale as 'The Absentee.' The humor and pathos of the Irishman at home she made an inexhaustible source of delight. Miss Sydney Owenson (Lady Morgan), who was much under the influence of Madame de Staël, wrote in hysterics of the O'Donnels, the O'Briens, and the O'Flaherties; while the Irish novel preserved its steadier tone in the sketches of the Banim brothers (John and Michael), and William Carleton. Indeed, the severest realism of the period is to be found in Carleton's 'Hedge School' and 'Poor Scholar,' of the collection known as 'Traits and Stories of the Irish Peasantry.' Samuel Lover in 'Handy Andy' (1842) wrote the broad comedy of Irish life; and Charles Lever caricatured the Irish dragoon.

Outside the Irish story, Maria Edgeworth was a force of considerable magnitude. Her 'Belinda' and Frances Burney's 'Cecilia' were the earlier types of two extraordinary pieces of literary abandon by Benjamin Disraeli and Bulwer-Lytton. The former's 'Vivian Grey' (first part, 1826) was written to startle by its brilliant and unrestrained cynicism. Vivian is a smart stripling of no real attainments, who tries the experiment of rising in the world by playing the part of an intellectual Don Juan. If a young lord has just published a poem, he will tell him that Goethe has reviewed it in the last number of *The Weimar Literary Gazette*, and add, 'It is really delightful to see the oldest poet of Europe dilating on the brilliancy of a new star on the poetic horizon.' If a sentimental miss is collecting autographs, he will give her offhand Washington Irving's, and then ask: 'Shall I write any more? One of Sir Walter's, or Mr. Southey's, or Mr. Milman's or Mr. Disraeli's? or shall I sprawl a Byron?' If she encourages his addresses, he will fascinate and frighten her by proving what an admirable plan it would be for all younger brothers (he is a younger brother) to sell themselves to the devil; and in a jugglery with words for which she is unprepared, he will bring her to the point of proposing to him, just as she is called from the veranda. By his coolness, impudence, and flattery, Vivian pushes his way into society, invited or uninvited, and becomes the agent of a political coalition which seems about to oust the ministry, when his intellectual legerdemain is exposed, and the impostor makes his exit to the Continent. Bulwer's pyrotechnic display in 'Pelham' (1828) is no less dazzling. The hero is in his externals a new ideal of a gentleman. At a time when the fop let his hair fall in ringlets to his shoulders, covered his shirt-front with a galaxy of studs, and threw a heavy chain around his neck; and browns, greens, and blues were the fashion in coats, — Pelham casts aside his jewellery, brushes out his curls, puts on black waistcoat and black trousers, and steps into a Cheltenham drawing-room, to be stared at, to mystify, and astound by his reckless talk, and to commit, without the least danger of discovery, the delightful blunder of speaking of Hesiod as an imitator of Shenstone. Entering politics, Pelham has a hand in driving out the Tories and in bringing in the Whigs, but through the ingratitude of the new Premier, whom he has brilliantly served, he misses what he was aiming at—a seat in Parliament.[1]

The novel of high life that thus skimmed the surface of things fell into the hands of women, and degenerated into trash and rhapsody. The number of these fashionable fictions that poured from the press during the thirties and immediately thereafter, I do not dare estimate. To Carlyle they appeared as 'shiploads.' The best of the class are the one hundred or more novels and tales written by Mrs. Catherine Gore between 1824 and 1862. About many of them that have come in my way is an air of profound learning. Not infrequently three languages are represented in a motto standing at the head of a chapter; while the language within is a mixture of aristocratic English and stock French phrases. Mrs. Gore's subject was commonly club life, ennui, fribbledom, and the political questions of the hour. The writer who had rejuvenated this kind of fiction, and given it a political bias, transformed it. Disraeli's 'Coningsby' (1844) is a remarkable piece of plausible reasoning. In it, the relations of Church and State, parliamentary

---

[1] 'There is "Pelham," it is true, which the writer of these lines has seen a Jewess reading in the Steppe of Debreczin, and which a young Prussian baron, a great traveller, whom he met at Constantinople in '44, told him he always carried in his valise.'—Geo. Borrow, Appendix to 'Romany Rye.'

abuses, the failure of utilitarianism, the part a popular
press should play as an educating force, and ways of
invigorating a weakened royalty and a weakened aristocracy, were all shrewdly canvassed by a wise and
magnanimous Hebrew; and a new programme was
announced as a guide to the Young English party,
of which Disraeli was the head. With this publication, the political novel which had grown out of the
older fashionable tale was established and came
into vogue.

Between 1820 and 1840, society had its jester
in Theodore Hook. He is the Mr. Gay of Disraeli's 'Coningsby,' who is invited to dinner parties
for his stories that make the guests hold their sides
and roll under the table, and the Mr. Wagg of
'Pendennis,' who goes about among 'the fashionables
and eccentrics,' and then cuts them up in his effusions.
These personalities, which run all through 'Sayings
and Doings' (1824-30), and gave them a high flavor
to his contemporaries, are now fast growing indistinct; and Hook appears as a trafficker in hoaxes and
word-plays. Of 'Sayings and Doings,' 'Gervase
Skinner' may be read as an example of Hook's
manner. Skinner is 'a skinflint on principle,' who by
mistake is imprisoned in a lunatic asylum, 'clipped,
washed, and waistcoated,' and at length mulcted of
£2000, and an annuity of £150, by Mrs. Fuggleston
— an adventuress of the stage — and her jealous
husband. A scene especially noteworthy for what
Dickens afterward made out of it is the one where
Mrs. Fuggleston, 'uttering a piercing shriek,' falls
senseless into Skinner's arms, and is discovered lying
there. And a wholly new character is the loquacious

gentleman whose thought jumps the ruts of the conventional sentence. He first appeared in 'Gervase Skinner' as the stage-manager Kekewich, and afterward in 'Gilbert Gurney' and 'Jack Brag.' Kekewich is becoming enthusiastic over Mrs. Fuggleston, the actress : —

'Wonderful woman, sir!' said Kekewich; 'full of talent as an egg's full of meat — husband a stick — must have him — part of her articles — pity she married — fine creature, depend upon it — plays Ophelia in high style — finds her own dresses, silk stockings, and all — symmetrical figure, sweet temper, and coal-black hair, down to the small of her back — great hit for me — short life and a merry one — snapped up for the London houses — manager sent down a doctor of divinity and two physicians to see her at Leek — nabbed her — snapped her up like a lamb from my flock,' etc.

There was a time when everybody, from King George the Fourth down to the boys on the streets of London and New York, knew by heart the phrases of Pierce Egan. The production that gave him this popularity, extending from the highest to the lowest, was 'Life in London; or, The Day and Night Scenes of Jerry Hawthorn, Esq. And His Elegant Friend, Corinthian Tom, Accompanied by Bob Logic, The Oxonian, In Their Rambles and Sprees through the Metropolis.' The work appeared in monthly shilling numbers, beginning with July, 1821, and was illustrated by Cruikshank when at his very best. Three observations should be made on this novel. It is one of the very earliest examples of a series of sketches published in monthly parts; which was afterward the usual method of Dickens and Thackeray. Second, it introduces into fiction the cockneys, their haunts and their speech. The cockney called his watch *ticker, tattler,* or *thimble;* his spectacles, *four-eyes, barnacles,* or *green specs;* his brain, *upper-story;* his hat, *tile, castor,* or *uppercrust;* his umbrella, *spread, summercabbage,* or *water-plant;* and in his pronunciation interchanged the sounds of *v* and *w.* The humorous chronicler of his slang italicized or capitalized it, that it might not escape the most rapid of readers. There were also word-plays, palpable and obscure, from which a Shakespeare might have learned something; and that they might be grasped by the weakest of intellect, they, too, were made to stand out boldly in italics and capitals. Third, 'Tom and Jerry' is a picture-novel, a joint production of author and artist. The reader of it is uncertain whether the drawings are there to illustrate the text, or the text is there to explain the drawings. The novel was at once dramatized for London and New York; and many imitations followed, in which the scenes were sometimes in London and sometimes transferred to Paris. It was concluded by Egan himself in 1828, under the title, 'Finish to The Adventures of Tom, Jerry, and Logic in their Pursuits through Life in and out of London.' The gay adventuress of the first part commits suicide; Bob Logic dies in wretchedness; Corinthian Tom breaks his neck in a steeplechase; Jerry, now reforming, retires to the country for good, where he marries Miss Rosebud, and becomes a highly respected justice of the peace.

It was at this juncture, while the humorists were experimenting here and there, with burlesque, caricature, and cockney, that the young Charles Dickens published the first instalment of 'The Pickwick

Papers,' a little pamphlet of twenty-six pages of text, in pale green wrappers. The first number was issued in April, 1836; the twentieth and last in November, 1837. At first, Dickens wrote his text as the letterpress to Robert Seymour's 'cockney sporting plates,' evidently having in mind something like 'Tom and Jerry.' Seymour dying after the publication of the first number, Dickens changed his plan greatly, subordinating for the future the illustrations to the letterpress. Such in brief was the origin of 'Pickwick.' It soon became the topic of conversation among all classes, who laughed over its unexpected situations, and word-plays such as, 'Mr. Pickwick proceeded to put himself into his clothes, and his clothes into his portmanteau'; its phrases entered popular speech, where some of them, as 'in a Pickwickian sense,' still remain; in the course of time it found its way into nearly every European language; and historically considered, its publication was a turning-point in the course of English fiction.

'Pickwick' was not so well received by the critics, who saw in it imitations of contemporary humorists. There were indeed some echoes. Mr. Samuel Pickwick was in a way anticipated by 'the fat knight' in 'Tom and Jerry,' and at least hints for Wardle and the Dingley Dell adventures were naturally found in the country scenes at Squire Hawthorn's. Oddly enough, too, in view of the usual explanation for the name of Dickens's hero, the word Pickwick as the name of a place occurs in Egan. Hook certainly furnished Dickens with several minor incidents, situations, and one character. The misadventures of Pickwick have their analogues in the career of Skinflint. Particularly

close is the resemblance between Skinflint's being
found with Mrs. Fuggleston in his arms, and Mrs.
Bardell flinging herself into Pickwick's, 'with a cata-
ract of tears and a chorus of sobs.' Kekewich is the
first edition of Mr. Alfred Jingle. This process of
pointing out the sources of Dickens might be carried
much farther, were anything to be gained by it, back to
Smollett and Addison. But all that is worth insist-
ing upon is that in Hook, Egan, and their brother
humorists is the literary background to 'Pickwick.'
Just as Scott had taken the Gothic and historical
romance, impossible and insane, and made of it 'Waverley'; so Dickens, working in the novel of farcical
situation, transformed it, making of it a distinct
species. The minor humorists were weak in what the
rhetoricians call invention. They worked again and
again the same situations; of characters in any full
sense of the term, they had few; and when they
touched low life, their imagination deserting them,
they presented it in its crass vulgarity. Dickens possessed immense creative power. 'Pickwick,' containing some sixty distinct situations and more than three
hundred and fifty characters, is of all English novels
the one of largest scope. Though these characters are
mostly the humors of comedy, they are not merely
such. Sam Weller is the embodiment of all that is
delightful in the London cockney. Dickens wrote
with the mind's eye upon the customs and manners,
the men and women of his time, which his imagination, seizing hold of, lifted into the world of the grotesque. This has been the home of the very greatest
humorists — the creators of Don Quixote, Falstaff,
and Uncle Toby. In full sympathy with his material,

as one who knew London and the hardships of its slums and prisons, he invested his narrative, be it farce or comedy, with a tragic cast and a noble humanity.

2. *Charles Dickens and the Humanitarian Novel*

The humanitarian novel, with which the name of Dickens is preëminently associated after the publication of ' Pickwick,' is the popular section of an extensive humanitarian literature, and as such it is the most available record of a deep and far-reaching philanthropic movement, which had its beginnings in the eighteenth century, and rose to its sentimental culmination some fifty years ago.   When the nineteenth century opened, the English penal code, to speak most respectfully of it, was a brutal anomaly.   Statutes of the Plantagenets and the Tudors, ludicrous for their tragic severity, were still nominally in full force. During the reigns of the Georges, the number of capital offences increased in steady march from sixty-six to above two hundred.   The readiness of the ministry to create at any time a felony without benefit of clergy, was one of the grim jests of Burke.   Among the acts punishable by death were pocket-picking and shoplifting, in each case to the amount of five shillings.   The moral and sanitary condition of British prisons was, to use the lone adjective of a Parliamentary report, ' dreadful.'   While the Gothic romancers were horrifying the public by detailed accounts of refractory nuns incarcerated in vaults for the dead, the real tombs, where real men and women were being buried alive, were the Marshalsea and Newgate; of

which and other jails and prisons one may read in
the Dantesque descriptions of John Howard. With
the invention of the power-loom arose new social
problems. Workmen in factories were paid barely
enough to afford mere subsistence in barns or in
cellars; and in the train of evils came the employment of women and children through long days, in
some cases from five in the morning until seven in
the evening. Workmen united, and Parliament sup-
pressed the trade unions. They rose in riot in consequence of famine and the high price of food products,
resulting as they thought from a new corn law; the
response of the government was a suspension of the
habeas corpus act, and the passage of laws practically
prohibiting public meetings for considering grievances.

Philanthropists in and out of Parliament had for a
long time been doing what they could for the amelioration of the lower and criminal classes; and in the second quarter of the nineteenth century their endeavors
were in large measure successful. Foundling hospitals had long been established, and societies for taking
distressed boys out of the street and educating them.
Laws were passed restricting the labor of women and
children. The slave-trade, and afterward slavery, was
abolished. Prisons were becoming penitentiaries, and
the penal code was reformed. The elective franchise
was enlarged. Corn laws were repealed. Parliament
appropriated money for public education, and standard
literature was published in cheap form. The list of
philanthropists and reformers is long and glorious,
Wilberforce, Romilly, Mackintosh, Brougham, Peel,
Lord Ashley, Cobden, and Bright.

The humanitarian movement gave us the humanitarian novel, and in turn the novel probably accelerated the movement. Philanthropic motive was not absent from our earliest eighteenth-century fiction. It appeared in Defoe, Fielding, and Goldsmith, combined with the picaresque escapade; and in Mackenzie, combined with a plaintive sentimentalism. It was a more conscious aim of the pedagogic and the revolutionary novelists, the popularizers of social theories. There are pages in Godwin's 'Fleetwood' which a reader cannot fail to remember; for example, the account of the dreary and despairing life of young children in the silk factories of Lyons. But the Godwin novel of theory, with its humanitarian tendencies, received a check from Scott. Scott brushed aside in jest all social and philanthropic schemes, having no faith in them; and consequently his romances are free of them. He represents the conservative recoil from the French Revolution and its philosophies, and he carried with him the world of fiction. It was not until he was dying at Abbotsford that the philanthropists showed any marked disposition to take possession of the novel. An approximate date of this appropriation is the publication of 'Paul Clifford' (1830), in which Bulwer-Lytton elaborated the thesis, that 'a vicious prison discipline and a sanguinary criminal code' do not prevent crime at all, but really help to turn out criminals. The truth of his contention was fully corroborated by the investigation of Parliament five years later.

In *Bentley's Magazine* for January, 1837, Dickens began the publication of 'Oliver Twist,' which, though differing in details and somewhat in aim from 'Paul Clifford,' is built on similar lines. It is a picaresque

story humanized, and given a realistic setting in the
London slums. After the publication of the two immediately succeeding novels of adventure — 'Nicholas
Nickleby' and 'Old Curiosity Shop' — Dickens became
a sort of professor of humanitarianism; and he held
his position for nearly thirty years, disturbed now
and then by a critic or reviewer who questioned his
knowledge. The light of that knowledge, which was
indeed somewhat false and misleading, and the light
of an imagination of strange and alluring splendor,
he turned upon a great variety of English scene and
character, but especially upon workhouses, debtors'
prisons, pawnbrokers' shops, hovels of the poor, law
offices, dark streets and dark alleys, all the London
haunts and lurking-places of vice, crime, and pain.
His theme was always the downtrodden and the oppressed. He was their advocate; for them each of
his novels after 'Pickwick' is a lawyer's brief. He
did not believe it possible for the lower and criminal
classes to raise themselves by the elective franchise
to a higher moral and intellectual plane. To him
Parliament was the dreariest place in the world, and
he kept out of it. He sought to arouse the conscience
of the British public, and he left the issue with themselves. He accordingly attended, often acting as chair-
man, meetings of philanthropic societies, where gov-
ernmental abuses and the condition of criminals and
the poor were to be canvassed, visited jails and prisons, holding long conversations with the keepers, and
went on addressing the ever increasing audience of
his novels. Through him spoke the heart and conscience of Britain, which had found no responsive
voice in Scott.

Though the novels of Dickens have their *raison d'être* in this quickening of the social sympathies, it will not do to insist upon faithfulness to truth in details; we must grant him greater freedom in dealing with facts than we are called upon to grant to any other modern humorist of the first order; greater freedom, it is often maintained, than art can reasonably expect. Satire—and the Dickens novel is always satirical, running the entire scale from light burlesque to fierce invective — satire is likely to be misplaced so soon as it becomes a profession. The attacks of Dickens on science and political economy are hysterical curiosities. Of all the abuses lashed or burlesqued in his novels, none later than those in 'Oliver Twist' were in the strictest sense real. The rest of his novels that purport to deal wholly or in part with contemporary vices, are really historical, representing, so far as they are true to fact, England of the Fourth George rather than England of Victoria. They are completely oblivious of what was done in the first twenty years of Victoria, in educating the mass of the English people, in reforming prison discipline, in lessening the law's delay, and in regulating the hours of labor. As Walter Bagehot pointed out to Dickens in 1858, there must be a government routine; there must be formal proceedings for courts of law; there must be disagreeable and irritating confinement for criminals. Hardship and injustice in individual cases have always accompanied the most careful and merciful administration of law. In spite of all precautions, a cruel schoolmaster will get himself enthroned somewhere; and there is no way of preventing a hard-hearted gentleman who has the necessary capital, from building a cotton mill and operating it, or of preventing a sleek villain from reading law and opening an office. But when Dickens had thus discovered some persisting imperfection of the social state, it became for him the germ of a structure as delightfully fantastic as a tale from the 'Arabian Nights.' For example, he has made up his mind to satirize the delays in the Court of Chancery. To this end he describes London in the grasp of November fog and rain, and then passes in easy transition to Lincoln's Inn Hall, where sits the Lord High Chancellor, with a foggy glory around his head, listening to lawyers who, like the men and women in the muddy streets, are tripping one another up — on slippery precedents. The object of government should be to despatch business. Dickens imagines a 'red-tape' establishment whose maxim is 'how not to do it,' and proceeds to construct his Circumlocution Office. The workhouses are notoriously mismanaged ; and, for the purpose of ridiculing them, Dickens represents the overseers of the poor as seriously contracting ' with the waterworks to lay on an unlimited supply of water, and with a corn factor to supply periodically small quantities of oatmeal.' And when he has once hit upon his fancy, he logically completes it down to the shrinking bodies of the paupers and the coffins ever becoming narrower and shallower. Accept the premises of Dickens, and every detail follows.

The immense audience of Dickens in England and America certainly did not stop to question him, though in course of time they had some misgivings. At first they were spellbound by the humor of 'Pickwick'; then, with the publication of 'Old Curiosity Shop,' their hearts were touched by the illness and death of little children. The outcasts in Bret Harte's roaring camps dropped their cards to listen to the tale of Nell; Landor thought that 'upon her, Juliet might for a moment have turned her eyes from Romeo'; and Poe wrote of 'Old Curiosity Shop': 'These concluding scenes are so drawn that human language, urged by human thought, could go no farther in the excitement of human feelings.' The effect of Dickens's pathos has, during the lapse of a half-century, undergone change; it seems to be of a fanciful world far removed from the actual. It no longer moves to tears, but awakens rather a pleasing æsthetic emotion, because of its poetic qualities, most completely manifest in the marvellous description of Paul Dombey's death. Of this pathos, so far as it has a literary source, Sterne is the father. The wanderings of Nell, holding the hand of her aged grandfather, along the lanes, through graveyards and villages, is the story of poor Maria with fresh details. There would seem to be *a priori* no reason why we should not accept in literature fanciful pathos as well as fanciful humor, but in the long run we do not; possibly because there is sufficient pathos in life as it is. The time comes when both the public and the critic express their want of sympathy with all premeditated emotion by calling it sentimentalism.

Against the current offhand condemnation of Dickens's sentimentalism history, however, will surely protest. It belongs to his time, having appeared, for example, in Bulwer's 'Eugene Aram' (1832), several years before Dickens had thought even of 'Pickwick.' When literature, under the influence of a changing public sentiment, begins its swing from romance or a coldly picturesque treatment of life to depicting the heart and the affections, it does not stop till it reaches sentimentalism. From reason as the guide, to the heart as the guide, the rebound is sudden. It was so in the eighteenth century; it was so in the nineteenth century. Dickens and Richardson are exact parallels. Moreover, as in the case of Richardson, the elemental feelings underlie the pathos of Dickens. There is nothing in life more fundamentally pathetic than the death of children. One generation demands that the scene be related briefly; another that the novelist linger over it in sentences cadenced and alliterative. That is the main difference.

On its personal side the sentimentalism of Dickens is a phase of his idealism. The terms romanticism and idealism have come to be, to an extent, synonymous, for the reason that a romancer is likely to be an idealist, and conversely, an idealist is likely to be a romancer. The English romantic movement began, so far as the novel is implicated in it, in a renaissance of feeling; it passed through a phase of adventure, and in Dickens it reverted to a literature of feeling. Scott is our type of romanticist in highest feather. His prime characteristic is a spirit of adventure, historical and imaginary. But in the mind of the idealist there may be no bias toward adventure. The inner life, first of all, he seeks to embody in his art, and with a direct or an implied moral purpose. His theme is the worth of our thoughts, imaginings, affections, and religious instincts; the need of a trust in our fellow-men, a faith in the final outcome of human endeavor, and a belief in immortality. He is a conservative defending the ways of Providence. Certain aspects of this idealism were not absent from Scott —honor, fidelity, courage, magnanimity. These virtues, however, are in Scott's romances not so much in and for themselves, as for majestic effect. The distinction between romance and idealism may be best comprehended by bringing into mental juxtaposition any one of Scott's historical novels and 'The Tale of Two Cities.' Both will be found to be grandly picturesque; the parallel extends no farther. The inner life depicted in Scott is cold, conventional, and illogical; Dickens preaches a sermon on the sublime text, 'Greater love hath no man than this, that a man lay down his life for his friends.'

Dickens thus restored to the novel the idealism which departed with Richardson and Fielding. For all the squalor, sin, and pain in the novels of Dickens, the impression left on reading any one of them is, that he believed as implicitly as Leibnitz that this is the best of all possible worlds. This is a proposition which metaphysicians have found rather difficult of proof, and it may be as far from the truth of the matter as arrant pessimism. But that Dickens should have held to such a faith, after passing through the degradation and the disappointments of his early life, and that he should have expressed it in literature, is most inspiring. His faith in the better element of human nature, in its possible triumph, in its readiness to grasp the helping hand outstretched to it, was boundless. His novels are a tribute to the human species, to the vast army of beings who live and struggle for a period, and then fall unremembered to give place to others. Read 'Paul Clifford' and 'Oliver Twist,' and note the difference between these two picaresque fictions. Paul becomes a highwayman; Oliver emerges from the den of Fagin uncontaminated. Read, too, 'Candide' and 'Martin Chuzzlewit,' and likewise note the difference between these two novels, each of which deals in its own way with the famous hypothesis of Leibnitz. The cynicism of Voltaire is brilliant and telling; but it is Mark Tapley that we like to follow, as he wanders over the earth seeking to relieve distress, that he may have some occasion to be 'jolly.' In Mark Tapley is Dickens's philosophy of life reduced to its lowest terms.

A most delightful manifestation of the idealism of Dickens is his humor. None of the novels after 'Pickwick' was conceived so completely in the spirit of farce as was that; and Sam Weller one can hardly think of as being surpassed. But on the whole the humor of Dickens broadened and deepened in the immediately succeeding novels, especially in certain sections of 'Old Curiosity Shop' and 'Martin Chuzzlewit,' where humor was united with pathos in a sort of tragi-comedy. Mr. Richard Swiveller, who, after being 'staggered' for years, fell in with the small servant, dubbed her the Marchioness, and taught her to play cribbage and drink hot purl, is the Don Quixote of blackguards. The disreputable workhouse nurse, Sairey Gamp, moving about the stage haunted by the imaginary Mrs. Harris, is Dickens's supreme achievement in humor. In 'David Copperfield,' where in the Peggotty and Barkis episodes farce is held in some restraint, Dickens wrote pure comedy.

Wherever there is humor and satire, there is, if not reality itself, a sense of reality; there must be events and characters that touch the real at some points. The men in whom no humor is found are the out-and-out romancers and the out-and-out naturalists. The region where humor dwells is somewhere between the real and the ideal; in an imaginative treatment of real life. The realistic reaction against Scott was initiated by the minor humorists, and the culmination of that purely humorous literature was 'Pickwick.' In the way of burlesque of romance, Dickens carried the reaction farther. In the opening chapter of 'Martin Chuzzlewit,' he ridicules 'leather-jerkined soldiers' and 'the enormous amount of bravery, wisdom, eloquence, virtue, gentle birth, and true nobility, that appears to have come into England with the Norman Invasion.' 'Oliver Twist' is a protest, in the name of 'stern and plain truth,' against the unreal housebreakers and highwaymen of Harrison Ainsworth : —

Here — in 'Oliver Twist ' — are no canterings upon moonlit heaths, no merry-makings in the snuggest of all possible caverns, none of the attractions of dress, no embroidery, no lace, no jack-boots, no crimson coats and ruffles, none of the dash and freedom with which ' the road ' has been, time out of mind, invested. The cold, wet, shelterless midnight streets of London ; the foul and frowsy dens, where vice is closely packed and lacks the room to turn ; the haunts of hunger and disease, the shabby rags that scarcely hold together : where are the attractions of these things ?

In these and other novels of Dickens, the door to realism is opening. Dickens, however, was not greatly inclined to remonstrate with his contemporaries, and his realism in the main came about naturally, as he followed the bent given his talent by his early life and reading. He began his literary career as a reporter. His short 'Sketches by Boz' have the air of the eighteenth-century quiet observer and newswriter. He talks to apprentices, loiters about hackney-coach stands, visits the circus and pleasure gardens, explores Newgate, where he converses with the murderer to be hanged in the morning, and is a spectator at the execution; he elbows his way along crowded thoroughfares, gets a glimpse at a shabby wretch, whom he follows through alleys to a cheap boarding-house or a gin-shop, and then he writes up what he has seen. The same reportorial air is about his long novels, which are groups of incidents. The main difference is that, while in his sketches he writes down his observations fresh from experience, in his novels he draws upon his memory. The former came nearer the literal impress of real life, without, however, quite reaching it; the latter have a greater infusion of imagination. No one who has not examined the matter can have the faintest conception of the very large body of personal experiences underlying the novels of Dickens, not only 'David Copperfield,' but even 'Hard Times,' where you would least expect to find them. In this richness of descriptive detail, based upon what Dickens had actually seen, is one aspect of his realism.

As in the treatment of fact, so in character-building, the essence of Dickens's art is grotesque exaggeration. Like Smollett, he was on the lookout for some oddity which for his purpose he made more odd than it was. But he had a way of observing the very oddity that marks some quality of mind, often a peculiarity of an occupation or a profession. To Sam Weller all men are boots; every movement and word of Seth Peck-sniff betrays his hypocrisy; Micawber is the incarnation of impecuniosity; and Mrs. Gamp of the lie so often repeated that it passes for truth. What he meant by his characters it was a habit of Dickens to indicate by the names he gave them; as Lord Mutanhed, the Artful Dodger, the Barnacles, and Mr. Hamilton Veneering. They are, all of them, humors highly idealized, and yet retaining so much of the real that we recognize in them some disposition of ourselves and of the men and women we meet. The number of these humorous types that Dickens added to fiction runs into the thousands; it is by far the largest single contribution that has ever been made.

Dickens was from the very first a check to mediæ-valism. After he began writing, knights and ladies and tournaments became rarer. He awakened the interest of the public in the social condition of England after the Napoleonic wars. The Scott novel had come swollen with prefaces, notes, and appendixes, to show that it was true to the spirit of history; the Dickens novel came considerably enlarged with personal experiences, anecdotes, stories from friends, and statistics, to show that it was founded upon facts. Instead of the pageant of the Middle Age, we now have, in the novels of those who have learned their art from Dickens, strikes and riots, factories and granaries and barns in blaze, employee shooting employer, underground tenements, sewing-garrets, sweating-establishments, workhouses, truck-stores, the ravages of typhus, enthusiastic descriptions of model factories, model prisons, model cottages, discussions of the new poor law, of trade unions, of

Chartism, and of the relations of the rich and the poor. The new characters are operatives in factories, agricultural laborers, miners, tailors, seamstresses, and paupers. Patience, longsuffering, gentleness, in stalwart or angelic form, is oppressed by viragoes, tall and bearded and of flashing eyes, or by gentlemen of bloated red faces. Dickens never advocated in his novels any specific means of reform. The novel is now stated as a problem, which the author solves, or indicates the way to the solution. Disraeli set the example of this broader social treatise in his 'Sybil' (1845), the subject of which is the condition of labor in the years immediately following the first Chartist riots. One sentence of his, in which he condensed his appreciation of the Liberal party, is memorable: 'The great measures of Sir Robert Peel, which produced three good harvests, have entirely revived trade.'

The year 1848 was for England, as for the rest of Europe, a time of alarm. In that year workmen from all parts of England congregated in London in very great numbers, and presented to Parliament a mammoth petition, in which they made known their demands. In every nook and corner of the metropolis Wellington had his soldiers in hiding. The workmen for the time were cowed; but whether they were remaining quiet, waiting for an opportune moment for attack, or had given over their projects in despair, was uncertain. Some saw in the immediate future only anarchy; others an approaching millennium of peace, fraternity, and good-will. Charles Kingsley, from his country parsonage at Eversley, was looking toward London with a heart palpitating with interest, wonder, and alternating hopes and fears. He was up in the morning at five o'clock, writing first 'Yeast' and then 'Alton Locke' before the heavy parish duties of the day. These two social sermons are red-hot ingots, hissing with passion and indignation. Kingsley believed that labor had great grievances, and he laid them bare. He also pointed out the moral mistakes of workmen, dwelling particularly on their atheism and unbelief; he stated what seemed to him to be the real attitude of the upper classes toward the downtrodden, and finally announced his programme for bringing about harmony and contentment. The Church of England was, in his view, the only mediator between employer and employee. And by the Church of England he was careful to make plain that he did not mean the existing aristocratic church looking Romewards, but a reformed church, liberal enough to administer to the spiritual needs of rich and poor. The comment of deepest insight that has yet been made upon Kingsley's Chartist fictions is in a letter which Carlyle sent the author after reading 'Alton Locke.' Carlyle praises 'the exuberance of generous zeal' and 'a certain wild intensity,' and adds: 'Of the grand social and moral questions we will say nothing at present; any time within the next two centuries, it is like there will be enough to say about them!'

While Kingsley was preaching his impassioned sermons to the Chartists, Mrs. Elizabeth Gaskell was depicting scenes in the manufacturing towns of the North. 'Mary Barton' was published in 1848; and 'North and South' in 1855. Mrs. Gaskell wrote from personal observation; she consulted no reports for statistics, and made no special tours in search of uncommon occurrences. As the wife of a

dissenting minister at Manchester, her visits of charity
gave her easy access to the homes of workmen, to neat
suburban cottages, and to the cellars of the city, where
women and children in darkness and fetid air were
dying of typhus and consumption. Strikes, the mysteries of trade unions, and cheap groceries were familiar facts to her. And the heart of that mill-owner
living in the mansion on the hill was an open book,
for she had followed his career from boyhood. She
was wise enough to offer no final solution of the
problem of labor and capital, beyond trying to inspire
employer and employee with the spirit of her own reasonableness.

   To the cause of humanity, the United States contributed Harriet Beecher Stowe's ' Uncle Tom's Cabin.'
The negro, as has been observed, was an important
figure in fiction around the year 1800, when he was
regarded as the most available specimen of man in
the state of nature. In the adventures of the sea, for
example in Marryat's, he again appeared, now amid
the scenes of his real life in the West Indies. It is
noteworthy, however, that the abolition of slavery in
Great Britain and her colonies was accompanied by
no great emancipation novel. The nearest approach
to it was Henry Senior's belated ' Charles Vernon '
(1848), which gave a plain account of the ill-treat-
ment and neglect of the slaves in the West Indies
some forty years previous, and of which, as in Mrs.
Stowe's novel, the heroine was a quadroon. ' Uncle
Tom's Cabin,' depicting slavery as it actually existed, in
its mildest and its most inhuman forms, in the border
states and on the southern plantations, electrified the
United States, Great Britain, and all Europe almost

simultaneously. Specifically an appeal to the humanity of the southern slaveholder, it was in reality an address to the religious instincts of Christendom; and it touched those instincts as no other novel has ever done.

The humanitarian mood continued to color a large section of popular fiction down to the death of Dickens in 1870. By that time there was no conceivable abuse or shortcoming of organized society that had not had its satirist. But meanwhile Thackeray, Trollope, George Eliot, and others were in open dissent from the school of Dickens.

CHAPTER VI

The Return to Realism

1. *William Makepeace Thackeray*

WHEN the humorists and humanitarians abandoned cathedrals and ruined castles for London slums and the factory towns of north England, they let the novel down from the picturesque heroic to the matter of contemporary life. And while there can be no doubt that in individual instances they performed a noble work in uncovering social wrongs inherited from the past, they had nevertheless created in fiction and society an atmosphere of false sentiment about criminals and blackguards and the attitude of the upper to the lower classes. Carlyle visited a model London prison in 1850, and found it as stately and cleanly as a ducal palace. He tasted the bread, the cocoa, soup, and meat, and pronounced them ' of excellence superlative.' Thackeray also knew of workhouses and prisons that in all appointments of health and comfort surpassed the most ancient foundations of learning. And yet the reformers in no wise abated their efforts. Thackeray protested in the name of truth against them all, and against the history of fiction since Fielding. By his ridicule and his creative work he brought the novel once more into the stream of realistic tendency, where since 'Pickwick' it had not kept a steady course.

Thackeray was a critic of rare insight, detecting latent absurdities in literature and conduct, and bringing them to light. This critical attitude, though remaining with him to the very last, was most buoyant in his sketches for *Fraser's Magazine* and *Punch*, and in that brief afterpiece 'Rebecca and Rowena.' Thackeray rewrote 'Ivanhoe' for Scott, marrying Wilfred to Rebecca, and making them the ancestors of an amazingly rich Hebrew family, with this marriage as the only blot in the scutcheon. Bulwer's first novels he reviewed seriatim, exposing their artificiality, sentimentalism, and jugglery with virtue and vice; and in what was said of 'the agreeably low' and 'the delightfully disgusting' of 'Paul Clifford,' were implicated Ainsworth and Dickens. On various occasions he ridiculed 'the milk and water' virtues of G. P. R. James, his conventional good morals, his poetic justice, and his 'perfectly stilted and unnatural' style. Of the Disraeli political and fashionable novel, he drew a slight sketch, in which, after the very manner of Disraeli, were exalted the Hebrew moneylender, the beauty of 'burning auburn' hair, and the comforts of the Ghetto. There was no escape even for his friend Lever, whose dragoon had been very familiar with the Emperor Napoleon and too prone to shrieks of delight over stale anecdotes. In the course of these extravaganzas appeared 'Barry Lyndon,' a superb mock heroic in defence of gambling, which stands in the same relation to Thackeray's other work as does 'Jonathan Wild' to Fielding's. 'The Book of Snobs,' belonging to this period, is in the same vein as the burlesques, the subject of ridicule being not so much literature as the affectations of society.

In January, 1847, was issued the first number of 'Vanity Fair.' With much good humor, Thackeray was now presenting his contemporary novelists with his ideal of a novel so well as he could express it. To them was conceded somewhat, particularly the historical background. The events of 'Vanity Fair' are assumed to have taken place at the Waterloo period. And all the novels Thackeray wrote thereafter, if not distinctively historical, as ' Esmond' and 'The Virginians,' have the historical semblance, going back, as do ' Pendennis,' 'The Newcomes,' and ' Philip,' to Thackeray's early life. 'Vanity Fair' and the rest also show the influence of Lever's military novels. Thackeray's heroes are men who had fought at Blenheim, Quebec, Waterloo, or in India. He rarely described in detail historical and military events, but commented upon them shrewdly. What the public wanted to know, who had had a superfluity of Waterloo stories, was what happened at Brussels in the weeks preceding the battle; what was going on at the period in London, in the mansions of bankers and merchants in the vicinity of Bloomsbury and Russell Square; and how a dull young colonel and his smart wife could live on nothing a year at No. 201 Curzon Street, May Fair. Thackeray told them, treating his subject with great tact and with full deference to decorum. He brought to his work no conscious philosophy of the good, the beautiful, and the true. An arbitrary reconstruction of life in accord with sentimentalism, philanthropism, or the Leibnitz formula had for him no allurements. His principle was that he must accept the world as he found it. 'It does not follow that all men are honest because they are poor; and I have known some who were friendly and generous, although they had plenty of money. There are some great landlords who do not grind down their tenants; there are actually bishops who are not hypocrites; there are liberal men even among the Whigs, and the Radicals themselves are not all aristocrats at heart.'

The imaginative reader of 'Vanity Fair' and the group of fictions around it has no difficulty in hearing the voice of Thackeray addressing his brother novelists, as among many things he says to them: Your plots and characters do not conform to the real. Mr. Bulwer, you are a sheer sophist. You take as a hero Eugene Aram, and by concealing his real character in fine language, italicized and capitalized, you would make me believe he is a much-abused scholar and schoolmaster. My dear brother Dickens, though you once thought me incompetent to illustrate your 'Pickwick,' I like it beyond measure; but your knowledge of young women and little boys has its limits. The British damsel is not commonly gentle, demure, and ingenuous; she is more likely to be a flirt, to be very deceitful, and may be delightfully wicked. Little boys are, as you represent them, very wise, but not quite in your spiritual sense; at least they were not so when I was a youngster at Swishtail Seminary. I will now paint you a picture of life as it is. To please you and your audience, I will give you two good and amiable characters: they shall be called Amelia and Dobbin; and I will take them, not from Belgravia or Newgate, but out of

Russell Square, from the moral middle class, where we
find more commonly than elsewhere the patient and
devoted daughter, wife, and mother, and the constant
lover and husband. In contrast, I will show you that
women may be rogues, — and he laughs in his sleeve at
Miss Rebecca Sharp, already thinking perhaps of that
scene (one of the three or four greatest he ever wrote)
in which Becky's husband suddenly appears and
strips her of her jewellery. I will present you, too,
with some men as I have observed them in Bohemia,
and at Lord Steyne's, with not much of the heroic in
them. or none at all; for example, Sir Pitt Crawley,
and his son Rawdon, who will at length sell himself
for the governorship of an island, like dear old Sancho
Panza, and death from yellow fever. Perhaps one of
these gentlemen in motley had better be a coward also,
—and Jos Sedley fleeing from Brussels flits through
Thackeray's imagination. And finally, in contrast to
your Lovel, Sir Walter, let us have George Osborne,
who shall be kept from deserting his wife for an adventuress by the rumble of Napoleon's cannon, calling
him to the battle-field to be shot dead.

And folded with Thackeray's monologue over his
literary brethren, is an address to the public, in which
he tells them that they are frittering away their lives
in buying tinsel and gewgaws at the tawdry booths of
vanity fair. Thackeray illustrates his allegory by
creating characters of many types, all of whom obtain
for their schemes and frettings and heartburnings
nothing worth the having. The elder Sedley amasses
a fortune, only to die, a childish old man, in poverty
and sorrow. The elder Osborne attains to a 'proud
position' in the tallow trade, only to lose his son

George, and to be found on a morning lying by his dressing-table in utter helplessness. Amelia, poking her pretty head out of a Bloomsbury window, waits and watches there for her George, who will come to laugh at her perplexities. Sir Pitt Crawley, while the corpse of his wife still lies unburied in a darkened chamber, proposes to Becky; but she is already married to Rawdon. Poor Jos Sedley attained to his desire, and then passed from the earth, very soon after taking out an insurance policy in favor of Becky. Honest Dobbin served for Amelia more than double the time of Jacob for Rachel. And how small the reward! for it was only Amelia.[1]

'Vanity Fair' is the expression of a mood. In instinctive recoil against the representation of life in false lights, especially the inner life of feeling and motive, Thackeray purposely overdrew for humorous effects. Becky Sharp, Jos Sedley, and Lord Steyne are exceptional characters; in short, they are caricatures, and were intended to be so. With the thoroughly good and respectable Amelia and Dobbin, the reader is in no sort of sympathy, and the suspicion is inevitable that Thackeray did not wish to make them attractive. He left it to his readers, saturated with the literature of the angels, to balance the account of life in their own minds. Moreover, in those passages of 'Vanity Fair' where Thackeray

---

[1] Of 'Vanity Fair,' Thackeray wrote to his mother : 'What I want is to make a set of people living without God in the world (only that is a cant phrase), greedy, pompous men, perfectly self-satisfied for the most part, and at ease about their superior virtue.' — Introduction to the biographical edition of 'Vanity Fair.'

recurs to his text and thus explains his meaning
of *vanitas vanitatum,* the drift of his social satire
seems to lie within well-established and almost conventional bounds. His attitude toward social vice
is much like that of the eighteenth-century essayist.
Like Addison and Fielding, he does not ridicule
life in and of itself. He conceives of the ends
and aims of the life of his contemporaries — particularly and almost exclusively the middle class, to which
he himself belonged — as nothing better than the false
gayety and glare of vanity fair. They fall prostrate
before rank and title, and do not know a real gentleman when they see him. They marry for wealth or
social position; and when married and disillusioned
they give great dinners beyond their means to keep
up the farce. Income and name gone, they attempt
a solution of the problem of living without labor.
They run into debt, never intending to pay their bills,
and flit about from place to place, hanging upon the
skirts of society. The curtain is rung down on an
ostentatious funeral, a popular preacher, and a humbug
eulogy. Of course, 'Vanity Fair' is not an ethically
harmonious transcript of the ways of the middle class.
We must grant to Thackeray the reactionary mood
and the satirical license. Beyond this, we must allow
something to form and tradition. 'Vanity Fair' is
of the picaresque novels. the prime characteristic of
which has always been the holding up to view the
seamy side of life, — rents, rags, and uncleanness.
Viewed in its large historical relations, the novelty
of 'Vanity Fair' consists in its being a magnificent
adaptation of picaresque fiction to modern society;
and in its rogue being a woman, — a peculiarity of

only two notable picaresque novels before Thackeray, 'La Picara Justina'[1] (1605), by Lopez de Ubeda, and 'Moll Flanders' (1722), by Defoe.

In 'Pendennis,' begun almost immediately after finishing 'Vanity Fair,' Thackeray took his stand by Fielding, defending 'the Natural in Art,' and announcing that he was going to present the public with a new 'Tom Jones.' His specific intent was an exact account of the doings of a young man, at school, at college, in the inns of court, and at the clubs, as he had observed them. But if 'Pendennis' be compared with its prototype, certain points of difference are clear. Tom Jones yields to temptation. Arthur Pendennis and George Warrington, bundles of high manly qualities and very great weaknesses, are for a time led astray by passions which they afterward overcome. Thackeray admits frankly that there are some passages in the careers of his gentlemen that will not bear telling. Fielding concealed nothing; 'Tom Jones' is a study in the nude. Thackeray reluctantly draped his figures, out of respect to conventions he was inclined from time to time to ridicule.

After 'Pendennis' Thackeray turned to an extent against himself; and the novels he then wrote, though historically of less significance, are the ones that win our love. There is, it is true, an unmistakable unity of tone pervading every scrap of his work. He never lost delight in unmasking affectation, sham sentiment, and hypocrisy of every sort. On the other hand, he was always reverent, even given to hero-worship when there was at hand an object worthy of wor-

[1] Translated from the Spanish, under title of 'The Country Jilt,' 1707, by J. Stevens.

ship — Shakespeare, Wolfe, or Washington. He was
kindly, charitable, tender, and withal slightly condescending. To think of fierce moral indignation
behind the ' Burlesques ' and ' Snobs ' or even
'Vanity Fair,' as did Charlotte Brontë, is not to understand them rightly. As a breaker of images his
weapon was banter. But — and this is the drift of his
development — in the later novels, the kindly, tender, and religious side of Thackeray came more and
more to the front. He grew less objective, weaving
his stories out of his heart and his dreams. The
change is first of all visible in the subjects he chooses.
Two of his novels, 'Esmond' and 'The Virginians,'
are now out-and-out historical; he leaves his own time
and the life of which he had been a part for the life
he had been living in his library with Addison and
Steele, Dr. Johnson, Richardson, and Fielding; and
he reconstructs that life. He abounds in recondite
literary allusions, and writes laments over the classic
fictions of his youth, which his later contemporaries
have forgotten. Marked as are the differences between 'The Virginians' and 'Henry Esmond' and a
novel by Scott, they are nevertheless histories, and
have all the ideality of romance except wild adventure.

'The Newcomes' and 'The Virginians' are novels
of sentiment or feeling, possessing the finer spirit of
Sterne. In them are Thackeray's famous deathbed
scenes: Colonel Newcome, in the dress of the poor
gray friars, summoned into the presence of his Master, and answering with *adsum*, the word he had
used at school; the remorse and madness and broken
French of the dying Baroness of Bernstein in ' The

Virginians,' once the smart and beautiful Beatrix
of 'Henry Esmond.' In these scenes Thackeray is
surely playing upon our emotions in the manner of
Sterne. Perhaps his most tragic situation is Clive
Newcome growing away in his intellectual and moral
sympathies from his father, a gentleman of another age.
'The old man lay awake and devised kindnesses, and
gave his all for the love of his son; and the young
man took, and spent, and slept, and made merry.'
The pathetic climax to the situation is when the Colonel with broken heart one day goes into Clive's study
and stammers: 'I — I am sorry you have any secrets
from me, Clive.' In Thackeray's first novel, as we
have seen, rogues and gentlemen in motley were the
real characters; in his second novel attention was
fixed upon two characters, lamentably weak but having a dash of sterling manhood in them. They were
both novels without heroes. Thackeray's later aim
was to portray great and commanding goodness of
the heart in characters like Ethel, and Colonel Newcome, Colonel Esmond, and Harry Warrington; and
by means of them to draw attention away from worldly
meanness. He dwells upon pardon, renunciation, for-
giveness, reconciliation, disinterested friendship, and
the separation of parents and children by sea and
death; and bows his head in awe before the inex-
plicable course of events and the mysteries of life
and death.

Of the style with which Thackeray invested his
thought, it came, so far as there is any historical explanation of it, along with much in his way of thinking,
from the eighteenth-century humorists — Addison,
Steele, Fielding, and Sterne — and from those burlesque

writers contemporary with his youth, among whom were Theodore Hook and Pierce Egan. Historical considerations, however, do not count for much in considering that sinuous style of his, adapting itself to plain narrative, and rising at will into eloquence, or meandering into the delightfully colloquial, or shunting off into the unexpected humorous turn. Not so careful in his syntax as Fielding, he is yet in his easy mastery of language and of grand and simple rhythm with the greatest of the Elizabethans.

In construction his success was variable. He wrote and published in parts, and of this method there are inevitable consequences. He proceeded in a leisurely go-as-you-please manner, strewing the way with characters he wished to rid himself of, by running them through, giving them a fever, or letting them drop in an apoplectic fit. To one or two notions he held fast. No ghastly death would he allow, no drownings nor strangulations; the corpse must look comely. And that the novel might have a pleasant ending, there must be at least one happy marriage in the last chapters and the restoration of a lost or sequestered fortune. From the standpoint of structure, 'The Virginians' and 'Philip' are the weakest of Thackeray's work. 'Vanity Fair' and 'The Newcomes,' epic in their immense scope, are more rigidly dramatic than they are usually said to be; beneath their apparent carelessness of manner is 'an art that nature makes.' Once Thackeray wrote his entire novel before the publication of any part of it, and the perfect form of 'Henry Esmond' has been the despair of his fellow-craftsmen. Dickens's novels we called groups of incidents; Thackeray's are confidential conversations.

Thackeray assumes the rôle of showman. He exhibits his characters, banters and scolds them, and talks through them as if they were Punch and Judy and he the ventriloquist; and, suddenly stopping, he turns to his audience, telling them all about the figures on the wires, and all about themselves. Characters, author, and reader are ever coalescing and separating like moving shadows. This procedure is denounced by the more modern builders as militating against the conservation of character; and probably therein lies the danger. Let the actors play their parts and the author keep silent; that is the maxim. But in any specific case the method must be judged by its success. Rawdon Crawley and Becky Sharp are among that small company of characters in fiction that really grow from page to page. Certainly nothing is more tiresome than commonplace moralizings. But Thackeray's thinking was so cosmopolitan and his feelings of so exquisite a quality that, when we think of him, his asides and comments are what return oftenest upon the memory. By means of them he awakened into ripple all those pleasing emotions of wit and humor and satire and loveliness and gentleness and reverence, common to the enlightened humanity for whom he, distinctively a man of letters, wrote. In his most ideal moods he was always a realist of the spirit, because of his sanity.

2. *Bulwer-Lytton in the Rôle of Realist, George Borrow, Charles Reade*

The return to realism in the nineteenth century was essentially a return to the manner of the great novelists of the eighteenth century. The minor humorists and Dickens went back in the main to the caricature of Smollett. Thackeray was to fiction a second Fielding. The product of the new realism, however, was quite different from the old. Dickens and Thackeray had their own rich experiences and observations, and both were captivated by the historical setting of Scott. If we were to have Smollett and Fielding once more, why not Sterne also? Sterne did appear again in the equivocations of Pierce Egan, in the gestures and grimaces of Dickens, and in the pretty sentimental scenes that Thackeray built up and pushed over. But the fully premeditated restoration of Sterne is a debt we owe to Bulwer-Lytton. Immediately after the rise of Thackeray, this talented novelist, who always kept his finger on the public pulse, writing of philosophies, criminals, fairies, ghosts, and Norman barons, as the heart-beat of his patient seemed to point the way, turned his attention to Quixotic characters of country life. 'The Caxtons' appeared in 1849, and its double continuation under the title 'My Novel; or, Varieties in English Life,' in 1853.

The scenes of these novels are English villages in the old days before railways, when the crotchets and the kindly absurdities of country manners had not yet been toned down by intercourse with London. The characters are a broken-down military captain, a gentleman with brain bewildered by useless knowledge multiplied beyond measure by syllogistic reasoning from whimsical hypotheses, old-fashioned squires and parsons, quack doctors, refugees, beautiful young women created for young members of Parliament, and a cabinet minister and leader of the House of Commons. The action is carried on in sentences and chapters short and abrupt, and frequently by dialogues arranged in dramatic form. Humorous pity is awakened by a lame and dyspeptic duck which the elder Caxton allows to walk about with him and which in kindness he tickles under the left ear; in a donkey that has been thrashed for munching a thistle and is consoled by the parson with a 'rose cheeked apple'; and in a poor moth, which, in seeking warmth by the Caxton fireside on a cold October evening, barely escapes a tragic end.

While there is undoubtedly in these two novels considerable autobiography and personal observation, especially in election scenes and the accounts of the actual working of government, Bulwer did not appreciably raise the quality of the realism of current fiction. He was too plainly imitative; and he took as his model not a realist, but a writer who had played fantastically with real life. Dickens and Thackeray were not primarily imitative. In certain peculiarities of manner, but not in matter, they were of the eighteenth century. In Bulwer were both the manner and the matter of Sterne. Perhaps the main historical interest in these sixteen hundred and odd pages of Bulwer's is that they show how the literary weathercock had veered round toward realism. Similar evidence we have in Dickens. 'The Personal History of David Copperfield,' which closely followed 'The Caxtons,' was a substitute for an autobiography; and as its early title indicates, it was in aim, whatever may be our opinion of the outcome, a transcript of actual experiences.

Among the strangest and most fascinating semi-autobiographies of the period were George Borrow's 'Lavengro' (1851) and 'The Romany Rye' (1857), one continuous novel of gypsy life and philological eccentricity. Borrow was the fierce critic of romance. Putting together the scattered shreds of his remarks, we have from him a history of the later romantic movement running in this wise: Sir Walter Scott, who boasted of a descent 'from the old cow-stealers of Buccleuch,' and who wrote 'in the sorriest of jargons,' befuddled the heads of his readers with many volumes of 'Charlie o'er the water nonsense.' And what has been the social influence of Scott's romancing? A certain mere external gentility of decorum and manner, a worship of rank, a pride of birth, an immense amount of cant of various sorts, and a conspiracy at Oxford to Romanize the Church of England. Capricious as was Borrow's social satire, there was in it salutary truth. The public needed to be addressed with a frankness that Thackeray was unwilling to venture upon, before it could free itself from the slough of sentiment and sham. And Borrow saw what literary criticism has since maintained,[1] that the Oxford movement was a working of the romantic spirit; that long before Newman went over to Rome, the mediæval priest had already, in the imagination and sympathy of Scott's readers, taken possession of Canterbury and York.

Borrow carried his readers back over the romantic revival to the adventures of Defoe. But hanging over his books is a dreamy, poetic glamour wanting in the

[1] See the essay on Newman by L. E. Gates, in 'Three Studies in Literature,' N.Y., 1899.

old picaresque novel. Borrow's gentleman, unconventional, courteous, generous, brave, and true as steel, is a young man who abandons the city for the trade of a strolling tinker and blacksmith, wandering along the hedges and lanes of England, and pitching his tent at night in lovely dingles. What Borrow admired was health, strength, and virility; a robust man who could enjoy to the full ' the good things which it pleases the Almighty to put within the reach of his children during their sojourn upon earth.' Intensely human and passionate, his heroine Isopel Berners, ' with her long beautiful hair streaming over her magnificent shoulders' as she sits with Lavengro in the gypsies' dingle, brewing tea or trying to decline an Armenian noun, possesses the ideality of the mighty Scandinavian queens. To the gypsy camp, the blacksmith's forge by the roadside, and the making of a horseshoe, Borrow lent the magic and the mystery of Celtic poetry.

Much akin to Borrow in eccentricity, robust combativeness, and a love of adventure, was Charles Reade. Reade affected, particularly at first, the manner of Sterne, emphasizing his sentences by giving each one a paragraph, and dropping capriciously the threads of his narrative and taking them up at will, sometimes a hundred or two pages on. He recognized no barriers between the drama and the novel; writing sometimes a play, and then turning it into a novel, and then again reversing the process. He was very fond of bringing into the novel certain conventional scenes of melodrama, such as the virtuous heroine listening unseen in the background, who rushes in and assumes a statuesque pose between an enraged mother and a disobedient son. In short, when he wrote he had in his mind's eye the actors on the stage, and the galleries applauding. Aware of this, he gave as sub-title to one of his novels 'A Dramatic Tale,' and spoke of another as a 'Dramatic Story by courtesy Novel.'

For these dramatic effects, Reade made use of current types of fiction. 'Peg Woffington' (1852) is a delightful episode in the history of the stage, and from the artistic point of view solely, it is the most perfect novel as a whole Reade wrote. 'Christie Johnstone' (1853) has many resemblances to the work of Maria Edgeworth, and specifically, in its treatment of the listlessness and staleness of high life, it is indebted to Miss Edgeworth's 'Ennui.' 'It is Never too Late to Mend' (1857) and 'Hard Cash' (1863) are didactic novels, of which the former was directly inspired by 'Uncle Tom's Cabin,' and was almost equally popular. 'The Cloister and the Hearth' (1860) is a belated historical romance. 'Griffith Gaunt' (1866) is an adaptation of the sentimental criminal novel, of which the type is Bulwer's 'Eugene Aram.' Moreover, like others who felt the humanitarian impulse, Reade did not believe that fiction should be written simply to please, but that it should contain matter for instruction and edification. Accordingly all his novels, even the historical ones, deal with social questions, and usually in the controversial manner. 'Christie Johnstone,' for example, is an attack on hero-worship, a fashionable cult of sham and humbug gods established by the most arrant of shams and humbugs. Over against lords and ladies lisping Carlyle, Reade sets the picturesque life of Edinburgh fishwives. In the portrayal of these plain folk, he aimed at the specific representation; maintaining that the artist has no business with abstractions, with streaks of black paint and streaks of white paint bearing the names of men and women, and that the salt of life is preferable to the spice of fiction.

Reade's novels are documentary. In preparation for them he went through a laborious process, gathering and arranging facts and incidents from his reading into huge commonplace books; and with these books before him, he compiled his novels with the same anxiety for truth that he would have displayed had he been preparing a thesis for a doctorate at the University of Göttingen. Even in his descriptions of romantic scenes which he had never viewed with the physical eye, he strove for accurate local color. He never speaks like Kingsley of 'the fragrant snow of blossoms' in the tropics; he rather takes pains to inform his audience that in Australia, 'the flowers make a point of not smelling, and the bushes that nobody expects to smell or wants to smell, they smell lovely.' For 'The Cloister and the Hearth,' he read, say his biographers, 'not only volumes, but book-shelves and libraries.' The novel is a scholar's endeavor to restore to the imagination of the nineteenth century, the form and the spirit of the fifteenth; to portray the dawn of the Renaissance, when mediævalism with its asceticism and narrow outlook on life was just beginning to give way to the human feelings: mighty passions of friendship, devotion, love, and jealousy, such as we have in the most splendid of Italian *novelle*. The unsuccessful attempt to adjust the mediæval ideal to the Greek ideal, and the strife and the conflict in which the mediæval wins outwardly but not inwardly in the heart, are depicted in the career of Gerard, and incidentally in the life of a venerable pope, who has written novels in imitation of Boccaccio, and is now abandoning theological controversies and the Bible for an illuminated Plutarch; Renaissance friendship in the adventures of Gerard and Denys; deathless devotion in Margaret; and mad love and jealousy most grandly in the Princess Clælia. The romance was not written only for these high colors. On the humble characters Reade bestowed equal care; on innkeepers, burgomasters, peasants, adventurers, 'the obscure heroes, philosophers, and martyrs'; on the hardships, struggles, and weaknesses of a Dutch family with its nine children, from which sprang a Clement and then Erasmus.

3. *Anthony Trollope*

These leaders in the return to realism — Thackeray, the Bulwer of 1850, Borrow, Reade, and Dickens before them — had many characteristics in common. They were all satirists in the way of banter or invective; they all possessed strongly marked personalities which they projected into their work; and this is their charm, for they were all manly men. But they were not dramatic in the high sense in which Jane Austen was. They were humorous, in the old Elizabethan meaning of the word; their emotions led the way, and their pens followed. If they were in a lyrical mood, they wrote poetic prose; if their sense of justice was ruffled, they wrote in grand indignation; whenever they saw an opportunity to ridicule, then, with the exception of Reade, they always took it. The way to stricter realism lay in the novelist's separating himself from his characters; in his withdrawal, so to speak, behind the scenes, so that the drama might play itself out unmolested. This was the contention and the practice of Anthony Trollope.

Trollope's notion of a novel was in many respects the same as that of his contemporaries. In his view, the novel was a salutary and agreeable sermon, preached to recommend the virtues and to discountenance the vices. But he objected to the manner in which this kind of sermon was put together by the social reformers. He accused Reade of not comprehending his subject; and in the most savage piece of satire he was capable of, he rebuked Dickens for creating vices in the middle and upper classes, merely for the sake of attacking them. He even maintained that the literary dishonesty of the reformers had been bad for art; that droll beings with no blood in their veins were made to pass for men and women, that pathos had become 'stagey and melodramatic,' that the comic style created by Dickens 'in defiance of all rules' and affected by his school was 'jerky' and 'ungrammatical.' Are there not, Trollope inquired, real men and women here in England, and humor and pathos in life as it is?

Trollope was more in accord with Thackeray, with whom he was associated for several years in the most pleasing social and literary comradery. Indeed, he was, as it were, a son of Thackeray, from whom he inherited much of his art and his outlook on life, without, however, the father's genius. He unmasked his rogues like Thackeray, but with less abandon. Ideal characters of goodness, nobility, and absent-minded-ness had some attractions for him; and in this kind of character-building he occasionally fell little short of his master. Witness Josiah Crawley, who cannot explain how a certain check came into his hands, and Septimus Harding, who when excited hugs to his heart an imaginary violoncello. The old romantic device which Thackeray revived, of letting the same charac- ters appear again and again in successive novels, Trol- lope managed with fine effects, for he took into account the modifications wrought by increasing age and chang- ing surroundings. In sentence structure he regarded Thackeray as a model. Though he is not so delightful in his style as Thackeray, his sentences are simpler and more easily read, as if he also had in mind Macaulay. For all this, he brought, but with less vehemence, the same charge against Thackeray as against Dickens. At any period, it was his opinion, there can be to the hon- est man of letters only a small place for satire; with Thackeray satire had become a manner and all men snobs. Of the romantic spirit there was, of course, hardly a trace in Trollope. To him as a boy 'Ivanhoe' was one of the best of novels, but that enthusiasm for Scott was forever quenched by the utter failure of his one experiment in historical fiction. Raphael's ma- donnas, he wrote in substance when in middle life, were justified for Church purposes, but the real matrons that once walked the earth are Rembrandt's.

It was Trollope's boast that he far surpassed all his English contemporaries in the literary output. He cer- tainly published enough — thirty-odd novels besides as many tales; and most of the novels occupied three volumes. He accomplished so much by a method that he recommended to all who wish to pursue successfully the literary career. Wherever he might be, in the drawing-room of the Athenæum Club, in a railway carriage, or on the ocean, he seated himself for three hours as a limit, with his watch before him; and regularly as it marked the quarter hour he turned off two hundred and fifty words, undisturbed by the stares of those about him. He kept two or three novels going at the same time; when one was finished, he began another on the next morning, without plan or thinking of it previously at all; sometimes he had several novels in his desk awaiting a publisher. It would be superfluous to add that the result was a vast amount of tameness and commonplace. His Irish stories were out of date; his political romances had been forestalled by Disraeli; and many of his tales of English life crept very close to the ground.

Better workmanship, however, is to be found in 'The Warden' (1855), 'Barchester Towers' (1857), 'Doctor Thorne' (1858), 'Framley Parsonage' (1861), 'The Small House at Allington' (1864), and 'The Last Chronicle of Barset' (1867), consisting, all told, of only thirteen volumes, and known as 'The Cathedral Stories' or as 'The Chronicles of Barsetshire.' However rapidly these novels may have been written, they are not mere desk work. 'The Warden' came to Trollope as an inspiration, while he was one day standing 'on the little bridge in Salisbury.' After sketching the opening chapter, he left the development of the story to a year's meditation. Its successors would naturally fall together in his imagination more easily and rapidly. The scenes of the entire series are laid in the cathedral town of Barchester and the surrounding villages; the characters are the clergy and their families, country doctors, and the gentry. Before this, cathedral life had only incidentally made its appearance in English fiction, as in Kingsley's 'Alton Locke.' Trollope added to England a new shire and discovered a new theme.

Of these Chronicles, the first two are the most closely threaded together, forming, in fact, one continuous novel. Very few new characters are introduced into the second, and most of the scenes lie close and compact in or near the cathedral close. The first point of interest is Hiram Hospital, very similar, it would seem, to Leicester Hospital, well known to visitors at Coventry. Early in the fifteenth century, one John Hiram, a wealthy wool-stapler, left in trust a house and certain meadows and closes near the town for the support of twelve superannuated wool-carders. The property through the centuries increased greatly in value, and the wool industry died out in Barchester. So, instead of wool-carders, the bishop, who had control of the estate, usually gave these twelve places to the aged poor, whatever may have been their occupation. According to the terms of the will, each inmate received his breakfast and dinner and sixpence a day; and the residue of the income, now amounting to eight hundred pounds a year, was to be given to a warden. The position, at the time of the story, was regarded as a sinecure by those seeking reform in Church and State, especially by Dr. Anticant, Mr. Sentiment, and the *London Jupiter*, under which names Trollope thinly veils Carlyle, Dickens, and the *London Times*. The present incumbent, the Rev. Septimus Harding, has for years ministered to the physical and spiritual wants of the brotherhood, never dreaming that he has been doing wrong in receiving pay for his services. But when the reformers discover him, and he sees himself pictured out as a winebibber and hypocrite, he resigns his office, in spite of the pleading and protests of his friends; and in course of time the hospital is given over to the plunder of the Rev. Mr. Quiverful, a type of the poor parson who truckles to authority for the sake of bread for his starving wife and fourteen children. The Episcopal palace is occupied by a bishop of whose character, though it is not strongly drawn, we see enough to know that he is worthy of his place. The good bishop lives in the most intimate relations with Mr. Harding, who, besides being warden of the hospital, is precentor to the cathedral. Nine miles away is Plumstead Episcopi, the residence of Archdeacon Grantley, the bishop's son and Mr. Harding's son-in-law, with whom the fathers have much to do in mollifying his aggressiveness. This Dr. Grantley, now in the very prime of life, and waiting patiently for the death of the dear old bishop, on which event he expects to remove to the palace, is a fine creation. He is in no sense a bad man, but he is worldly and ambitious, and insists, while the bishop is still living, on ruling the diocese. He is dignified in bearing, elegant in dress, and when in the pulpit he is 'a noble ecclesiastic.'

The bishop dies, and, owing to a change in ministry at the very time, he is not succeeded by his son-in-law, but by Dr. Proudie, who becomes, however, bishop in name only, for Mrs. Proudie rules the palace. The new bishop brings with him down from London as his assistant Mr. Obadiah Slope, an Evan-

gelical reformer, who is allowed to preach the installa-
tion sermon. He takes the occasion to attack the
cathedral service, which has been brought to the
perfection of art and beauty by the patient labor
of the precentor, Mr. Harding. All the clergy of
the diocese hear that sermon and leave the cathedral in hubbub and indignation. Now war — open,
determined war — is waged against Mr. Slope, under
the leadership of Dr. Grantley. Mr. Slope is pro-
hibited from preaching again in the cathedral, and
after a time is forced to leave Barchester. The archdeacon has won, he thinks, a brilliant victory. But
the reader of 'Barchester Towers' knows that Mrs.
Proudie in the stillness of night won that victory.
Mr. Slope had been Mrs. Proudie's favorite ; but when
she saw that he was conspiring with her husband to
weaken her authority, she rose to the fury of a Medea,
and Mr. Slope received his passports. What occurred on
that memorable night, when the bishop was punished
for intriguing against his wife's authority, Trollope
leaves us to imagine from the crushed, trembling,
doglike, and aged face of the bishop on the next morning. Shakespeare had his shrew, but at length Pe-
truchio tamed her; Mrs. Proudie remains glorious in
her triumph through volume after volume. With
author and reader she was for years a fascination.
Finally she met her match in the Rev. Josiah Crawley,
who in her own palace and in the presence of her husband turned 'his great forehead and great eyebrows'
full upon her and silenced her meddlesome tongue with
the simple utterance, 'Peace, woman!' 'The bishop
jumped out of his chair at hearing the wife of his bosom
called a woman. But he jumped rather in admiration

than in anger.' This scene in 'The Last Chronicle of Barset' was the beginning of the end. When one morning the news was brought to Plumstead that Mrs. Proudie died last night standing erect by her bedpost, Mrs. Grantley 'dropped from her hand the teaspoonful of tea that was just going into the pot,' and the archdeacon remarked, 'What a relief!' thinking of the poor bishop as well as of himself.

The novelty of Trollope's clergy is in the common-sense standpoint from which they are viewed. Having never associated with bishops, deans, and archdeacons, he built them up (to use his own expression) out of his 'moral consciousness.' A bishop is as likely to enjoy the luxury of being henpecked as the man on 'Change. If an archdeacon has grown up in affluence he will likely be given to display and high living. Just as in the wide world there are all sorts and conditions of men, so there are the same motley personages within the rustling gown and cassock. Sermons may not be masterpieces of eloquence and reason; they may abound in 'platitudes, truisms, and untruisms.' Such was the sound position, now extremely commonplace, that Trollope took for the purpose of his realistic art, and such was the position that long before him had been taken by Chaucer, but forgotten by the reading public.

As to Trollope's characters outside of his clergy, many of them are merely figures of pasteboard. Some of them, however, are a part of his best work. Madame Neroni, for example, who heartlessly unmasks Obadiah Slope in his love-making; and Bertie Stanhope, the smart young gentleman who sports with the passions of Mrs. Proudie,

and gets from the enraged Juno the melodramatic
'Unhand it, Sir!' Best of all, perhaps, are his young
women: Eleanor Bold, the widowed daughter of Mr.
Harding, and Grace Crawley, who is married to a son
of Archdeacon Grantley. These young women and
many others are what we conceive the English girl
to be: not too fine for everyday wear, solid, substan-
tial, and withal good-looking enough. They are the
very type of Wordsworth's ideal, and are the fore-
runners of Mary Garth and Diana Merion.

Trollope's plots, so far as he may have any, are
conventional. Finding from experience that a novel
would not sell without a dash of love-making, and
believing that one plot was as good as another, he hit
upon two situations he thought true to real life; and
he employed them over and over: a young woman
vacillating in her choice between two or more professed lovers, or a young man deciding after much
concluding which of two girls he shall marry. Upon
the novel of mystery and difficulty in which Wilkie
Collins was an adept, he looked in wonder, and once
dabbled with it, only to mar the beauty of his most
tragic last chronicle of Barset. Dispensing for the
most part with the 'wearing work' and the 'agoniz-
ing doubt' of the skilful plot manipulator, he sits
down comfortably and writes about his cathedral
folk; men and women come and go; he relates
what they said and did, and draws full-length portraits of them. His main regret is 'that no mental
method of daguerreotype or photography has yet been
discovered by which the characters of men can be
reduced to writing and put into grammatical language
with an unerring precision of truthful description.'

With his mind concentrated upon his characters, he looks them full in the face, perplexed by no ethical or philosophical medium. By virtue of this directness, he is the great chronicler of English fiction.

4. *Charlotte Brontë*

We have followed the steps by which, from Scott and the romantic school, the novel returned to a point very near where it was when left by Jane Austen. In the last stage of this reaction, the direct influence of Jane Austen was potent. Signs of an awakened interest in her appeared in 1833 — the year after Scott's death — when her six novels found a place in Bentley's 'Standard Novels.' The assertion of Macaulay in 1843, that she ranks with Shakespeare in the dramatic delineation of character, put the seal on a Jane Austen cult. Five years later George Henry Lewes wrote: 'Astonishing as Scott's powers of attraction are, we would rather have written "Pride and Prejudice," or "Tom Jones" than any of the Waverley novels.' Trollope, speaking in his Autobiography of his early literary opinions, says: 'I had already made up my mind that "Pride and Prejudice" was the best novel in the English language, — a palm which I only partially withdrew after a second reading of "Ivanhoe," and did not completely bestow elsewhere till "Esmond" was written.' And the art of his novels speaks more emphatically than his Autobiography.

Charlotte Brontë excited amazement when she told her correspondents and literary acquaintances that she knew nothing of Jane Austen. After reading 'Emma,' she sent a criticism of it to the 'reader' of her publishers, in which she said: 'She [Jane Austen] ruffles her reader by nothing vehement, disturbs him by nothing profound. The passions are perfectly unknown to her; she rejects even a speaking acquaintance with that stormy sisterhood.' Thackeray expressed with sanity the moods of the spirit. Charlotte Brontë awoke the 'stormy sisterhood' of passions, and turned fiction into the channel of tragedy. In her procedure, she made some use of the heroics and the melodrama of Gothic romance. Rain pours, hurricanes blow, and moons rise throughout her novels; and in two of them there are mysteries — the maniac in the upper story of Thornfield Hall, and the nun that walks by night in the garden of a Brussels school — which are duly explained as Ann Radcliffe would have explained them. To these romantic incidents, Charlotte Brontë was driven by the pressure of publishers, who refused the novel she first wrote, on the ground that it was commonplace. Her descriptions of scenery, however wild, were nevertheless from observation; as the Yorkshire moors 'washed from the world' in 'whitening sheets' of rain, and the cold autumn evening in Brussels when from her lattice she 'saw coming night-clouds trailing low like banners drooping.' But whatever decorations she may have employed to gain a hearing, she described herself and the aim of her work when she said: 'I always, through my whole life, liked to penetrate to the real truth; I like seeking the goddess in her temple, and handling the veil, and daring the dread glance.'

Charlotte Brontë passed most of her brief life of thirty-nine years on the moorland wastes of Yorkshire, in the little village of Haworth, where her father was curate. She was sent away a few miles to two boarding-schools, in one of which she was for a short time a teacher, and then she went out twice as governess. She declined two proposals of marriage; and what was more out of the common order of events to one of her humble lot, she was for two years a pupil and teacher in the Pensionnat Héger in Brussels. Thus circumscribed were her experiences down to her first appearance in literature. When she became famous, she went up to London, where she first saw her publishers, the critics, and Thackeray. Through similar excursions from home and a correspondence with men of letters, she came into contact with varied opinions and beliefs, — but too late. To the end, the horizon of her vision never extended far beyond 'the solitary hills.' The life and the literature of the south she could not appreciate. To her, Shakespeare, except in a few of his histories and tragedies, was indelicate, and she was afraid of him. She expected to find in Thackeray a stern Hebrew prophet of dauntless and daring mien; she returned to Haworth still believing in him, but bewildered by his want of seriousness and his admiration of Fielding. Of all that is French in the character and the manners of Englishmen she had no comprehension whatever.

The men and women with whom she had grown up in the north were of a different race; being the descendants of the Scandinavian freebooters. Their characteristics in distinction from the men of the south are well known. Back in the fourteenth century, John of Trevisa contrasted the soft speech of Wessex with the sharp, piercing, and grating utterance of Northumbria. In the Elizabethan romance of

'George a Green' were described the village games
of the West Riding, in which 'crowns pass current.'
The men of the north are still hard of feature,
and abrupt and brusque in manner. For the graces
of society they care little. But beneath their rough
exterior beats the warm heart of the primeval
barbarian. Manners different from theirs Charlotte
Brontë regarded as affectations. What she saw of
the outside world in Brussels and in London served
merely to remind her that fate had dealt with
her cruelly, in consigning her to a life apart. Her
spirit rebelled, flashing up in bitter sarcasm and
irony.

The scenes and the characters of 'Jane Eyre' (1847)
and 'Shirley' (1849) are of Yorkshire; the scene of
'Villette' (1853) and its first sketch, 'The Professor,'
is laid in Brussels. Into these novels Charlotte Brontë
put the portraits of her friends and her imagined
enemies, and her own travails of the spirit. That
this is true, every piece of fresh information concerning her more and more confirms. And yet her novels
do not lie outside the trend of English fiction, detached
and isolated. In them she is remonstrating against
the novel of the circulating library. When she began
writing, the heroes and heroines of novels prepared
for young ladies and gentlemen were made ideally
perfect. The approach of the heroine was announced
by the rustling of voluminous muslin, whose quality
was described as the whitest and finest. When she
came tripping in in sandals, long ringlets were seen
falling over a drooping head and a swan neck, and
she was declared tender, soft, languishing, and innocent. The hero was the pink of kindness and gra-

ciousness; and when, after three volumes of courtship, he won a reluctant bride, he was told to be never cross or wayward with her. The best novels of this species — a lingering on of the 'Sir Charles Grandison' tradition — were those written by Mrs. Anne Marsh-Caldwell. Even Anne and Emily Brontë were careful to keep their heroines beautiful in 'Wildfell Hall' and 'Wuthering Heights,' though to no such extreme. The Brontë sisters, after the sewing, knitting, bread-making, and general housekeeping of the day, when all was quiet in the Haworth parsonage, used to sit down and talk over their stories as they were progressing. On one of these occasions, Charlotte told Anne and Emily that they were 'morally wrong' in adopting the conventional heroine, and said to them, 'I will show you a heroine as plain and as small as myself, who shall be as interesting as any of yours.'

Jane Eyre was the new heroine. It is her character alone that fascinates, — her fiery spirit, her hatred of self-righteousness, and her love of truth. An orphan, cruelly treated in childhood by her aunt on whom she is dependent, Jane is sent away to school, becomes a teacher and governess, and finally marries Edward Rochester, the father of one of her pupils. This situation — a young woman entering life under social disadvantages, and after many struggles winning the place she deserves — is clearly the one introduced into fiction by Marivaux and established by Richardson. It was, in 1847, more than hackneyed. The novelty was in the management of the situation, and in the hard details taken from the life of a real governess. Pious moralizings, scenes of idyllic

friendship and love-making, there were none. Their
places were taken by malice, hate, and a love of
infinite tenderness, uncouth in its earlier manifestations. The aim was to represent a young woman who
should speak and act the truth under all circumstances, with no thought of the consequences to herself or others. A little girl, Jane Eyre looks her aunt
full in the face and tells her she hates her for
her cruelty ; and when asked by a Pharisee what she
must do to escape punishment after death, she replies,
'I must keep in good health and not die.' At a charity
school, where the famished girls are fed on burnt
porridge and rusty meat, and go to bed too tired to
dream, and rise in the morning to wash themselves in
frozen water, she squares her conduct likewise by
truth, enduring reprimand and infamy, while hoping
for a new and easier servitude. A governess at Thornfield, she is still her own keeper in her relations with
Rochester, who is equally no conventional hero. He
is over forty years old, his nose is big, his nostrils are
full and open; his mouth and jaws are grim and
sinister, his chest is too massive for his legs. He is
haughty, domineering, and tyrannical. He is nevertheless Jane's ideal of a gentleman. She can sit by him
and hear him tell in detail the story of his escapades
in Paris and elsewhere, and then declare that she loves
him and is ready to marry him. What this man,
who would have been the villain in the old novel, has
done under misguidance and temptation does not
greatly distress her, for she sees in him a better self.
She goes to the altar with him; and when the marriage rite is there interrupted, she still clings to him,
and leaves him only when her conscience tells her it

is right to do so. When that moment of decision comes, she does not hesitate to choose vagabondage to degradation. When Rochester loses a hand and an eye in trying to rescue from fire his maniac of a wife, Jane returns to him, after her wanderings; watches over him, marries him, and loves him the more for his mutilated arm and 'cicatrized visage.' It is no marriage of the world or of the flesh; it is of the spirit.

'Jane Eyre,' published under the name of Currer Bell, was understood neither by the critics nor by the public. Who is this Currer Bell? — man or woman? The audacity of the novel points to a man; its little details of dress to a woman; but then a man may get these minutiæ from his sister or wife. If a woman, she is unsexed. Perhaps she may be Becky Sharp, who is taking revenge for her treatment in 'Vanity Fair,' — then appearing in monthly numbers. Doesn't Rochester strike you as a caricature of Thackeray? So rumor ran. In the interim 'Jane Eyre' was being widely read on both sides of the Atlantic. Here in the New England states it produced for some months what a reputable critic of the time called a Jane Eyre fever. Young women played the part of Jane Eyre, denouncing hypocrites and moralists in sentimental paradoxes; and young men swaggered in the presence of ladies. In England the novel was denounced as immoral and irreligious. The boorish manners therein depicted and its strange love-making were unknown outside of the north; and there they occasioned no criticism, for they belonged to the common order of things. No book was ever written with sincerer motives, or sprang more directly from an

aching heart. It was a criticism of the vast structure
of modern manners built up on Norman convention-
alities, in the light of the truth of a simpler civilization. 'Jane Eyre' was of its time. The *Zeitgeist*
had reached the great northern moors. While in
the south laboring men were organizing, massing,
and demanding their rights, and clergymen and
politicians in easy circumstances were preaching
to them Chartism and social millenniums, the same
democratic voice was coming from the north out of
the very heart of its people: 'Millions are condemned
to a stiller doom than mine, and millions are in silent
revolt against their lot. Nobody knows how many
rebellions beside political rebellions ferment in the
masses of life which people earth.'

'Shirley' (1849) is milder in tone; in it Charlotte
Brontë is not quite herself. Much disturbed by criticism of 'Jane Eyre,' she undertook to profit by it,
particularly by the advice of George Henry Lewes,
who told her to avoid poetry, sentiment, and melodrama, and to read Jane Austen. She now sought to
daguerreotype Yorkshire life and scenes; and this is
the way she did it. For an enveloping plot of exciting incident, she went back some forty years to the
commercial troubles with the United States, and to
the contest between mill-owners and operatives over
the introduction of labor-saving machinery. She thus
made for herself an opportunity to describe the bat-
tering of a woollen mill by starlight, and the shooting
of the manager. In this setting she placed Yorkshire
men and women with whom she was acquainted, — her
sister Emily, her father, her school friends, one of her
lovers, and the neighboring curates. Incident, too,

she reproduced from life, with varying degrees of modification. The novel is thus an historical allegory. It is hardly necessary to observe that it is constructed on false notions of art and on a complete misunderstanding of Jane Austen. It is, however, as a description of externals the most careful and most sympathetic of all Charlotte Brontë's work, and is still the novel of hers most liked by Yorkshiremen, who see themselves there. The portrait which has the most unusual interest is the minute study of Emily Brontë under the name of Shirley Keeldar. In all her moods and loves and changes of feature under excitement, Charlotte represents her, — her indolence, her passion for fierce dogs and the moors; the quivering lip, the trembling voice, the eye flashing dark, the dilating nostrils, the sarcastic laugh, the expansion of the frail body in indignation, and her wild picturesque beauty when visited by one of her rare dreams, such, for example, as the vision of Nature, the Titanic mother.

'Shirley' failed to please Lewes, who was expecting another 'Pride and Prejudice.' To his flippant criticism Charlotte Brontë replied cavalierly, and became herself once more. 'Villette' has never been quite so popular as 'Jane Eyre,' for its scenes are not English, and to the critic its mechanism is crude and amateurish. Its main situation is a reproduction of that in 'Jane Eyre,' with a new setting and new incidents. The obstacle that kept Jane Eyre and Rochester apart was difference in social position; that between Lucy Snowe and Paul Emanuel is religion. In 'Jane Eyre,' society was viewed from the standpoint of a governess; in 'Villette,' as it appears to a school-teacher who has some difficulty in managing her pupils. In

her first novel Charlotte Brontë's style was wildly,
glowingly Celtic; in 'Shirley' it was rhetorical; in
'Villette' it is more subdued in tone, and rendered
more intense and compact by brief and forcible meta-
phor. This change in style has its correlative in
deeper and more intense feeling. The defiance of
'Jane Eyre' has exhausted itself and settled into
despair. States of mind are now subtly analyzed
that verge upon madness. The debits and the credits
in the account of life are reckoned up, and the books
will not balance, for there is so little to be set over
against pain and grief.

We have in Charlotte Brontë a realist of the feelings, trailing, however, the bright colors of romanticism. Her descriptions of the outside of things, of
men and manners, we have not much dwelt upon, for
the reason that they proceeded so often from prejudice and incomplete knowledge. Roman Catholics
and Methodists, the patrons of boarding-schools, and
English and French girls, we cannot believe were as
she saw them. At any rate, her significance in the
course of fiction is that she delineated the intense
moods of her own heart and imagination, which have
their *rapport* in the moods of the race. In 'Jane
Eyre' and 'Villette,' photography of manners has
passed into that inner photography which Trollope
lamented as an art beyond his power of vision. The
next epoch-making step in internal realism was taken
by George Eliot, when she dealt with states of conscience and feeling psychologically, arranging and
defining them with an attempt at scientific precision.

CHAPTER VII

THE PSYCHOLOGICAL NOVEL

1. *Elizabeth Gaskell — The Ethical Formula of the Psychologists*

BETWEEN Charlotte Brontë and George Eliot is, however, Mrs. Elizabeth Gaskell, whose factory novels we have briefly described. To her work there is another and a less polemic side. Hardly aspiring to the title of novelist, she frequently reminded her public that she was writing only tales. These tales were told in the first person, and for the moral edification of her own sex. In form and aim they are accordingly of the Edgeworth type. Indeed Mrs. Gaskell may be said, in a general way, to have performed in them the same noble service to her contemporaries that Maria Edgeworth did to hers. She entered into the thoughts and wayward moods of children with true insight; she gave us the first English nurses and housekeepers of hard common sense and racy wit, the Nancys and the Sallys. Her style, too, at times is most felicitous, as when she says: 'Edith came down upon her feet a little bit sadder; with a romance blown to pieces' — a sentence which in the natural course of events should have been written by George Meredith. One province she discovered and made her own — feminine society in out-of-the-way towns and villages before the encroachment of railroads and penny postage. Of this life 'Cranford' (1853) is the classic. Here is described

the old-style etiquette, the genteel poverty, the formal
calls, and evening parties, of a village wholly in the
possession of the Amazons — widows and spinsters —
where no men are tolerated, except the country doctor,
who is allowed to stay there occasionally over-night
when on his long circuit.   Old maids spend their time in
tea-drinking and stale gossip, and in chasing sunbeams
from their carpets.   Before going to bed they peep
beneath the white dimity valance or roll a ball under
it, to be sure no Iachimo with 'great fierce face' lies
concealed there.   So ends the day of trivialities and
Gothic fears.   'The Moorland Cottage' (1850) will always have a special interest, for George Eliot in 'The
Mill on the Floss' revivified some of its incidents and
characters : the water, Maggie, the stubborn 'little
brown mouse,' her tyrannical brother Edward, and her
fault-finding mother.

'Ruth' (1853), which probably long ago departed
from the imagination of novel readers, occupies a very
important position in the history of English fiction,
for it follows certain ethical lines more ostensibly than
any previous novel — what may be called the doctrine
of the act and its train of good or evil.   'All deeds,'
says Mrs. Gaskell, 'however hidden and long passed by
have their eternal consequences.'   The doctrine was
not new to literature, for it was not new to observation.
Macbeth hesitated to assassinate Duncan, for he feared
there might issue from the deed a series of extremely
disagreeable events over which he could have no control.
This ethical theory,[1] which Carlyle and likewise

---

[1] For a full exposition of this ethical theory, see the study on
George Eliot, by M. Ferdinand Brunetière, in 'Le Roman Naturaliste,' Paris, 1892.

Comte were popularizing, Mrs. Gaskell employed for unifying her plot. Ruth is an attractive sewing-girl, who at the age of sixteen is betrayed by a young gentleman and abandoned. At the point of suicide, she is rescued by a Dissenting minister, who takes her and the child into his home, where at the suggestion of his spinster sister, she passes for a widow. In the course of time Ruth's offence and the parson's deceit are suddenly and unexpectedly revealed, and then follows the retribution. The respectable part of the parson's congregation deserts him; and Ruth, shunned by the village folk, becomes nurse to patients in typhus fever, from one of whom (who turns out to be her former lover) she is infected, and dies. Mrs. Gaskell works her scenes up to crises, where some one must make a decision as to his course of action, to what she once called 'the pivot on which the fate of years moved'; and then she studies the influence of the act on a small group of characters. The motives and the constraining circumstances that lead to the decision are analyzed in detail. We know precisely why Ruth makes her early mistake and why the parson conceals it; and two pages are devoted to cataloguing the reasons why a country gentleman takes his candidate for Parliament to a luxurious house by the sea to pass Sunday.

When we speak broadly, we call all novels of the inner life psychological. The old romances were psychological, because of their craft of love; so too was Richardson, because of his minute record day by day of the fluctuations of a woman's heart; so too Thackeray, and brilliantly, in his Beatrix and Rebecca; and Trollope in his delicate analysis of the aged warden's conscience. Charlotte Brontë was preëminently psychological in the portraits of Lucy Snowe and Paul Emanuel. But 'Ruth' announces the approach of the psychological novel in a restrictive sense. The outward sequence of its incidents is the correlative of an inner sequence of thought and feeling, which is brought into harmony with an ethical formula and accounted for in an analysis of motive. Mrs. Gaskell did not possess the clearness of vision, the equipment of knowledge, and the breadth of horizon requisite for completely satisfying this definition of the psychological novel. What she did in part was fully accomplished by George Eliot.

2. *George Eliot*

Like Shakespeare, with whom she has often been compared, George Eliot (Marian Evans) was born in the English midlands. Her early life was passed in and near Nuneaton and in Coventry. Brought up in the strictest Evangelicism, she came into contact in Coventry with the positivism and the destructive Biblical criticism which were filtrating into English thought; and, after a severe spiritual struggle, she broke away completely from the faith of her childhood. The first intimation she gave that she might turn to novel-writing as a profession was in October, 1856, when she wrote for *The Westminster Review* a delightfully audacious analysis of the current fashionable and religious novels by lady novelists. In *Blackwood's Magazine* for January, 1857, appeared the first part of 'The Sad Fortunes of the Rev. Amos Barton.' The career of George Eliot the novelist, thus

begun, covers twenty years. So violent a change in
her manner is marked by 'Romola,' that it is an aid
to criticism to divide her novels into two groups. To
the first group belong 'Amos Barton,' 'Mr. Gilfil's
Love-Story,' 'Janet's Repentance' — which were published together in 1858, under the title 'Scenes from
Clerical Life,' — 'Adam Bede' (1859), 'The Mill on
the Floss' (1860), and 'Silas Marner' (1861). The
second group comprises 'Romola' (1863), 'Felix Holt'
(1866), 'Middlemarch' (1871–72), and 'Daniel Deronda' (1876).

At first George Eliot took Elizabeth Gaskell as her
model in the externals of her art and in the choice of
her subject. These external resemblances are manifest in the names of characters: Mary Barton becomes
Milly Barton; and Maggie Brown, Maggie Tulliver.
The 'Scenes from Clerical Life' are tales like Elizabeth Gaskell's; 'Adam Bede' and 'Ruth' are both
studies in the consequences following the erring of
a passionate moment. 'The Mill on the Floss' and
'The Moorland Cottage' are both novels of childhood
and early youth. For an historical setting both novelists went back to the manners of an 'elder England,'
to the time when Coleridge and Wordsworth were
boys, and people laughed at the 'Lyrical Ballads.'
Note well, however, the point of dissidence. After
reading 'Ruth' in 1853, this is George Eliot's criticism: 'Mrs. Gaskell seems to me to be constantly
misled by a love of sharp contrasts, — of "dramatic"
effects. She is not contented with the subdued coloring, the half tints, of real life.' In this passage
George Eliot laid her finger upon the very defect of
Mrs. Gaskell as a realist so soon as she attempted to

depict life with which she was not thoroughly acquainted. Ruth is the soul of goodness, and her
betrayer is the soul of villany. George Eliot had
seen too much of life, and observed character too
closely, to fall into the error of dividing men and
women into angels and demons. The criminal novel
as written by Bulwer-Lytton and many others, she regarded as romance. She had nothing in common
with Thackeray. Between her and Dickens the
bond was closer than criticism has yet taken note
of. Dickens taught her, as he has taught every English novelist since his time, the art of minute observation. Moreover, when describing the death of Milly
Barton, she cadenced her sentences in the very Little
Nell manner. But though always a friend of Dickens
and profoundly impressed by his sad and worn face,
she nevertheless criticised his portrayal of the inner
life as transcendental and unreal. What her own
aims were in distinction from those of her contemporaries, she told her first publishers, and often repeated
to her audience: she would give a sympathetic rendering of common life as we have it in Dutch painting,
and in a style held in firm intellectual restraint.

In the first group of her novels, she confined herself
mostly to her experiences and observations as a Warwickshire girl. By the church at Chilvers Coton,
near Nuneaton, is the tomb of Milly Barton, bearing
another name. With her sad fate George Eliot was
perfectly familiar. At a short distance, in the Wed-
dington churchyard, lies the body of the inebriate
Dempster who ruled at the Red Lion. His dark
career, the riot he instigated against the Evangelical
Tryan, and the patient suffering of his wife, are all

well-known traditions about Nuneaton. The characters and the incidents in 'Adam Bede' have to some extent their prototypes in family history. The first two volumes of 'The Mill on the Floss' are somewhat autobiographic, Tom Tulliver being Isaac Evans, and Maggie George Eliot herself. Likewise George Eliot's scenery is either that of Warwickshire, or of Derby and Stafford, where she visited when a child.

The charm of this early work is her perfect æsthetic sympathy with midland life. She was able, without any air of benevolent condescension, to place herself on the level of her characters, to see things just as men and women of the class she depicts would see them, and to talk just as they would talk. The workshop of Jonathan Burge and the kitchen at the Hall Farm are apparently as interesting to her as to Adam Bede and Mrs. Poyser. With Maggie Tulliver, she becomes a child, who quarrels with her brother, and runs away to the gypsy camp. As Maggie grows up, George Eliot's mind grows with her; she is tempted with her, and goes with her to the Red Deeps, where she sits listening to the 'hum of insects' and watching 'the heavenly blue of the wild hyacinths.' She is with Silas Marner as he counts his gold at midnight; and thence she passes to a Christmas ball at the Red House, and to the racy gossip of the Rainbow Inn. It is curious that it should have been left to George Eliot to do justice to Dissent, and to those members of the Established clergy who were not in orthodox standing on account of their Evangelical tendencies. Ever since Smollett, the irregular clergy of fiction had been hypocrites or grotesque figures. So faithful were George Eliot's portraits of them, that the Dissenters believed the 'Scenes from Clerical Life' were written by one of their number; and in fact a Dissenter was found who acknowledged himself as their author, and thus enjoyed for a short time a brilliant literary reputation for which unaided he had struggled in vain. It is true George Eliot's irregular clergymen are narrow; they do not include in their scheme of salvation Roman Catholics, and they have some doubts about the future happiness of Protestants who cling tenaciously to the Establishment. But they are sincere; and from them comes the only inspiration that quickens the moral sense of the country folk. One of the characters made most attractive in 'Adam Bede,' is Dinah Morris, the Methodist exhorter, who, as she stands on a summer evening in 'an amphitheatre of green hills' pleading with the villagers of Loamshire, sees in vision bending from above Christ in heightened form, weeping, and stretching out his arms to the rough and weary faces before her. Instead of making light of the hallucination of the scene, George Eliot remarks that such a faith was to them 'a rudimentary culture.'

Another result of the flexibility of George Eliot's imagination is the dramatic quality of her pathos and humor. Of course, humor and pathos in any novel are in their last analysis personal. There are, however, different ways of expressing humor and pathos. Our master humorists of the old school, Fielding and Thackeray, made no attempt to conceal the origin of their emotions. To do so was not in accord with their purpose. When they think that it is not sufficiently clear that they are speaking their sentiments through their characters, they pause and throw in a paragraph or a chapter *in propria persona*. George Eliot, too, is always present as an interested spectator, but she keeps herself distinct from her characters and her drama. She was profoundly convinced of 'the difficulty of the human lot,' and that conviction is what makes her novels so pathetic in their conclusions. But her pathos does not appear to come from herself; it rises from the situations she chooses, and is thus apparently of life itself. She saw the humorous side of the doings of vicars and parsons, housewives, and loiterers at the Red Lions and at the Rainbows. But we are not to suppose that the racy and proverbial sayings of these people are from shreds of conversation remembered from childhood. Not at all; they are of George Eliot's own mintage, receiving only their stamp from the tone of the midlands. They are so intimately associated with her characters, that when they are excerpted, their piquancy is gone. George Eliot completed the work of Wordsworth: in the spirit of a measureless humanity, he dealt with the pathos of the pastoral life; she mingled its pathos and its humor.

Of 'Romola,' George Eliot, who was a nice critic of her own work, said: 'I began it a young woman — I finished it an old woman.' This remark is indicative of the differences between the two groups of her novels. The first novels were written between the ages of thirty-seven and forty-one, and in rapid succession; the later novels, between the ages of forty-two and fifty-seven, and in slow succession. George Eliot exhausted her Warwickshire material quickly. For the last volume of 'The Mill on the Floss,' she made an excursion to Gainsborough. For 'Romola,' she visited Florence, and read all that came in her way on Florentine art and manners and history in the fifteenth century, ploughing her way through thick quartos. In 'Felix Holt' and 'Middlemarch,' she returned to the midlands, but the freshness and glory of Warwickshire scenery was departing. 'Daniel Deronda' opens in a brilliant Continental gambling *salon*, and, after passing through the woods and parks of Surrey, loses itself in the London Jewry and the cabala. Its scenes and incidents come largely of special study and preparation. Moreover, in commonplace men and manners George Eliot is losing her interest; the eye that has looked outward quite as much as inward is now concentrated on mental and moral facts, and out of herself she creates her characters to illustrate her psychological discernments.

This change was brought about in the main by two influences — Walter Scott and Auguste Comte. When hardly eight years old, George Eliot came under the enchantment of 'Waverley,' as she has told of it in the motto to the fifty-seventh chapter of 'Middlemarch.' This early delight in Scott, which afterward gave way to the moralists, began to assert itself anew in middle life. There is more romance in 'Romola' than in 'The Fortunes of Nigel.' Concerning the second influence, she wrote in 1867, 'My gratitude increases continually for the illumination Comte has contributed to my life.' The following sentences from the 'Système de Politique Positive' (1851–54) would suggest that the illumination she received was not wholly ethical: 'The principal function of Art is to construct types on the basis furnished by Science.' . . . 'Art controls the Ideal, indeed, by systematic study of the Real; but only in order to furnish it with an objective basis, and so to secure its coherence and its moral value.' This is the æsthetic code that inspired 'Romola,' 'Middlemarch,' and 'Deronda'; it is the code of philosophical idealism, which has very little in common with the Dutch realism elaborated and defended in 'Amos Barton' and 'Adam Bede.'

Notwithstanding all these differences between her earlier and her later work, George Eliot was from first to last a philosopher and moralist. All her novels and tales are constructed on the ethical formula of Mrs. Gaskell's 'Ruth.' For the way in which she thought out and applied this doctrine of the act and its train of good and ill, the only appropriate epithet is magnificent. She explained chance and circumstance, giving to these words a new content. All happenings, she showed, are but the meeting and the intermingling of courses of events that have their source in the inner history of mankind. This invisible medium in which we move is outside of time. The past is here in what was done yesterday; the future is here in what is done to-day; and 'our finest hope is finest memory.' Whatever may be her method of telling a story, — whether she begins at the beginning or breaks into the midst of her plot and in due time gathers up its threads, — George Eliot always comes quickly to an incident which discovers somewhat the moral quality of her characters; and then she proceeds slowly with their self-revelation. Arthur Donnithorne, stepping one day into Mrs. Poyser's dairy as if by chance, speaks to 'a distractingly pretty girl' in the charming attitudes of making butter; and she blushes in reply. These are incidents which in most novels we should pass by as of no moment. But in this case there is meaning in the word simply spoken and the responsive blush. Clandestine meetings follow; and the bitter soon begins to mingle with the sweet. The generous young gentleman thinks that he can turn the ill consequences of his conduct from the dairymaid upon himself; he is soon illumined on this point, and lives to see in the wreck of himself and of others for which he is responsible that 'there's a sort of wrong that can never be made up for.' When a little girl Gwendolen Harleth 'strangled her sister's canary-bird in a final fit of exasperation at its shrill singing which had again and again jarringly interrupted her own'; and atoned for her cruelty, as she imagined, by buying for her sister a white mouse. That incident, which in its startling self-revelation haunted her memory like a bad dream, was but typical of her career as a young woman. She went on imagining that she could make life conform to the pressure of her own desires. A short experience as the wife of Mr. Mallinger Grandcourt humbled her to the dust, where she lay 'with closed eyes, like a lost, weary, storm-beaten white doe, unable to rise and pursue its unguided way.' And when she did rise, she found it necessary to discard her cruel egoism and to adjust her conduct to the presence of others.

Again, on a fair spring morning in 1492 a shipwrecked stranger awoke in Florence. He was a beautiful Greek of sunny face, who was on his way to Venice, where he hoped to sell some jewels intrusted to him, and with the proceeds to ransom from the Turks his foster-father, to whom he owed all his culture and attainments. He disposed of some of his jewels at once in Florence, and then asked himself. Why should I trouble myself about my father, who likely died long ago? why should I run the risk of a possible capture of myself? why not remain here, where I am assured of pleasure and an easy career? He yielded to the temptation, and from that moment began his descent to treachery and broken vows. He betrayed all who placed their trust in him, Romola, Tessa, and Savonarola. Regardless of others, he attempted to steer his course so that there might be no grating rubs against the shingle. For a time he succeeded. But one day Tito awoke on the banks of the Arno to feel the great fingers of Baldassarre pressing upon his throat.

As a study in moral decay, 'Romola' is undoubtedly George Eliot's sternest effort. The novel does not, however, take so complete possession of one as 'Middlemarch' with its English scenes and characters. 'Romola' is a tragedy of crime, the successor to 'Adam Bede,' which is a tragedy of youthful passion. 'Middlemarch' is a tragedy of lost ideals. Dorothea Brooke is a beautiful, plainly dressed Quakeress. She has read the lives of Hooker and Milton, learning how the former was henpecked, and the latter was deserted by his wife Mary, and abused by his daughters. She would have liked, she often repeated, to have been the helpmate of the sweet and loving Hooker; and she would have gladly sat and read to the blind Milton. She meets Mr. Casaubon, and to her he is a Milton or a Hooker living in the present. He proposes and she accepts him at once. A few weeks later she is with him at Lowick Grange; and finds the copying and sifting for a genius not quite what she thought it to be when she used to pity the poor Hookers and the blind Miltons. She fails miserably in her *rôle* as martyr. Edward Casaubon, of sallow face and blinking eyes, has labored a lifetime, weary days and wearier nights, over a 'Key to All Mythologies.' There was nothing ignoble in the impossible ideal he set for himself when a young student many years ago. But in his pursuit of Egyptian divinities, he loses his grasp upon the delights of the present moment. He will correct the error of overstudiousness, by marrying a young and beautiful wife. He will burst the barriers of his virgin affection that has long been pent up like the waters of a mountain lake, and let it overflow in wild torrents. The day of astonishment comes, when he sees that that impetuous and refreshing stream of his love is a tiny, insignificant rill losing itself in the arid sands of a withered and desolate nature. He becomes jealous of Will Ladislaw, and then uneasy and irritable. At length his heart loses the rhythm of its beat, and finally ceases to beat at all. Edward Casaubon sought to remove what to his vision was a mistake far back in his career, and the hoped-for cure was his death.

Dr. Lydgate, a young man twenty-seven years old, comes to Middlemarch with the intention of carrying forward the researches of Bichat, a distinguished French anatomist, who, after opening new vistas in biological science, suddenly died in the midst of his labors. It is not long before Dr. Lydgate is very unexpectedly called upon to cast the deciding ballot as to who shall be chaplain to an infirmary. That ballot also decides what his own career is to be. In his arrogant egoism, he suppresses forever his intellectual selfhood; he turns his back upon a kind-hearted friend, and unwittingly places himself under the thumb of Mr. Bulstrode, the banker and hypocrite. The want of balance between his intellect and his passions leads also to certain other acts on which he had not counted. He is soon married to Rosamond Vincy. His practice gradually decreasing owing to his connection with Bulstrode, he has not the wherewithal to satisfy creditors pressing payment for furniture, plate, and jewels. And the paradise of 'sweet laughs' and 'blue eyes,' over which he had been dreaming ever since he first saw Miss Vincy, proves to be a disastrous illusion. At the age of forty, Dr. Lydgate, of magnificent possibilities, is thoroughly disenchanted. Instead of completing the unfinished work of Bichat, he has become a fashionable physician at bathing-places, and distinguished himself by writing a treatise on the gout. In the prime of life, his hair still brown, now and then conscious of visitations from his earlier self, he comes to the close of his career.

Is there not another picture to be set over against these scenes of frustrated plans? Undoubtedly there is; but the imagery of light is not so effective as the imagery of darkness. George Eliot has her paradise as well as Dante. Of a fine act she says, 'It produces a sort of regenerating shudder through the frame, and makes one feel ready to begin a new life.' And as a large motive to it she says, 'That things are not so ill with you and me as they might have been, is half owing to the number who lived faithfully a hidden life, and rest in unvisited tombs.' That was a fine act of Mary Garth's when she stoutly refused to 'soil the beginning' of her life by burning

the will of Mr. Featherstone. And she became one
of those strong, honest mothers of our race, such as,
says George Eliot, Rembrandt once loved to paint.
Silas Marner, when his greed for gold and his com-
passion for a starving and freezing child came into
conflict, took in Eppie and nursed her as a mother.
Over that scene George Eliot wrote: 'In old days
there were angels who came and took men by the
hand and led them away from the city of destruction.
We see no white-winged angels now. But yet men
are led away from threatening destruction; a hand is
put into theirs, which leads them forth gently toward
a calm and bright land, so that they look no more
backward; and the hand may be a little child's.'
Felix Holt, the champion of radicalism, of great
Gothic head and barbaric shoulders, swerved neither
to the right nor to the left, unregardful of the solici-
tations of expediency. Esther Lyon, without much
knowledge of the world, had to choose between wealth
and ease on the one hand, and poverty and duty.
Sorely perplexed by the conditions of her choice, she
chose rightly when she came to see them clearly.
Felix and Esther had their reward, if in no other way,
in that peace of memory which is the basis of hope.

It was not by mere accident that 'Adam Bede' and
'The Origin of Species' appeared in the same year.
George Eliot, as well as Darwin, is of the great scientific movement of the nineteenth century. Comte
built up a system of social and practical ethics, and
attempted a science of history, taking his analogies
from the facts of biological science. Taine went a
step further, and applied the results of Comte's inves-
tigations to historical criticism. George Eliot took

the ethical system of Comte, modified it much by a study of the great moralists of the past and present, and incorporated her conclusions in the novel. Like the scientist, she meant to deal only with phenomena and their laws. She takes into her study the Donnithornes, the Titos, and the Lydgates, and applies to them the intellectual scalpel and the intellectual microscope. With that keen scalpel of hers she lays bare the brain and heart; with that microscope she examines every nerve vibration; and with a trained ear she counts the heart-beats. As Dr. Lydgate once hoped to do, she 'pierces the obscurity of those minute processes which prepare human misery and joy, those invisible thoroughfares which are the first lurking-places of anguish, mania, and crime, that delicate poise and transition which determine the growth of happy or unhappy consciousness.' Her great law of conduct is the act and its consequences. Character, in her view, is not fixed; it is an evolution. We have, as it were, two selves. From the one comes the voice of duty proclaiming that our salvation lies in 'daring rectitude,' in meeting bravely every circumstance of life; from the other comes the insinuating voice of passion and egoism, which if heeded leads the deluded spirit on to the city of destruction. Which self shall be triumphant rests with ourselves. By our deeds we are saved or lost; by them we create in our own hearts an inferno or a paradise.

George Eliot gave prose-fiction a substance which it had never had before among any people. That her ethical system has logical inconsistencies we may admit. While intending to keep close to empiricism, she really admits transcendentalism in what she says about the inner and better self, and the command of duty, which she at least once calls a divine voice. Undoubtedly, too, the very greatest of English moralists was free from conscious systems; by deep intuition he displayed the emotions that sway men to action. But there has been only one Shakespeare. When systems become antiquated, the work that was reared upon them falls. Positivism was antiquated some years ago, and evolution has taken its place. George Eliot is, however, connected with the theories of her time more in appearance than in reality. In her ways of thinking, there is less of Comte than of Wordsworth and Thomas à Kempis, both of whom taught renunciation as a command. Between Dante and George Eliot there is a suggestive analogy. Dante expressed himself in the terms of the grotesque philosophy of the Middle Age. Thomas Aquinas is no longer read, while the fame of Dante increases more and more every day. Why? because the scholasticism of St. Thomas is only the vesture of Dante's own profound meditations, which each generation for itself may translate into its own language. So of George Eliot. Her moral discernments, often clothed in the language of positivism, are nevertheless imbedded everlastingly in the inherited thought of the ages. With a precision and a minuteness never possible before her time, she worked out the Hebrew formula, that they who sow the wind, shall reap the whirlwind; which was likewise the Greek idea, that when a wrong is done, the Eumenides, daughters of earth and darkness, will awake from their sleep and avenge it. And with the terrible earnestness of Æschylus, she reiterated the tragic corollary: 'We can conceive no retribution that does not spread beyond its mark in pulsations of unmerited pain.'

3. *George Meredith*

George Meredith is not a disciple of George Eliot. In fact, his first essay in fiction slightly antedates hers. 'The Shaving of Shagpat,' a pleasant Oriental entertainment, she appreciated for *The Westminster Review* for April, 1856. 'The Ordeal of Richard Feverel,' George Meredith's first regular novel, appeared in the same year as 'Adam Bede.' Twelve novels, not counting tales, have thus far followed: 'Evan Harrington' (1861); 'Emilia in England' (1864), afterward changed to 'Sandra Belloni'; 'Rhoda Fleming' (1865); 'Vittoria' (1867); 'Harry Richmond' (1871); 'Beauchamp's Career' (1876); 'The Egoist' (1879); 'The Tragic Comedians' (1880); 'Diana of the Crossways' (1885); 'One of our Conquerors' (1890); 'Lord Ormont and his Aminta' (1894); 'The Amazing Marriage' (1895).

From the first, George Meredith has been a psychologist. Thus he writes when well on in 'Richard Feverel': 'At present, I am aware, an audience impatient for blood and glory scorns the stress I am putting on incidents so minute, a picture so little imposing. An audience will come to whom it will be given to see the elementary machinery at work; who, as it were, from some slight hint of the straws, will feel the winds of March when they do not blow.' From this passage will be seen how like to George Eliot's conception of the novel is Meredith's; only his is subtler than hers, for she never asks us to feel the winds of

March when they do not blow. Both deal primarily
with the invisible life, the events of which they would
'render as consequent to your understanding as a
piece of logic, through an exposure of character.'
Both have their 'memorable crises' — the expression
is Meredith's as well as George Eliot's; in both is the
energizing of the scientific spirit in literature.

The audience Meredith felt assured of in 1859 has
hardly come to him, and he seems to allude to the fact
in the closing paragraph of 'The Amazing Marriage.'
Why has there been no rush pell-mell toward him?
Probably not because of the reason he implies — his
subject-matter — so much as because of his obscurity.
There are in his earlier novels passages of unsurpassa-
ble poetic beauty: Richard and Lucy in the woods by
the lake; the purification of Richard as nature and
the storm speak to him; Wilfrid and Emilia by Wilming Weir; and most marvellous of all in its rich,
Oriental luxuriousness, the London scene between
Richard and Mrs. Mount, the enchantress. A master
of color and melody when he wills, Meredith has
mostly cast his lot with those who have whimsically
misused the English language; he is of the company
of Sterne, Carlyle, and Browning. He does not speak
directly, his aim being 'a fantastic delivery of the
verities'; and to be at pleasure utterly unintelligible
is one of the graces of his style. He began by speaking through maxims and aphorisms, and he still
speaks through them. They are not witty sayings
like Mrs. Poyser's, which give truths in half-lights;
they come from the meditation of a phrase-builder;
and in them is concentrated his criticism of contemporary life. He says, for example, 'Men may have

rounded Seraglio Point; they have not yet doubled Cape Turk,' and leaves it to you to think out what he means. He is fond of quaint and finely drawn allegory, going so far as to describe a 'Philosophical Geography,' with its Rubicon and Acheron, which stands in the same relation to morals as Scudéri's chart to the analysis of love. Even to his fit audience, though few, Meredith was for a long time perplexing. His purpose was not apparent, and perhaps because he himself had not clearly defined to himself what he wished to do. The illumination came when in 1877 he published a lecture in plain English, entitled 'On the Idea of Comedy and of the Uses of the Comic Spirit.' After-light came from the prelude to 'The Egoist' and the initial chapter of 'Diana.' Since these prolegomena, there has been no sufficient reason for not following Meredith in the main drift. 'The Egoist,' which soon followed the essay on comedy, is the type of the Meredith novel, containing all that may be found in the rest, except that the poetry, romance, wit, and pathos of some of the earlier novels are here held in greater restraint.

Meredith has given the novel a new heroine. Before him three types of woman had prevailed in our fiction. The heroine was usually the lady of chivalry. While she was in reality the slave of her husband or lover, he was ostensibly her worshipper. This lady of the castle still exists in our social ideal; and as a consequence she has stood in the foreground of our fiction. In contrast to her, Thackeray placed the rogue of the Spanish novel. In the lighter forms of fiction the woman of farce was omnipresent, to be pommelled by satire, jest, and innuendo. From these three ideals, there had been some notable breakings-away, in Jane Austen, Charlotte Brontë, Trollope, and George Eliot. In Meredith we have their utter repudiation. His women are never rogues, nor are they flawless; they are obnoxious to ridicule, and he ridicules them. They are always beautiful, because they are healthy. They can dance, but they like the open air best; they are lithe of limb; they run and jump, and fall of exhaustion; they have fresh faces and they eat well. Their heads are furnished with brains and with a dislike of losing their identity; they fight for their independence and win. If they find it necessary, they clip the locks of their lovers and husbands, and abandon them to the Philistines. Then, arm-in-arm with the men they love, they proceed to a jolly dance down what the world calls 'the halls of madness.' Such is the composite portrait of Emilia, Clara, Diana, and Aminta.

Meredith is at war with sentimentalism. This word of vague content he defines enigmatically in the first chapter of 'Diana': 'The sentimental people *fiddle harmonics on the strings of sensualism,* to the delight of a world gaping for marvels of musical execution rather than for music.' Benevolence, kindness, charity, — all the altruistic virtues, — are sentimentalities, unless the heart goes with the act. So too are equally self-pity and the 'sham decent.' The present social code determining the conduct of sex to sex has its foundation in sentimentalism. It has come to us from the bepraised age of chivalry, which was the age of barbarism. All our nice sexual etiquette is only 'a fine flower or a pinnacle flame-spire,' starting up from sensuality. The best that can be said of it is that the

beast veiled is better than the beast uncovered.
Very severe is Meredith on the folly of those boys
and girls who meet in the pale moonlight to part
forever or to swear eternal love. Wilfrid and
Emilia are sitting by Wilming Weir at evening, and
this is a piece of their conversation with Meredith's
comment: —

'You are my own, are you not, Emilia?'
'Yes; I am,' she answered simply.
'That water seems to say "for ever,"' he murmured; and
Emilia's fingers pressed upon his.
Of marriage there was no further word. Her heart was
evidently quite at ease; and that it should be so without chain-
ing him to a date, was Wilfrid's peculiar desire. He could
pledge himself to eternity, but shrank from being bound to
eleven o'clock on the morrow morning.

The egoism of Willoughby, in 'The Egoist,' is one of
the various manifestations of sentimentalism. It is
not because of genuine passion that he proposes to
Constantia Durham and Clara Middleton; his feeling
toward them is only a kind of agreeable nerve irritation
from the presence of fine form and bearing. All his
talk to Clara about their being all in all to each other
and their keeping themselves unspotted from the world,
is the sickly animal speaking in him. So too his demanding of her that she shall be his not only in life
but in death; so too his straightening himself up erect
as the letter I, when it is rumored that he is engaged to
a widow. Why should not a man marry a widow?
Meredith would ask. It is a morbid sentiment that
makes widows unmarketable. The main thing in
marriage is suitability as common sense points it out:
in the ideal union husband and wife are 'capital

comrades,' like Weyburn and Aminta. What is disagreeable to Meredith is an unhealthy animalism,
which, however much it may stalk behind form, is
nothing more than bestiality. Are not Meredith's discernments true to fact? Is not sentimentalism born
of the beast and unreason? No one can much doubt
it, who has read the 'Confessions' of Rousseau. On
the other hand, says Meredith in substance, the senses
have their right uses, and reality is of infinite sweetness. And what are the right uses of the senses? and
what is the sweetness of reality? — these questions
he has answered in his strong athletic heroines,
in whom the animal has received the stamp of the
spirit.

Though shunning all unsound feeling and self-
imposed misery, Meredith maintains that there is
pathos in his novels. He and George Eliot have best
expressed the new view of tragedy which presided at
the birth of the modern novel. According to the old
view, as we have it in our national drama, there can
be technically no tragedy without at least one violent
death. To-day we distinguish less mechanically.
Death in and of itself is no longer tragic. It is tragic
only in certain circumstances, as when a man falls in
the midst of worthy labors, or leaves behind him
children unprotected and unprovided for. On the
other hand, we see the intensest pathos in life itself;
and science has enforced common observation. The
tragedy is not in the cries of Prometheus bound,
but in Prometheus not yet bound, says George
Eliot; in 'a solitude of despised ideas,' in 'the fatal
pressure of poverty and disease.' Thus the tragedy
of Dr. Lydgate is not in his death so much as in his

failure as a man. The tragedy of Meredith is less obvious and less pronounced than George Eliot's. He has no inferno through which his characters slip from circle to circle, but rather a purgatory through whose fires he marches them for their purification. It may be that a great social wrong has been committed; then Richard Feverel must pass through a severe ordeal. It may be that a young woman in her ignorance and thoughtlessness has promised to marry or has in fact married a man for whom she can have no affection; the act must be atoned for, as in the case of Clara and Aminta. The tragedy of Meredith is almost always held in firm barriers, and its darkness is pierced by the approach of morning; as in that scene in the park when Clara pleads with Willoughby for freedom.

'You are cold, my love? You shivered.'
'I am not cold,' said Clara. 'Some one, I suppose, was walking over my grave.'
The gulf of a caress hove in view like an enormous billow hollowing under the curled ridge.
She stooped to a buttercup; the monster swept by.

As in this conversation, the tragedy of situation and character with Meredith frequently passes into grave comedy. He has written tragi-comedies. The sub-title of 'The Egoist' is 'A Comedy in Narrative.' By comedy Meredith does not mean farce and gayety, but serious social ridicule on the border-land of the tragic and comic states. He makes a very nice distinction between humor and comedy. We usually roughly class Cervantes, Fielding, Sterne, and Thackeray together as humorists. But are not Cervantes and Fielding comic writers, and does not professional

humor date from Sterne? Cervantes and Fielding
ridicule folly: the former, among many follies, the
reading of romances of chivalry; the latter, among
many follies, clean-cut ethical maxims, the conduct of
contemporary men and women and their education,
and the presumption of taking as the subject of a
novel a class of men and women concerning whom
you are in the densest ignorance. It is a correction
of manners they aim at in the light of comic consciousness. Sterne fiddled the harmonics for amusement. The cast of Thackeray's mind was that of the
comic writer. His setting out to correct Dickens, to
teach him how to write a novel, by making its heroine
Becky Sharp instead of Little Nell, Meredith would
call a comic situation. But there is another element
in Thackeray, which came from Sterne, — a literary
sentimentalism. This mingling of sentiment and
comedy is humor; it lacks, according to Meredith, the
high seriousness of Fielding; and its force as a social
corrective is lost. Comedy he conceives of as a Muse
watching the actions of men and women, detecting
and pointing out their inconsistencies with a view to
their moral improvement. She never laughs aloud, she
only smiles at most; and the smile is of the intellect,
for she is the handmaid of philosophy. For the
frailties of human nature she has no ridicule, for she
is no pessimist; for individual men she has no lash-
ings, for satire is not comedy. She 'is impersonal and
of unrivalled politeness,' occupying herself with the
unnatural and conventional codes we have built up for
ourselves, and she leads the way to a higher civilization. She may be called the humor of the mind, in
distinction from the humor of Sterne and Thackeray,

which is the humor of the heart; and the heart is sensation and material.[1]

Do you not experience 'a tremble of the laughing muscles,' Meredith would ask, when you contrast the conduct of Willoughby with what it would be, were he not in love with himself? He insists on a woman's marrying him after she has fled from him; and will release her from the engagement only on condition that she shall consent to marry his cousin, with whom in his blindness he is not aware she is desperately in love. He boasts of the bravery of the Patternes, citing as an example of it an act of heroism performed by a Lieutenant Patterne in the navy, and sends him a check. When the 'thick-set, stumpy marine' makes his appearance at the Hall in a pouring rain, without gloves and umbrella, Sir Willoughby is 'not at home.' He would not marry into the aristocracy, because 'he doubted the quality of their blood.' The woman he marries must swear to be his eternally, for he fears that he may die first, and his spirit be harassed by the scandals that pursue widows. He tells Clara that he is no poet, and she replies that she has not accused him. Should you tell Meredith that his comedy is elusive and over finely wrought, he might reply, using one of his favorite words, that you are obtuse.

Himself a product of science, Meredith has spoken very disrespectfully of her. We went to her, he says, for light, and she told us that we are animals. And

---

[1] While there is much truth in Meredith's contentions, they are nevertheless based upon a questionable psychology. It is a fanciful procedure to detach the intellect from the feelings, and then to place it above them.

is there not an element of truth in what he avers? The first great scientific discoveries the contemporaries of Comte and Mill welcomed with hopes and enthusiasms no longer intelligible; society in its inner life, they thought, was to be revolutionized. Men who like Meredith are the connecting links between those days and the present have become disillusioned. The path taken by science has not been what they supposed it would be. Its ends have been mainly practical; it has ministered unto physical comforts; it has led to agnosticism. Not one whit has the spirit within been purified and made nobler by it. Egoism, for example, in its thousand phases is as rampant now as it was fifty years ago.

'Art,' says Meredith, 'is the specific.' He does not believe in that form of realism which lays claim to an actual transcription of manners. Life is too short for that, and nothing is to be gained by it. What, let it be asked, is the value of the numerous stories of New England and the Tennessee mountains, and of all provincial fiction? So far as they are true to fact in dialect and local color, they are documents for the linguist and the historian. Their value as art, beyond a transient amusement, which in a decade becomes ennui, depends wholly upon the extent they rise from the particular to the general and everlasting truths of human consciousness and conduct; upon the extent their characters are broadened by imperceptible gradations from the individual to the type, never being quite the one nor quite the other. Such types the characters of Meredith have been mostly since 'Sandra Belloni.' Not life in its wearisome vastness nor a patch of it is his aim, but 'a summary' of it. He works as a philosopher; he mingles with society, and believes that he detects certain maladies, and he aims at the artistic presentation of them. The malady of men is a primeval egoism in their attitude toward women. Consequently many of Meredith's men are egoists. His great feminine characters are also types, and in a measure homologues. They are women as they would be if emancipated, verging into women as they are, faultily educated and hemmed in by historic conventions. Meredith would be another Menander or Molière: he would probe life with a clear perception, and, by pointing out our absurdities, show us what we are.

CHAPTER VIII

The Contemporary Novel

1. *Henry James and Impressionism*

By the contemporary novel is meant the novel of the younger generation of writers. George Meredith, of the present and the past, has carried on the literary tradition of George Eliot. But he belongs essentially to a time when science amused itself with broad generalizations, when its methods were synthetic rather than analytical. Hence his impatience with the course of speculation since the advent of Darwin. Science has become more and more exact; in withering irony and sarcasm, it has excluded the so-called spiritual from its consideration or has reduced the spiritual to the material; beyond perception it refuses to go; it has found its working hypothesis in the theory of evolution; and as to minor formulas, it proceeds warily. Literature has watched science eager for instruction; it has aimed at scientific exactness of perception. Where it has not done this, it has, by theory or practice or both, insisted that imagination should be subordinated to observation.

The romancer of fifty years ago seated himself in a retired nook of England, behind ivied walls and shuttered windows, and described the life and scenery of the Spanish main. When raised to competency and leisure by the sale of his books, he visited the places he had described, and found them wonderfully like what he had seen in his imagination. His descendant of to-day does not so. He visits the country he intends to illustrate ; he jots down outward characteristics and minutiæ of manners, customs, dress, and scenery, and sets them into some kind of frame, labelling the result a novel. In individual instances he has accompanied pilgrims to famous shrines or followed the soldier to the battle-field, writing in full detail of all he saw. His counterpart is the tourist with a pocket camera. Other novelists have made prolonged studies of character and manners in some well-defined district. We have novels, and hosts of them, of village and town life in England, Scotland, Ireland, New England, the South, the West, Australia, India, and Africa, written not by men and women who have left their homes in search of material. These novelists, themselves a part of what they depict, have aimed at living cross-sections of life. They have, as it were, their specialties, like the scientist, the professional man, and the merchant. We read them for information or amusement, pleased to learn how our cousins are living in distant places. Though interest in this kind of fiction must eventually become local and provincial, undoubtedly there are pieces written by these specialists that will become classics, just as ' Cranford ' has already become a classic.

From this universal realism has issued — under the influence of Ivan Turgénev and Alphonse Daudet — an artistic presentation of the matter of real life often called impressionism, of which one of the exponents in criticism and fiction is Henry James. 'A novel,' he has said, 'is in its broadest definition a personal, a direct impression of life: that, to begin with, constitutes its value, which is greater or less according to the intensity of the impression.'[1] He describes only what he sees, but not all that he sees. The following from the 'Tragic Muse' (1890) is what is seen at a glance: 'What Biddy discerned was that this young man was fair and fat and of the middle stature; he had a round face and a short beard, and on his crown a mere reminiscence of hair, as the fact that he carried his hat in his hand permitted it to be observed.' And speaking of the women with this man, Biddy says: 'One of them was an old lady with a shawl; that was the most salient way in which she presented herself.' This is not photography, which, making no distinction between one detail and another, gives a crude impression of them all; it is art. Out of a possible multitude of details, James selects the striking or significant pose and incident. Moreover, he 'strains the visual sense' that he may observe nuances the camera refuses to reproduce, laying claim to a superior faculty of perception. When we read Howells we wonder that we have not seen in the commonplace what he sees. In the case of James, we wonder that there is so much to be seen; and question whether what he sees is really there. For example, the Tragic Muse has wretchedly failed in her first performance. One of the spectators nevertheless still believes in her : —

He remained conscious that something surmounted and survived her failure, something that would perhaps be worth

[1] 'The Art of Fiction,' in 'Partial Portraits,' London and New York, 1888.

taking hold of. It was the element of outline and attitude, the way she stood, the way she turned her eyes, her head, and moved her limbs. These things held the attention ; they had a natural felicity and, in spite of their suggesting too much the school-girl in the *tableau-vivant*, a sort of grandeur. Her face, moreover, grew as he watched it ; something delicate dawned in it, a dim promise of variety and a touching plea for patience, as if it were conscious of being able to show in time more expressions than the simple and striking gloom, which, as yet, had mainly graced it. In short, the plastic quality of her person was the only definite sign of a vocation.

From this passage it will be observed that James looks at the externals of life through the eyes of the connoisseur of the fine arts, particularly of painting. As here his language is that of the studio; his most repeated words being, outline, color, style, form, and plastic fact. The impressionist is also a psychologist. George Eliot begins with inner states and inner events and works her way outward; sometimes never reaching the surface at all, as in the eleventh chapter of 'Deronda,' where she records parenthetically the thoughts of Gwendolen and Grandcourt, in the pauses of their first conversation. James begins on the outside and passes a little way beneath appearance, reading character through feature and movement of eyes, head, and limb. It is the manner of Richardson, to which is added the trained perception that has come with science.

James is inclined to play with the stern analysis of George Eliot. He evidently thinks that the 'crisis' has been overdone; and he would call attention to the fact that our conduct in the so-called 'sacramental moments' often leaves no visible trace. It is not customary with him to round off his plots; whether the novel is long or short, it is an episode. Men and women meet, have their tender experiences, and then go their way. Nothing happens in his novels, the critics used to say. The marriage expected in the last chapter does not take place; if the young man and young woman marry at all, it is to some one else. This apparent incompleteness originated among the modern realists in an attempt to correlate literature more closely with life as it is. But in the view of the impressionist there is no incompleteness; rather a higher morality than in the old novel, where virtue was rewarded and villany punished. 'The moral sense and the artistic sense,' James has written, 'lie very close together.'[1] In 'The Tragic Muse,' a portrait painter would marry an ambitious woman-politician; and a diplomat would marry an actress. James does not allow these events to happen. He marries the actress to a third-rate actor, and leaves the rest of his characters unmarried. For him to do otherwise would be insincere art, just as in real life a marriage between a man and woman having no common fund of ideas would be an immoral act. We should stick to the career nature seems to have marked out for us, accept the conditions, and struggle on to the end.

Though the impressionists have written novels of all lengths, they have chiefly cultivated the short-story. Short stories have been frequent in our literature ever since the Renaissance. Under the name of tracts they were given a wide circulation by Hannah More, a hundred years ago. A large number were written by Maria Edgeworth, and several by Irving. They received great encouragement in the middle of

[1] 'The Art of Fiction.'

this century from the editors of magazines. They
were beautifully wrought by Poe and Hawthorne,
who first gave them a style and an art of their own.
As written by Poe and Hawthorne, they were usually
brief narratives, best designated as short tales. More
recent writers have considerably enlarged the means
of procedure; sometimes they make use of narrative,
but more frequently of dialogue, and there are examples of the ingenious management of letters. On
the subject Professor Brander Matthews has written
a philosophical essay,[1] in which he claims for the recent short-story the right of being a distinct species of
the novel. It is to the regular novel, according to him,
what the lyric is to the epic; it is, in his words, 'a
high and difficult department of fiction,' because of
the extreme concision required and the inelastic laws
that govern it. Like the sonnet, it must be a unit,
giving expression to one emotion or a series of emotions possessing a unity of tone; its characters must
be few; its action must be simple; it tells something, but it suggests more. It satisfies a large body
of readers who do not have time to look at things
long or steadfastly. What is wanted is a momentary
impression of them, artistically delivered.

2. *Philosophical Realism: Mrs. Humphry Ward and Thomas Hardy*

While Henry James has been weaving a delicate psychological tissue, Mrs. Humphry Ward has held to
the firmer texture of the old-time novel. Like George

[1] 'The Philosophy of the Short-Story,' in 'Pen and Ink,' New
York and London, 1888.

Eliot, she has assimilated something of Wordsworth and Dante. She feels the weight of chance desires, and seeks refuge in the voice of duty. In the intense phrases of the 'Divine Comedy' she finds a natural vent to her spiritual moods. But between 'Middlemarch' and 'Robert Elsmere' (1888) is sixteen years. During this period the world of thought and speculation moved rapidly and far; and social theories took new and strange forms. Mrs. Ward has reflected these changes. George Eliot, though an agnostic, had, in common with others of her time, scruples against propagandism, as if she did not fully trust the conclusions of her intellect. Not so Mrs. Ward. She refashions the church on Christ as a human ideal, placing the Church of England by the side of 'the Brotherhood of Jesus,' in the spirit of criticism and proselytism. She delves in Christian origins, scrutinizing and weighing testimony with the confidence of her uncle Matthew Arnold, who re-wrote the Bible on his own lines. George Eliot's altruistic ethical formula was general in application, having a bearing upon conduct in all circumstances. Mrs. Ward, in a like altruistic manner, expounds what she calls industrial ethics. She takes up, as in 'Marcella,' contemporary social theories, criticises them, shows whither they lead, and comes forward with a solution of her own, which is a *via media*. The compass of her work has increased with each successive novel, until in 'Helbeck of Bannisdale' she has depicted the spiritual struggle of a devout Catholic in contact with modern unbelief. Everything she does is wrought at a high emotional pitch, where there is no temptation to laugh or even smile at absurdities.

Mrs. Ward is the inspirer of a popular group of novelists who have turned to current speculations for the purposes of open didacticism. They have discussed class distinctions, agrarian reforms, the intricate problems of labor and capital, the theory and practice of municipal government, etc.; and most sensationally, the social enfranchisement of woman, the failure of marriage, and the grounds for divorce. Like the revolutionary novelists at the close of the eighteenth century, they have embellished the political treatise for people who would not read it without the story of passion. Into their work has crept once more the humanitarian motive, and, as a few years will make clear, a sentimental note very like Rousseau's.

As science proceeds by experiment, which has been defined as 'provoked observation,' the novelist has asked, Why cannot literature do likewise? It is in France that the experimental novel first received its apotheosis. In 1869, Emile Zola wrote the 'Fortune des Rougon' (published in book form in 1871), the first of a long series of novels bearing the general title, 'Les Rougon-Macquart, histoire naturelle et sociale d'une Famille sous le second Empire'; the series closed in 1893, with 'Docteur Pascal.' In his critical writings[1] during the decade 1880–90, Zola formulated the body of principles which should govern the 'naturalist' or the 'experimental novelist.' The story as groundwork of the novel must never be invented out of one's head; it must be taken from direct observation, the newspaper, or some well-authenticated report;

[1] 'Le Roman Expérimental' (1880): English translation, B. M Sherman, London and New York, 1893.

it must be a piece of life itself.   For example, it may
be supposed that Zola reads of a young woman who,
when about to leap into the Seine, is rescued by the
police. He has an interview with her, finds out all
he can about her, the surroundings under which she
has grown up, and the character and occupation of her
parents. He studies similar cases, let us say ten or
twelve; then he makes his generalization, maintaining
that for a given set of environing and hereditary conditions, there is only one issue. To him there is no
uncertain quantity in the problem; he takes no account of a mysterious element in human nature, which
may rise and assert itself, for to do so would not be
scientific. He is now ready to write his *débâcle*. In
any single novel of Zola's, it is the visible environment that appears most to determine the outcome;
but read three or four of his novels as they fall
chronologically in the series, and it will be seen
that he has also sought to treat the other determining
force, character passing from generation to generation.
Certain corollaries follow from his method. There
is no artificial shuffling in the last chapter, no revolution of fortune, no happy marriages, no unexpected
inheritances, the climax is inevitable, for it is marked
out by nature. The author should never let his feelings interfere to turn events into a fantastic channel;
he should not assume the *rôle* of wit or humorist, —
life is too serious for that; he should speak as a scientist, telling precisely what he observes.

The difference between this so-called naturalism and
the older realism may be illustrated by a criticism
of some of our realists from the naturalistic point
of view. Fielding, as has been remarked, had

the naturalist's situation in 'Amelia,' a woman of some rank married to a gambling lieutenant who is unable to support her and her children. The issue nature has fixed; but Fielding, taking things into his own hand, disturbs the logic of events that the story may end pleasantly. The material Dickens worked is of superlative naturalistic quality. For example, the episode of Stephen Blackpool in 'Hard Times' possesses the inherent possibilities of Zola's 'L'Assommoir' or Hardy's 'Jude the Obscure.' The dissipated wife, the ruined home, and the hard-laboring husband are all there. Dickens, however, lights up his dark picture with sublime suffering, which the naturalists regard as a sham. Thackeray, when he should speak out plainly about Becky Sharp, hedges and becomes silent. Of the fiction of the last generation, 'Middlemarch' comes nearest to the experimental novel. George Eliot describes briefly the career of Dr. Lydgate as student, places him in a midland town, and then tells how he behaves. The determining forces of his conduct are, accordingly, his antecedents and his environment, plus an unexplainable personality. This is not satisfactory to the naturalists. They would eliminate every vestige of freedom whereby an individual becomes responsible for his acts. Naturalism is thus determinism.

Of philosophical realism of the kind just described, Thomas Hardy is the best English representative. Born in Dorsetshire, he has studied closely the peasant life of his native shire and those neighboring counties which together comprised the ancient kingdom of Wessex. Why he has left the madding crowd for the country folk, he explained in an essay pub-

lished in *The Forum* for March, 1888. Writing the
common language of his brotherhood, — equally well
understood in England, France, Germany, and Scan-
dinavia, — he says that the conduct of the upper
classes is screened by conventions, and thus the real
character is not easily seen; and if it is seen, it must
be portrayed subjectively : whereas in the lower
walks, conduct is a direct expression of the inner life;
and thus character can be directly portrayed through
the act. 'In the one case the author's word has to be
taken as to the nerves and muscles of his figures; in
the other they can be seen as in an *écorché.*' From
their views on the question of style, the naturalists
fall into two general classes. There are the extrem-
ists who — like Aristotle, the practical realist of an-
tiquity — let style look out for itself, on the ground
that any attention to it would result in a rhetorical
misrepresentation of fact. And there are the poets
who clothe the disagreeable narrative in the most
pleasing language at command. To the latter class
Hardy has the most affinity. The choice of words
and the arrangement of them in and for themselves,
he does not believe in. His aim is at an exact and
felicitous expression of his ideas and emotions; and
the first principle that he lays down to this end is the
'lucid order' of Horace. Style in this high sense he
would do his little toward bringing to ultimate perfection. When completed the novel should give, on
account of the harmony of the subject-matter and its
treatment, an æsthetic pleasure similar to that derived
from a fine painting.

Hardy struck the note of the newer realism in 'A
Pair of Blue Eyes' (1873), which is a lament, not

without much cynicism, over the clash of circumstance and individual effort. In 'The Return of the Native' (1878) is magnificently expressed his love of the dark and sinister in nature, and his feeling of the nothingness of human life in the presence of the everlasting heath. Here he began to speak of physical beauty — the face without its lines of care — as an anachronism, of life as 'a thing to be put up with,' of 'the defects of natural laws,' and 'the quandary that man is in by their operation.' In 'Tess of the D'Urbervilles' (1891), he gave freer utterance to the same mood, which had now become more intense. In 'Jude the Obscure' (1895), he threw off every semblance of restraint, writing a novel that his earlier admirers were unable to read.

'Tess of the D'Urbervilles,' his mightiest production, is a tragedy that at no period in our history other than these *fin de siècle* days could have been written; or, if written, could have been understood. And what is its novelty? Surely it is not the subject-matter, for recall 'Clarissa Harlowe' and 'Adam Bede.' It has been a tacit assumption in English tragedy that the dramatic hero must commit some deed from which he suffers. The deed may be a crime, as in 'Macbeth'; it may issue from a fault in judgment, as in the case of Brutus, or from a stubborn vanity, as in the case of Lear. That there are likely to be innocent victims of the deed may be admitted, and therein lies the deeper pathos of Shakespearean tragedy. The way George Eliot, somewhat like Shakespeare, traced the events of her sombre novels to free individual acts of will we have elaborated. The tragedy of 'Tess of the D'Urbervilles' begins in a crime and ends in a crime; Alec pays the penalty for his misdeeds. But Alec is only a subordinate character. Tess is the main and central character, who, from first to last, Hardy insists, is free from any wrong-doing. In this reversal of the traditions of tragedy both in our drama and our novel, Hardy is an innovator.

Tess stands in isolated weakness. She has a conscience and a will that may possibly be called her own, but against her are her father and mother, Alec, Angel, a conventional society, nature, hereditary tendencies, and a malicious course of events. With what happens to her she has nothing to do. In forced obedience to her parents she goes to Trantridge, the home of the spurious D'Urbervilles. The smutching of her innocence there is an act of treachery, for which she is in no wise responsible. Her love for Angel Clare, which results in the ill-starred marriage, is the working in her of a cruel law of nature, against which she struggles in vain. She returns to Alec to save her mother, brothers, and sisters from starvation. If it be said that at this point in her career there is a relaxation of will, Hardy has anticipated the remark by suggesting that her weakness is in part inherited, and in part the product of the enervating climate in which she has grown up. She puts a knife into the heart of Alec. Even this act is outside her normal character, for when herself she could not hurt a fly or a worm, and she wept at the sight of a bird in its cage; to it she was led by an 'obscure strain in the D'Urberville blood.' By her death she atones not for her own crimes, but for those of her race; for wrongs, to paraphrase Hardy, that her mailed ancestors, rollicking home from frays, had dealt upon peasant girls, say, back in the reign of King Stephen. Likewise the conduct of Angel Clare finds its explanation mostly in heredity. From the Evangelicism of his parents he had broken away, and taken refuge in Greek paganism; but when the crisis came, the 'creed of mysticism' rose to the surface and became master. That inherited subconsciousness he succeeded in stilling only by his sojourn in Brazil.

In harmony with Hardy's view of character as the resultant of heredity and environment, is his notion of events that lie outside and beyond us; of happenings, chance, fortune. The Immortals would appear to have become enraged at Tess, and to have predestined her hard career. At the very threshold of life she meets the wrong man. A few days before she marries Angel Clare, she pushes under the door of his bedroom a written confession, which slips out of sight under the carpet, where it remains concealed until found by Tess on the wedding morning. On a Sunday, Tess tramps fifteen miles to the parsonage of the elder Clare to seek protection; there is no answer to her ring at the door, for the family is at church. At just the wrong time she now stumbles upon Alec once more. A letter she despatches to Angel in Brazil is delayed, and he reaches home a few days too late. This ironical arrangement of events, Hardy declares to be 'a true sequence of things,' and asks, with a thrust at Wordsworth: Wherein can be seen 'Nature's holy plan'? Wherein a beneficent Providence? And coming to the prime events, he inquires: Why was Tess born? where are 'the clouds of glory'? 'To her and her like, birth itself was an ordeal of degrading personal compulsion, whose gratuitousness nothing in the result seemed to justify, and at best could only palliate.' This is the pessimism associated with the names of Leopardi and Schopenhauer. It is not within the province of literary criticism to argue either for or against it as a philosophical tenet. In the ferment of ideas in these closing days of the century, in our hasty adjustment of the new conceptions of science and experimental philosophy to life, pessimism has been accepted by millions either openly or tacitly. With an immense audience, Germanic, Latin, and Slav, Hardy is in perfect agreement.

On the other hand, he is out of joint with the codes of conduct sanctioned by a Christian civilization. His cynical thrusts at Sunday-school teachers and well-intentioned gentlemen in black we must pass by. By prolonged observation of the country folk, where the heart is less concealed than among the great, he has come to the conclusion that they are still pagan, as in the days when their ancestors worshipped Thor and Odin. On one occasion Tess hums the Benedicite, and finds in it rest and consolation. Hardy tells why: it is 'a Pantheistic utterance in a Monotheistic falsetto.' He watches the sun break through the August mists; and says: 'The sun, on account of the mist, had a curious sentient, personal look, demanding the masculine pronoun for its adequate expression. His present aspect, coupled with the lack of all human forms in the scene, explained the old-time heliolatries in a moment. One could feel that a saner religion had never prevailed under the sun.' Agnosticism he apparently welcomes, for if it is not a return to sun-worship, it is a blow struck at 'theolatry.' The novel is throughout pagan in tone; and its paganism climbs to its height in the impressive scenes of the closing chapters, where Tess rises at daybreak from a fallen altar of a Druidic temple, to be conducted to a cathedral city for trial and death.

Quite as important to Hardy's drama as the actors, are nature and all external objects. That intimate relationship with things as personalities, which older civilizations felt and which is possessed by children, Hardy has preserved. His scenes he does not describe; he makes one acquainted with them, as if he were introducing his friends. Seasons — he says, to paraphrase him slightly — have their moods; morning and evening, night and noon, have their temperaments; winds, trees, waters, clouds, silences, and constellations have their dispositions; and all speak in voices audible to the spirit. To Tess of Marlott, a sudden gust of wind through the roadside trees and hedges on a starlit night is 'the sigh of some immense sad soul, conterminous with the universe in space, and with history in time.' Upon Tess of the Var Valley, the trees look down with 'inquisitive eyes,' and the river reproaches her for living. As she moves through the meadows in the morning light, her head emerging from the low-lying mists, she is to Angel Clare the Magdalen, or Artemis, or Demeter. A rough table-land at evening is 'Cybele the Many-breasted' reclining with outstretched limbs. Salisbury plain at the approach of morning is a mighty being waking from sleep. In one great scene clothing is made sensible to the steadfast gaze, and in one still greater, even furniture is endowed with life. Thus marvellously Hardy interprets the external world through the moods of his characters. This manner has been condemned by Ruskin as fallacious, because of the conceits to which it leads. But it has the authority of Coleridge and Milton. And as managed by Hardy, things about his characters become a substitute for the Greek chorus of ancient counsellors and warriors sharing in the tragedy and commenting upon it, as it moves on, under the guidance of the Fates, to the certain disaster.

Any criticism of Hardy must be based on first principles, for it is impossible to question his fine workmanship. To him literary art owes a debt which at some time will be more highly appreciated than it is now. But he and the other philosophic realists since George Eliot have all failed to see the important distinction between science and literature. It may be granted that, so far as science can throw any light on the subject, our conduct is determined for us. And yet there is a voice from the depths of consciousness which says this is not the whole truth. Human nature is not comprehended by formulas and theorems. Whatever may be our speculative beliefs, we all behave as if we were in a measure free, and responsible for our acts. And so has literature thus far usually represented us. True, our novelists since Richardson have been disposed to call attention to restraining forces from the outside; and for that very reason the novel has expressed the modern view of conduct better than the drama has yet been able to do. Nevertheless, Richardson, Fielding, and George Eliot left indefinite the boundary line between freedom and restraint. Like Shakespeare and Milton before them, they did not attempt to give a fixed denotation to the words *fate, doom, fortune,* and *Providence,* any more than any one does in the language of common speech. Probably literature will have to let the matter rest where the greatest of the past were contented to let it rest. Toward the close of the last century a group of novelists experimented with determinism; the reading public revolted, and turned to the Gothic romance and then to Scott and Cooper. Something very like this, in a smaller way perhaps, is happening to-day.

3. *Robert Louis Stevenson and the Revival of Romance*

During the long period of realism from 'Pickwick' to 'Tess,' the spirit of romance, as is evident from our narrative, was not dead. Some of her old lovers, Harrison Ainsworth and James Grant, lived on and kept writing down to 1880. Charles Reade was uncertain whether he was a realist or a romancer, and so he called 'The Cloister and the Hearth' 'a matter-of-fact romance.' George Eliot's Gwendolen Harleth 'in sea-green robes and silver ornaments, with a pale sea-green feather fastened in silver, falling backwards over her green hat and light brown hair,' is a serpent wrought in the full details of Keats and the mediæval allegorists. But these are survivals. Forty-odd years ago, modern spiritualism gave rise to a literature dealing with the night side of nature. A chair stealing to the side of the story-teller as he sits by the fireplace smoking his evening pipe; the patter of invisible feet on the stairway as he mounts to his chamber; and a materialized spirit or two standing at the foot of the four-poster as he lies awake listening to the faint ticking of his watch, which in a moment is silent and in another drops from its resting-place with a thud to the floor — such were some of the current incidents. And in these latter days, romance has fed on the reports of the Society for Psychical Research. Of this pseudo-spiritualism, the classic is Bulwer-Lytton's 'Haunted and the Haunters' (*Blackwood's Magazine*, 1860).

The novel of crime has also found out new sources of horror, and its popular writer for above thirty years was Wilkie Collins. The quality of his work is well represented in miniature by 'A Terribly Strange Bed,' whose heavy tester slowly sinks down to smother the sleeper. He won his great popularity by 'The Woman in White' (1860); and thereafter novel after novel of the same kind followed, one of the best being 'The Moonstone' (1868). He always had a good story, which was a mystification so adroitly put together that the secret lay beyond guess to the end. It was he who handed over the detective story from Poe to the author of 'Sherlock Holmes.' Some thirty years ago began to be common the romance of science; the purpose of which was to decorate the most showy scientific discoveries. Examples of this kind of romancing are 'Elsie Venner' (1861), 'a medicated novel' by Oliver Wendell Holmes, and Bulwer-Lytton's 'Coming Race' (1871), in which was set forth the Utopia of an age of electricity. Bulwer's romance was also mildly socialistic; and as the facts of science became more and more trite, it was this socialistic phase that in a few years appeared the most striking. Witness 'Looking Backward' (1888), by Edward Bellamy, which was taken seriously by the reformers and at length by the author himself. In 1869 R. D. Black-more published 'Lorna Doone,' the first of his many similar picturesque fictions in rhythmic prose. More gorgeous still are the romances of William Black, of which 'A Princess of Thule' (1873) tells a pathetic love idyl of the Hebrides. In the eighties, H. Rider Haggard revived the marvels of the East. Though of singularly slight literary value, his fictions served as an antidote to the surfeit of realism. The real initiator of what is most beautiful and lovely in contemporary romance was William Morris. He wrote tales in verse, in prose, and in verse and prose commingled, and all in a simple and entrancing manner. Away from the stressful burdens of modern civilization, he directed the imagination back to the time when 'Geoffrey Chaucer's pen moved over bills of lading,' and thence to the Icelandic sagas. In these epochs, he discovered an earthly paradise beside 'a nameless city in a distant sea.'

The romancer who has won the affections of the present generation, both old and young, is Robert Louis Stevenson. Blackmore has appealed to youth at the sentimental stage. Morris has addressed the æsthetic sensibilities of the scholar who delights in hearing deliciously retold the old stories of Ogier the Dane and Sigurd the Volsung. Stevenson with a middle flight has reached both the scholar and the general reader. Women only has he failed to please; and there is good reason for this; for with love as a motive he dealt charily. It is true that love romance is present in many of his novels, in 'Prince Otto,' 'The Master of Ballantrae,' 'David Balfour,' and 'St. Ives'; and he finally came to the conclusion that it is 'the everlasting fountain of interest.' But love was not with Stevenson of prime consideration; adventure does not flow from it as the sole source, as in the case of 'Lorna Doone.' In the two romantic tales by which he brought his name before the public, 'Treasure Island' (1883) and 'Dr. Jekyll and Mr. Hyde' (1886), there is no love-making at all. What he did at first — and this is one of his innovations — was to awaken delight in adventure for its own sake, just as Defoe did. Chance and Circumstance which to the philosophers are at best unlovely, he writes with initial capitals, and says they are the divinities whom he adores. Events, which Hardy marshals so that they seem endowed with spite and cruelty, Stevenson made sing together as the morning stars. His gentlemen are always lucky, escaping from duels and wrecks with flesh wounds and a little wetting and hunger. As occasion demands, many subordinate characters are shot, or walk the plank, or sink into quicksands; but they are cowards or pirates whom no one is troubled to see disappear.

In fact, the incidents which Stevenson created, following in the footsteps of Scott, Dumas, Poe, and Borrow, are to an extent outside the realm of the moral law. He wrote an essay defending the 'a-moral' in art, that is, art which is neither moral nor immoral, but neutral — art which aims at the imaginative presentation of crime and adventure, and then looks upon its task as done. He makes a voyage along the Sambre and the Oise in a canoe as graceful as a violin; he crosses the Cévennes prodding a whimsical donkey which bears his luggage, and sleeping in a sack on the cold uplands under the light of the stars. He is captured by pirates, whose captain with black, curly whiskers he sends below, and raises the Jolly Roger on his own account. He is wrecked off the coast of Mull, and traverses the Highlands with an outlaw, dodging the king's troops. He enters out-of-the-way places in London and Paris which the police leave undisturbed, and from his explorations there he fashions new Arabian Nights. Most of all he goes in quest of hidden treasure, digging in an old monastery, diving into the deep sea, or sailing the Spanish main with a mutinous crew. What civilization most cares for is discarded, — ease, luxuries, and soft beds. And though his characters are so often after gold, yet their love of it is only a pretence to adventure; when they get it, they squander it or force it upon a chance acquaintance to whom they are indebted for a night's lodging or some trivial kindness. Stevenson was thus in all he wrote a boy, delighting in wild incident in and for itself; and he sought to set us back into our boyhood, when the moral sense was ill trained and we viewed nature naïvely. Stevenson (if it be permitted to read between the lines), when he stood in a broad highway swept white in the distance by the sunlight, thought of Dick Turpin and the exciting ride from London to York; when he went down to the sea, he saw to the westward the phantom ship of Kidd, and heard the ruffian crew calling to him over the water; when he felt his isolation, he could fancy himself going out on a star-lit night and shouting through his hands to the heavens peopled with his silent friends.

Stevenson was not of those who argue that if a man has something to say, he will necessarily say it well.

There are awkward ways of telling a story, and there are right ways. Stevenson always hit upon one of the right ways. A common convention of fiction since Fielding has been that the reader shall admit without question the ubiquity of the novelist. But Stevenson, with some exceptions, held to a point of view. He puts his narrative into the mouth of a character, sometimes a minor one, and permits him to speak of only what he himself has seen and experienced. It was furthermore his custom when the story possessed considerable length to let it be told by two or more persons, each relating a part. This is the method adopted in 'Treasure Island,' 'Dr. Jekyll and Mr. Hyde,' and with most cleverness in the 'Master of Ballantrae.' In this last case the story is in the hands of the faithful old steward Mackellar, who is a sort of editor and glosser. He tells what he knows personally of the Ballantrae tragedy; and to complete it, he breaks his narrative with long quotations from the memoirs of Chevalier Burke. Wherever he wished to do so, Stevenson did not hesitate to employ the special relation; that is, when a new character is introduced he may give, if he likes, an account of himself. Stevenson thus passed by the structural art of our greatest novelists and went back to Smollett and Defoe. He showed that the old episode, which was once so abused, is susceptible of a treatment that will please; that the critics since Aristotle who have condemned it were mistaken. By the use of it he was able to keep his main characters directly before the reader with no more effort than is apparent among those who have discarded it as loose art. For example, in 'Treasure Island' Jim Hawkins is always the hero, whether he or the Doctor relates what happened on that memorable voyage of the *Hispaniola*.[1]

Admirable as the structure of Stevenson's stories is his style. His syntax is of studied simplicity. His sentences are short clauses in coördinate relation, separated by semicolons and connected by *and* or *but*, expressed or implied, as he wishes quick or slow movement. Involved complex sentences he never wrote; his subordinate clauses are short, and are frequently dropped into the sentence within parentheses. In this way he gained compactness, an even flow, and a delightful rhythm. Quaint and smooth-sounding words were to him beautiful for themselves. He seems to have culled them from his reading of our classic literature, and to have stored them away in his memory, an exhaustless repository from which he could draw at pleasure for the formation of new and felicitous phrases. His prototype in our prose literature is Sir Thomas Browne.

The supremacy of Stevenson as a stylist in recent fiction his harshest critics have not denied him. But then, it is said, there is not much substance behind the dress. Those who speak thus must have in mind the novel that solves all social and religious problems. There is as much substance behind his style as behind that of any other English romancer. He was certainly not consistent with the dictum that romance should be 'a-moral.' In 'A Chapter on Dreams,' he gave with special reference to 'Dr.

---

[1] For the way former novelists frequently managed the point of view in narration, see the opening chapter of 'David Copperfield,' in which the hero relates verbatim conversations that took place before he was born.

Jekyll and Mr. Hyde' the genesis of much of his writing. Certain incidents and situations came to him in dreams, which he playfully ascribed to the wayward brownies. From elf-land hints of this kind he built up his stories when awake, himself laying claim only to the characters and the morality. Almost everywhere in Stevenson's work there is this duality. There are the incidents of pure romance, and there are the ethics. As a man Stevenson was a Puritan; as an artist he was a Bohemian. He wrote an essay on François Villon, in which he did scant justice to the author of 'A Ballad of Dead Ladies.' He wrote a story with Villon as hero, and was in full æsthetic sympathy with the instinct for housebreaking and stealing gold flagons.

Just as he possessed two selves, so he was pleased, as both artist and man, with the two selves of the psychologists. This notion of a double selfhood is at the basis of 'Markheim,' 'The Treasure of Franchard,' 'Prince Otto,' and 'Dr. Jekyll and Mr. Hyde.' Sometimes the evil self wins and sometimes the better. The problem of 'Dr. Jekyll and Mr. Hyde' is exactly that of George Eliot's novels. A man plays with his lower self whimsically, and finally falls under its complete thraldom. At first to do ill is voluntary; in the course of time it becomes involuntary. The point of difference is this: George Eliot treats the subject directly and analytically; Stevenson treats it romantically and picturesquely, making use of an effervescing liquor, under the influence of which the good doctor shrivels up so that his clothes are too big for him. The method of George Eliot may be more convincing than Stevenson's; but the uncompromising ethics are in Stevenson for all that. Even such stories as 'The Dynamiter' and 'The Suicide Club' have their application to society; for they are fantastic satires on the Irish hero and the sentimental pessimist. Stevenson's art is thus always human. With rare exceptions there is audible in it a lyrical note. At times it is a soft fluting; then again it rises to a reflective longing for what might have been, as in 'Will o' the Mill'; and sometimes it breaks out in an appeal to the stars for 'tolerance and counsel.'

To Stevenson more than to any one else we owe the recrudescence of the historical romance. His treatment of history was mostly in the spirit of adventure after the way of Dumas rather than after the way of Scott. His history may be only the web of a dream as in 'Prince Otto,' the hero of which, a descendant of Shakespeare's Prince Florizel, plays at being ruler over a petty German principality somewhere on the confines of Bohemia, and through incapacity for rule loses his crown, and the princess is Cinderella. 'St. Ives' is an account of the adventures of a French prisoner in Scotland and England during the later years of the Napoleonic wars. The historic period which most occupied Stevenson's imagination was that of the years following the second Pretender's struggle for the English throne in 1745. Historic battle scenes he did not describe, for that would have placed too great restraint upon his fancy; well-known historical characters he rarely more than mentioned, and for the same reason. What he depicted is Scotch social life; the tragedy of a house divided against itself in its loyalty both to King George and Charles Edward; and the poverty and desperation of the Highlanders after they were stripped of their arms and plaids. Escapes, broils, fights, and sword-play, there are in abundance. For stirring adventure like this, Stevenson maintained that only roughly outlined characters are necessary, for the reader himself at once becomes the hero. And yet in two of his romances, 'Kidnapped' and 'The Master of Ballantrae,' there is a more detailed study of char-acter than in Scott or Dumas. The two masters of Ballantrae and David Balfour are Meredithian, closely and surely analytical. They are, of course, out of the pale of realistic creation, for they are ex-traordinary and exceptional. Instead of taking the common run of men and telling us why they behave as they do, Stevenson began with a dream or with the Society for Psychical Research, showing whimsical ways in which heredity is imagined to manifest itself, or what mad things a man may do who has a clot of blood, though only a speck, on the brain. Alan Breck, the agent of Prince Charles in the Highlands, is Stevenson's master character stroke. After killing his enemies, as they rush upon him in the round-house of the *Covenant*, and passing his sword through their dead bodies, Alan sits down to a table, sword in hand, and breaks forth into a victorious Gaelic song composed on the moment. Then he takes off his coat, brushes it, and cuts off a silver button as a reward to David for services rendered. That insight into the make-up of the cavalier, Scott never surpassed.

Just as in the case of Scott, Stevenson has been accompanied and followed by several historical romancers, among whom are Conan Doyle, S. R. Crockett, Stanley Weyman, Anthony Hope Hawkins,

and S. Weir Mitchell; and by a group of Scotch emo-
tionalists and humorists, among whom are J. M. Barrie
and John Watson, who have spread the fame of Thrums
and Drumtochty.   Literary history is thus repeating
itself.

4. *Rudyard Kipling*

Since the death of Stevenson, the most striking
figure in our fiction has been Rudyard Kipling.
When his Anglo-Indian tales first found their way to
the western world, the critics associated them with
the empty adventures of Rider Haggard; but his succeeding publications have forced a readjustment of
opinion.   Kipling has seen an opportunity, and he
has seized it.   He is to India somewhat more than
Maria Edgeworth was to Ireland, and somewhat less
than Scott was to Scotland.   From Burke and Macaulay the public had derived a knowledge of the India
of Clive and Hastings, sufficient for argument and for
rhetoric.   An imaginative sense of India of the same
and a little later period appeared now and then in
Thackeray: in India Colonel Newcome won his laurels; and Jos Sedley is a type of the old civilian.
Of the new India of the Queen-Empress and Lord
Roberts of Kandahar, Kipling is the first worthy
interpreter.   Of this India he has confined himself
mostly to Punjaub, which he best knows; to its
sweltering heat, and the madness induced thereby,
its drenching rains and fever and cholera, its blinding
sand-storms and the picnics they spoil; the immense
perspective of a star-lit heaven, the filth and superstition of the natives, the love intrigues of civilians,
the haphazard process of law-making ; a village in-

vaded and blotted out by the beasts of the jungle;
the magnificent ruins of a city, where monkeys 'sit in
circles on the halls of the king's council-chamber'; and
barrack-room stories, in which the private tells of his
experiences, his practical jokes, and death grapples on
the battle-field with giant Afghans.

One of the remarkable things about all these tales
is Kipling's nearness to his subject; he does not write
from the outside of it; but as one who is a part of it.
In this he has perhaps been helped by a little Hindoo
mysticism.   In that beautiful poem, 'To the True
Romance,' he seems to hold that it is possible to get
beyond the sensuous appearance of things to their
heart, to arrive at

> . . . . that utter Truth
> The careless angels know.

This penetrating insight is most obvious when he
writes of animals.   In the Jungle Books he sustains
this sympathetic attitude for two volumes; he interprets the conduct of wolves, bears, panthers, monkeys,
serpents, and elephants, and translates their language into English.   In these fables he has given
fresh life and meaning to the mediæval bestiaries, incidents from which had lived on in modern literature
only as allegorical adornments for the poets.   It is a
happy coincidence that the beast fable should have
received its new dress from the jungles of India, one
of its earliest homes.   The fancy that endowed his
animals with speech, Kipling has now extended to the
cargo-boat and the locomotive engine.

In the selection and recombination of the matter of
real life for his purposes, Kipling is at will a realist

or a romancer. As a realist he is an impressionist,
suggesting his characters by a few epithets and leaving to the reader the completion of the sketch. When
he has done more than this, as in the case of Mulvaney,
he has revived the method of Chaucer, letting his characters reveal themselves by the tales they tell. He is
not a romancer in the sense in which Stevenson was,
who reared his fabrics on dreams; for he always has a
realistic setting, and says much about real things. He
is not a romancer in the sense in which Scott was, who
looked backward. He is the romancer of the present;
of the modern social order, on which shines from afar
a light as resplendent as that which shone on mediæval
society; for it is the same divine light of the imagination. Kipling feels the presence of romance in shot
and shell as well as in bow and arrows, and in red
coats as well as in buff jerkins; in existing superstitions as well as in the old; in the lightning express
as in the stage-coach; in a Vermont farmer as in
Robin Hood; in the fishing schooner as in the viking's
ship; in the loves of Mulvaney and Dinah as in Ivanhoe and Rowena; in the huge python as in the fire-
breathing dragon. This is his great distinction in an
age that has come to look on its marvels with dull,
passive eyes.

CONCLUSION

A TREATISE on fiction ought to close, like the old
heart-easing novels, with a look into the future. We
may be sure that the novel will conform, as it has done
since Arthurian romance, to the moods of human nature as they vary from epoch to epoch; that at one
time will prevail realism — the stern endeavor to
keep the imaginative product in harmony with the
actual; and at another time, idealism — the heightening of incident and passion for grand effects. What
is to happen in the first quarter of the twentieth
century, it would be most hazardous to prophesy.
Besides tearing down and building anew the internal
structure of the novel, the contemporary novelists
would seem also to have modified permanently its
outer form. Hardy has cut the three volume novel
down to one volume. The short-story has found
its own beautiful art; but it can never hope to
become a universal type, for it gives scant room.
Kipling, who has experimented all the way from
three to three hundred pages, is bringing into
fashion a novel of from twenty-five to fifty pages.
The paganism which characterizes the thought of
the contemporary novel has appeared at intervals in
our fiction from the time the Anglo-Saxon gleemen
sang of Beowulf and Grendel; it is in Sterne, in
the Gothic romancers, and in Scott. Where it is

not a morbid sentiment, it is manifest in a love of adventure and an exaltation of the strong man. To the novel of the future, Kipling, who is gathering to himself present-day tendencies, may be pointing the way.

APPENDIX

APPENDIX

APPENDIX

I

A LIST OF TWENTY-FIVE PROSE FICTIONS

THESE books, arranged in logical order, show in large out-line the development of the English novel. All of them may be found in ordinary public libraries or procured of the bookseller. For convenient reference, I have indicated good editions.

1. Morte Darthur, by Sir Thos. Malory. Books I., III., VI., XVII., XXI. Globe ed. (The Macmillan Co., London and New York.)

2. Rosalind, by Thos. Lodge. Cassell's National Library. (Cassell and Co., London and N. Y.)

3. Pilgrim's Progress, by John Bunyan. Temple Classics. (J. M. Dent and Co., London. Macmillan, N. Y.)

4. Robinson Crusoe, by Daniel Defoe. Bohn's Library. (Geo. Bell and Sons, London. Macmillan, N. Y.)

5. Roderick Random, by Tobias Smollett. Bohn's Library.

6. Clarissa Harlowe, by Samuel Richardson. Abridged ed. (Henry Holt and Co., N. Y. Geo. Routledge and Sons, London and N. Y.)

7. Tom Jones, by Henry Fielding. Bohn's Library.

8. Tristram Shandy, by Laurence Sterne. Abridged ed. Morley's Universal Library. (Routledge.)

9. The Vicar of Wakefield, by Oliver Goldsmith. Temple Classics. (Dent. Macmillan.)

10. Castle Rackrent, by Maria Edgeworth, ed. with The Absentee by A. Thackeray Ritchie. (Macmillan.)

11. Pride and Prejudice, by Jane Austen, ed. R. B. Johnson. (Dent. Macmillan.)

12. Waverley, by Sir Walter Scott. The Dryburgh ed. (A. and C. Black, London. Macmillan, N. Y.)

13. Kenilworth, by Sir Walter Scott. The Dryburgh ed.

14. The Pathfinder, by J. F. Cooper. The Mohawk ed. (G. P. Putnam's Sons, N. Y. and London.)

15. The Scarlet Letter, by N. Hawthorne. (Houghton, Mifflin and Co., Boston. Cassell and Co., London.)

16. Pelham, by Bulwer-Lytton, New Library ed. (Routledge.)

17. David Copperfield, by Charles Dickens, ed. by Charles Dickens the younger. (Macmillan.)

18. Vanity Fair, by W. M. Thackeray. Biographical ed. (Harper and Brothers, N. Y.   Smith and Elder, London.)

19. Barchester Towers, by Anthony Trollope, in Chronicles of Barsetshire series. (Dodd, Mead and Co., N. Y. Chapman and Hall, London.)

20. Jane Eyre, by Charlotte Brontë, illustrated by H. S. Greig. (Dent. Macmillan.)

21. Adam Bede, by George Eliot. (Harper, N. Y. Blackwood and Sons, Edinburgh.)

22. The Ordeal of Richard Feverel, by Geo. Meredith. The Author's ed. (A. Constable and Co., London. Chas. Scribner's Sons, N. Y.)

23. The Return of the Native, by Thos. Hardy. Crown 8vo ed. (Harper.)

24. Treasure Island, by R. L. Stevenson. (Scribner. Cassell and Co.)

25. The Brushwood Boy, by Rudyard Kipling, in The Day's Work. (Macmillan, London. Doubleday and McClure, N. Y.)

The means of enlarging the list will be obvious to the reader of this book. One should read other novels by Jane Austen, Scott, Dickens, Thackeray, Trollope, Charlotte Brontë, George Eliot, and Stevenson. Also the outlines

may be filled in as thus: Don Quixote after 1; Gil Blas
before 7; Evelina after 9; a Gothic romance before Scott;
Bulwer's *Last of the Barons* after 13; Kingsley's *Westward
Ho!* and Poe's tales after 14; one of Mrs. Gaskell's novels
after 19; a novel by Howells or James after 23. See the
indications for the student which immediately follow.

II

BIBLIOGRAPHICAL AND OTHER NOTES

The aim of the following notes is to furnish means for a still further study of English fiction. The arrangement follows the main text, the numerals denoting page. For critical works on fiction, the reader is referred to the list prefixed to J. C. Dunlop's *History of Prose Fiction*, revised ed., Lond. and N. Y., 1888; and for biography, excepting American writers, to the *Dictionary of National Biography*, Lond. and N. Y., 1885–99. As a foundation for the study of the modern novel, the student should become acquainted with what was done in fiction by the Greeks; for among them, just as in the Middle Age, the romance detached itself from the epic. See for a guide *Der griechische Roman*, by E. Rohde, Leipzig, 1876, and *A History of the Novel previous to the 17th Century*, by F. M. Warren, N. Y., 1895. For English translations of the Greek novel, *Greek Romances*, Bohn's Library. For some suggestions concerning the influence of Greek romance on mediæval romance, see *A History of English Poetry*, by W. J. Courthope, vol. i., Lond. and N. Y., 1895.

Introduction

The early use of the word 'romance' from Fr. *roman: Romania* i., 1–22; Chaucer's 'Rime of Sir Thopas,' and 'Death of Blanche the Duchess,' line 48 *et seq.* For 'novel' of same and later period : the *Flamenca* (thirteenth century), ed. P. Meyer, Paris, 1865; the *Decameron* of Boccaccio (fourteenth century), ed. T. Wright, Lond., 1873; and the *Palace of Pleasure*, Wm. Painter, 1566, ed. J. Jacobs,

Lond., 1890. Contemporary use: 'The Art of Fiction,' H. James, in *Partial Portraits*, Lond., 1888; 'A Gossip on Romance' and 'A Humble Remonstrance,' R. L. Stevenson, in *Memories and Portraits*, N. Y., 1894.

1. The Mediæval Romancers and Story-tellers

Catalogue of Romances in the Department of MSS. in the Brit. Museum, H. L. D. Ward, Lond., vol. i., 1883, vol. ii., 1893. *Historia Regum Britanniæ*, Geoffrey of Monmouth, ed. San Marte, Halle, 1854; Eng. trans. Bohn's Library. *Morte Darthur*, Sir Thos. Malory, ed. H. O. Sommer, Lond., 1889. For love-casuistry, see *De Amore* (about 1200) by André le Chapelain, ed. E. Trojel, Copenhagen, 1892, and Chaucer's *Troilus and Cressida*.

For romances of adventure and miscellaneous fictions, see *Ancient Engleish Metrical Romanceës*, J. Ritson, 3 vols., Lond., 1802; *Specimens of Early English Metrical Romances*, Geo. Ellis, 3 vols., Lond., 1805, revised by J. O. Halliwell, Bohn's Library; *English Metrical Romances*, H. Weber, 3 vols., Edinburgh, 1810; *Fabliaux or Tales*, modernized, G. Way, Lond., 1815; publications of the *Early English Text Society;* *Romances of Chivalry*, in facsimile, John Ashton, Lond., 1887; *Gesta Romanorum*, ed. S. J. Herrtage, Lond., 1879.

The Works of Geoffrey Chaucer, Globe ed., Lond. and N. Y., 1898. *Confessio Amantis*, John Gower, ed. R. Pauli, Lond., 1857.

6. The Spanish Influence

Amadis de Gaula, Ordoñez de Montalvo, Eng. trans. by A. Munday, completed 1620, abridged by R. Southey, 1803, latest reprint, Lond., 1872. The *Diana* of Geo. of Montemayor, Eng. trans. B. Yong, 1598. For bibliog. of picaresque novel, see *History of Spanish Fiction*, Geo. Ticknor, revised ed., Boston, 1866; and *Études sur L'Espagne*, A. Morel-Fatio, sér. 1, Paris, 1888. English trans. of *Lazarillo de Tormes* and *Guzman de Alfarache*, N. Y., 1890. *Don Quixote*, Miguel de Cervantes, Eng. trans. H. E. Watts, Lond., 1888.

It is believed that the picaresque novel has behind it lost
Spanish farces. The picaresque element is certainly very
noticeable in *Celestina*, a tragi-comedy by F. de Rojas, 1492,
Englished by J. Mabbe, 1631, reprinted with introduction
by J. F. Kelly, London, 1894. For the picaresque escapade
even in ancient fiction, see *The Golden Ass of Apuleius.*
(Eng. trans. Bohn's Library.)

10. The Elizabethans

For general bibliog., *The English Novel in the Time of
Shakespeare*, J. J. Jusserand, Lond. and N. Y., 1890. For
translations from the Italian, see paper by M. A. Scott in
Publications of the Modern Language Association of America for 1896. The most influential Greek romance was
Theagenes and Chariclea, trans. by T. Underdown, 1577,
revised 1587, reprint Lond., 1895. For jests, *Shakespeare
Jest-Books*, ed. W. C. Hazlitt, Lond., 1864. For miscellaneous
fictions, *Early English Prose Romances*, ed. W. J. Thoms,
2d ed. Lond., 1858; *Romances of Chivalry*, ed. J. Ashton,
Lond., 1887; and *Early Prose Romances*, ed. H. Morley,
Lond., 1889. For rogue stories, *The Fraternitye of Vaca-
bondes*, etc., by John Awdeley, ed. E. Viles, Lond., 1869.

There is no reprint of H. Chettle's *Piers Plain.* In fact, the
only extant copy of it (so far as I know) is in the Bodleian
Library at Oxford. For comparison with *Lazarillo*, it may
be of interest to observe here that the novel is a pastoral
in its setting, and that Piers the rogue is in turn servant to
(1) Thrasilio, a court braggadocio and flatterer, (2) Flavius,
a prodigal, (3) a broker, who ruins young gentlemen, (4) a
miser, and (5) Petrusio, an embodiment of treachery. Sitting
between two shepherds in the classic vale of Tempe, Piers
relates his experiences with these various masters during an
apprenticeship of seven years.

The *Arcadia*, Sir P. Sidney, ed. H. O. Sommer, Lond.,
1891. Complete Works of Robt. Greene, ed. A. B. Grosart,
Lond., 1881–86. Complete Works of Thos. Nash, ed. Gro-

sart, Lond., 1883–85.   The *Euphues*, Jno. Lyly, Arber reprints, Lond., 1868.   Complete Works of Thos. Lodge, Hunterian Club, 1883.

13. The Historical Allegory and the French Influence

Argenis, Jno. Barclay, Eng. trans. Sir R. LeGrys, 1629; More's *Utopia*, Eng. trans. Ralph Robinson, 2d and rev. ed., 1556; Arber reprints, 1869.   For the French romances of the seventeenth century, see Dunlop's *History of Prose Fiction; Geschichte des französischen Romans im xvii Jahrhundert*, H. Körting, Oppeln and Leipzig, 1885–87; *Le Roman au dix-septième siècle*, André Le Breton, Paris, 1890; *Manuel de la Littérature française*, F. Brunetière, Paris, 1898.   (Eng. trans. Boston, 1898.)   For English translations of Fr. romances, see Jusserand.

For the passage of mediæval love-casuistry into the modern novel, see the *Astrée* (1610?) by Honoré d'Urfé, pt. ii., bk. v.   Here are formulated twelve laws of love.

18. The Restoration

For literary coteries, see Jusserand, ch. vii., and 'The Matchless Orinda' in *Seventeenth Century Studies*, E. Gosse, new ed., Lond., 1895.

Aphra Behn, Works, Lond., 1871.   John Bunyan, *Grace Abounding*, Cassell's Nat'l Library; *Pilgrim's Progress*, Temple Classics.

22. Literary Forms that contributed to the Novel

BIOGRAPHY. — Margaret Duchess of Newcastle: *Nature's Pictures drawn by Fancy's Pencil*, Lond., 1656, containing amusing sketches of herself and her father; and *Life of Wm. Cavendish*, Lond., 1667.

LETTERS. — See *Le Salut d'amour dans les littératures provençale et française*, P. Meyer, Paris, 1867; *Amadis; Euphues;* Scudéri's *Clélie;* works of Aphra Behn; *CCXI Sociable Letters* by Margaret, Duchess of Newcastle, Lond., 1666; *Letters written by Mary Manley*, 1696, and novels of E. Hay-

wood, Lond., 1725. Also the *Letters of a Portuguese Nun*, ed. with a bibliog. E. Prestage, Lond., 1893, and the *Letters of Eloisa and Abelard*, trans. by J. Hughes, 4th ed. Lond., 1722.

CHARACTER BOOKS. — For bibliog., see appendix to Jno. Earle's *Microcosmography* (1628), ed. by P. Bliss, Lond., 1811. The *Characters* of Theophrastus were translated into Latin by I. Casaubon, Lond., 1592; Eng. trans. by J. Healey bears the date of 1616. *De Coverley Papers* from the *Spectator*, Globe ed., Lond. and N. Y.

27. Daniel Defoe

The Romances and Narratives of D. Defoe, ed. G. A. Aitkin, Lond. and N. Y., 1895, 16 vols. Reprint of 1st ed. of *Robinson Crusoe*, with a bibliog., A. Dobson, Lond. and N. Y., 1883. For translations and imitations, see *Robinson und Robinsonaden*, H. Ullrich, Weimar, 1898.

Gulliver's Travels by J. Swift, Temple Classics. For Swift on the purpose of the romance, see letter to Pope 29 Sept., 1725, in Works of Swift, ed. W. Scott, Lond., 1814., vol. xvii., p. 39.

31. Samuel Richardson

Standard ed. by Leslie Stephen, Lond., 1883, 12 vols. Source of facts of life and popularity, *The Correspondence of Samuel Richardson*, A. L. Barbauld, Lond., 1804, 6 vols. For additional light on Richardson's aims, postscript to Clarissa and preface to Grandison, and the two letters appended to 'A Collection of the Moral and Instructive Sentiments, etc., contained in the Histories of Pamela, Clarissa, and Sir Charles Grandison,' Lond., 1755. For genesis of Pamela, *Correspondence*, vol. i., pp. lxix–lxxvi. See similar story, told in three letters, in *Spectator*, No. 375.

For Richardson's relation to the drama, should be read particularly the plays of Thos. Otway, Colley Cibber, Richard Steele, and Geo. Lillo.

For the extensive vogue of Richardson, and the imitations of him on the Continent, see *Richardson, Rousseau und Goethe,* Erich Schmidt, Jena, 1875; and *Jean-Jacques Rousseau et les origines du cosmopolitisme littéraire,* J. Texte, Paris, 1895. (Eng. trans. by J. W. Matthews, N. Y., 1899.) For French estimate of him, see Diderot's *Éloge de Richardson;* and Rousseau's *Lettre à d'Alembert sur les spectacles.* For the German view, see *Correspondence,* vol. iii., 140–158. For the Dutch view, *Correspondence,* vol. v., 241–270. For Goethe on morality of, *Dichtung und Wahrheit,* bk. xiii. For Dr. Johnson on morality of, *Correspondence,* v., 281–285, and Boswell's *Life of Johnson,* ch. iii.

42. Henry Fielding

Works, ed. Geo. Saintsbury, Lond. and N. Y., 1893, 12 vols. For Fielding on his aims, see especially preface to *Joseph Andrews,* and the introductory chapter to book iii. For external nature in Fielding, *Tom Jones,* bk. i., ch. iv., and bk. xi., ch. ix. *Life of H. Fielding,* A. Dobson, Lond. and N. Y., 1883.

57. The Novel *vs.* the Drama

For the outer and the fundamental differences between the drama and the novel, see Goethe, *Wilhelm Meisters Lehrjahre,* bk. v., ch. vii.; Brunetière, *Les Époques du Théâtre Français,* Paris, 1892, *première conférence;* Brander Matthews, *Studies of the Stage,* N. Y., 1894, ch. i.; Henry James, *The Tragic Muse,* N. Y., 1890, ch. iv.; R. L. Stevenson, 'A Humble Remonstrance' in *Memories and Portraits.* On revolt of public and literature from regular tragedy, *David Simple,* S. Fielding, bk. ii., ch. ii.; and *Correspondence of Richardson,* vol. iv., 220.

63. Tobias Smollett

Works, ed. Geo. Saintsbury, Lond. and Phila., 1895, 12 vols. Smollett on his sources, preface to *Roderick Random.*

306 DEVELOPMENT OF THE ENGLISH NOVEL

69. Laurence Sterne

Works, ed. Geo. Saintsbury, Lond. and Phila., 1894, 6 vols. Standard life, by P. Fitzgerald, new ed., Lond., 1896. On Sterne's sources, *Illustrations of Sterne*, Dr. John Ferriar, Manchester and Lond., 1798. For bibliog. and influence, the article on Sterne in *Dict. Nat'l Biog.*

76. The Minor Novelists

No recent edition of *David Simple*. Facsimile reprint of *Rasselas*, ed. J. Macaulay, Lond., 1884. Facsimile reprint of the *Vicar of Wakefield*, ed. A. Dobson, Lond., 1885. Both contain bibliographies. For Goldsmith on the humor of Sterne, the *Citizen of the World*, Letter liii.

84. Novel of Purpose

PEDAGOGIC. — J. J. Rousseau's *Nouvelle Héloïse* and *Émile*, *Œuvres*, Paris, 1823–26. *The Fool of Quality*, by H. Brooke, Lond., 1859. *Sandford and Merton*, Thos. Day, St. Nicholas series, N. Y.

REVOLUTIONARY. — Of most of these fictions, there are no reprints. Novels of R. Bage, Ballantyne's Novelist's Library, Lond., 1824. Works of Amelia Opie, Boston, 1827, 10 vols. *Caleb Williams*, W. Godwin, Boston, 1876; *Nature and Art*, E. Inchbald, Cassell's Nat'l Library. On Godwin, see *The Spirit of the Age*, by W. Hazlitt, 1825. For current speculations popularized in these novels, *Vindication of the Rights of Woman*, Mary W. Godwin, 1792, reprint, Lond. and N. Y., 1891; and *Political Justice*, Wm. Godwin, 1793.

93. The Light Transcript of Contemporary Manners

Evelina and *Cecilia*, Frances Burney, ed. R. B. Johnson, Lond. and N. Y., 1893; works of Maria Edgeworth (New Longford ed.), 10 vols., Lond., 1893. For the change in manners in the half-century following Richardson, see Charlotte Smith's *Desmond* (1792), vol. ii., letter xii., pp. 172–173, where the immorality of Richardson is attacked. See also R. Cumberland's *Henry* (1795), bk. v., ch. i. Illustrative of the manners depicted by Frances Burney, see 'Diary and Letters of Madame d'Arblay, as edited [1842–46] by her niece Charlotte Barrett,' new ed., Lond., 1893.

98. The Gothic Romance

For the romantic revival, of which the Gothic and historical romances are a part, see *English Romanticism, Eighteenth Century*, H. A. Beers, N. Y., 1898; and the *Beginnings of the English Romantic Movement*, W. L. Phelps, Boston, 1893. *Longsword*, attributed to Rev. Thos. Leland in *European Magazine* for Aug., 1799, vol. xxxvi., p. 75; no recent ed. *The Old English Baron*, Clara Reeve, Cassell's Nat'l Lib. *The Castle of Otranto*, Cassell's Nat'l Lib. *Vathek*, Wm. Beckford, ed. R. Garnett, Lond., 1893. Reprint of Radcliffe's *Italian, Romance of The Forest*, and *Mysteries of Udolpho*, Lond., 1877. The *Monk*, M. G. Lewis, Phila., 1884. Latest ed. of C. B. Brown, Phila., 1877. Shelley's romances, in Works, Lond., 1875. *Frankenstein*, Mary Shelley, Routledge's Pocket Library, 1888.

110. The Historical Romance

On the survival of the seventeenth-century romance, see *The Female Quixote*, Charlotte Lennox, Lond., 1752; *The Phœnix* (a trans. of *Argenis*), by Clara Reeve, Lond., 1772; and Scott's general preface (1829) to *Waverley*. None of the historical romances of the period have been recently republished, except Jane Porter's, which may be found in the Oxford series, N. Y.

Some notion of the extensive vogue of the historical romance during the thirty years immediately preceding *Waverley* is afforded by the following incomplete list of tales more or less historical : —

The Recess, Miss Sophia Lee, 1783–86; *Warbeck*, 1786; *Alan Fitzosborne*, Miss Anne Fuller, 1787; *William of Nor-*

mandy, 1787; *The Son of Ethelwulf*, Anne Fuller, 1789; *Earl Strongbow*, James White, 1789; *John of Gaunt*, J. White, 1790; *Historic Tales*, 1790; *Adventures of King Richard, Cœur de Lion*, J. White, 1791; *The Duchess of York*, 1791; *The Foresters*, Jeremy Belknap, 1792; *The Minstrel*, 1793; *Memoirs of Sir Roger de Clarendon*, Clara Reeve, 1793; *The Haunted Priory*, Stephen Cullen, 1794; *An Antiquarian Romance*, Thos. Pownall, 1795; *The Duke of Clarence*, 1795; *Montford Castle*, 1796; *The Canterbury Tales*, Harriet and Sophia Lee, 1797–1805; *The Knights*, 1798; *The Abbess*, S. W. H. Ireland, 1799; *St. Leon*, Wm. Godwin, 1799; *A Northumbrian Tale*, 1799; *Midsummer Eve*, 1801; *Thaddeus of Warsaw*, Miss Jane Porter, 1803; *Astonishment!.!* Francis Lathom, 1804; *The Forester*, Sir S. E. Brydges, 1804; *The Swiss Emigrants*, Hugh Murray, 1804; *St. Clair of the Isles*, Elizabeth Helme, 1804; *Sherwood Forest*, Mrs. V. R. Good, 1804; *Gondez the Monk*, S. W. H. Ireland, 1805; *The Mysterious Freebooter*, F. Lathom, 1806; *A Peep at Our Ancestors*, Mrs. Henrietta Mosse, 1807; *The Fatal Vow*, F. Lathom, 1807; *Queenhoo-Hall*, Joseph Strutt, 1808; *The Husband and the Lover*, Miss A. T. Palmer, 1809; *Don Sebastian*, A. M. Porter, 1809; *Anne of Brittany*, 1810; *Scenes in Feudal Times*, R. H. Wilmot, 1809; *Ferdinand and Ordella*, Mrs. M. A. C. Bradshaw, 1810; *Edgar*, Mrs. Elizabeth Appleton, 1810; *The Scottish Chiefs*, Jane Porter, 1810; *Edwy and Elgiva*, John Agg, 1811; *The Lady of the Lake* (founded on Scott's poem), 1810; *Despotism or the Fall of the Jesuits*, Isaac D'Israeli, 1811; *Alonzo and Melissa*, Isaac Mitchell, 1811; *The Loyalists*, Mrs. Jane West, 1812; *The Scottish Adventurers*, Hector MacNeil, 1812; *The Border Chieftains*, Miss Mary Houghton, 1813; *Alicia de Lacy*, Jane West, 1814.

114. Jane Austen

Novels, Lond. and N. Y., 1895, 10 vols. *A Memoir of Jane Austen*, by her nephew, J. E. Austen-Leigh, 2d ed., Lond., 1871. For early appreciation of, R. Whately, *Quarterly Review*, Jan. 1821 (article entitled Modern Novels); Scott's *Journal*, 14 Mar. 1826, and 18 April, 1827; Macaulay's 'Essay on Mme. d'Arblay,' *Ed. Rev.*, Jan. 1843. For recent estimate and full bibliography, *Life of Jane Austen*, by G. Smith, Lond., 1890.

125. Sir Walter Scott

Convenient recent edition, with introduction by F. W. Farrar, Lond. and N. Y., 1898, 25 vols. Standard life of Scott, by J. G. Lockhart, 1837, often reprinted. For Scott on himself, see Lockhart, the *Journal of Sir Walter Scott* (1890), and the prefaces, especially to *Waverley*. For lively contemporary criticism of, see 'Novels by the Author of Waverley,' *Quarterly Rev.*, Oct. 1821, vol. xxvi., 109–148. On Scott's style, see T. Carlyle, in *West. Rev.*, Jan. 1838, vol. xxviii., 293–345 (article reprinted in *Critical and Miscellaneous Essays*); W. Bagehot's essay on the Waverley Novels, *Literary Studies*, vol. ii., Lond., 1879; and R. L. Stevenson's 'A Gossip on Romance,' in *Memories and Portraits*. For the literary and romantic treatment of history, see Coleridge on Shakespeare's historical plays in the Complete Works of Coleridge, Lond., 1871, vol. iv., 116 *seq.*

For Scott in Germany, see Gottschall, cited under *Cooper;* for Scott in France, *Le Roman Historique*, Louis Maigron, Paris, 1898.

136. Scott's Legacy

Novels of A. E. Bray, Lond., 1884, 12 vols. Works of H. Smith, Lond., 1826–44, 26 vols. Novels of G. P. R. James, republished in part by Routledge. Novels of W. H. Ainsworth, Library ed., Lond. and N. Y., 16 vols. Works of Bulwer-Lytton, New Library ed., Boston, 1892–93, 40 vols.

Novels of Chas. Kingsley, Pocket ed., Lond. and N. Y., 1895, 11 vols.

For Bulwer c⌐ his art, see preface to his historical novels. For Kingsley on his purpose in *Hypatia*, see letter to Rev. F. D. Maurice, 16 Jan. 1851, in 'Charles Kingsley, His Letters, and Memories of his Life,' ed. by his wife, Lond., 1892, ch. ix., 108–109.

149. The Romance of War

Stories of Waterloo, and *The Bivouac*, by W. H. Maxwell, Notable Novels ser., Lond. and N. Y. *The Military Novels* of Charles Lever, Lond. and Boston, 1891–92, 9 vols. Novels of James Grant, Lond. and N. Y., 1882, 34 vols.

150. James Fenimore Cooper and the Romance of the Forest and the Sea

Works (Mohawk ed.), N. Y., 1896, 32 vols. For life, see *James Fenimore Cooper*, T. R. Lounsbury, N. Y., 1883. Novels of Captain Frederick Marryat, ed. R. B. Johnson, Lond. and Boston, 1896, 22 vols.

Cooper's influence. Novels of W. G. Simms; novels of Captain Mayne Reid, and of W. Clark Russell, and sketches of Western life by Bret Harte, Hamlin Garland, and Owen Wister. See also Michael Scott's *Tom Cringle's Log*, ed. M. Morris, Lond. and N. Y., 1895. Cooper was at once imitated in French and German, and the imitations, translated into English, were popular both in Eng. and in the U. S. Karl Postl (pseudonym, Charles Sealsfield), a German refugee, travelled in the Southwest, and wrote several Cooper tales, among which are *Das Kajütenbuch* (1840) and *Süden und Norden* (1842–43), well known in their Eng. translations. For him and the influence of Cooper in Germany, see *Die deutsche Nationallitteratur des 19 Jahrhunderts* by R. von Gottschall, vol. iv. Gustave Aimard, when a boy, came to the U. S., and lived for ten years in Arkansas and the neighboring territories. He wrote, in French, tales of the South-

west, the Rocky Mts., and California. Among them in
Eng. trans. are: *The Prairie Flower*, 1861; *The Last of the
Incas*, 1862; *The Indian Scout*, 1862; *The Buccaneer Chief*,
1864, — all published in London.

158. The Renovation of Gothic Romance

Melmoth the Wanderer, C. R. Maturin, with memoir and
bibliog., Lond., 1892, 3 vols. *Tales of a Traveller*, W. Irv-
ing, Knickerbocker ed., N. Y., 1897. For Bulwer see p.
309. The Works of E. A. Poe, ed. E. C. Stedman and G.
E. Woodberry, Chicago, 1894–95, 10 vols. *A Tale for a
Chimney Corner* in *Tales of Leigh Hunt*, ed. W. Knight,
Lond. and Phila., 1891. The complete Works of N.
Hawthorne, Boston, 1895, 13 vols.

168. The Minor Humorists and the Author of 'Pick-wick'

Novels of Susan Ferrier, ed. R. B. Johnson, Lond. and
N. Y., 1893. Novels of J. Galt, ed. D. S. Meldrum, Edin.
and Boston, 1895–96, 8 vols., *Mansie Wauch*, D. M. Moir,
new ed., Edin., 1895.

Our Village, M. R. Mitford, ed. A. T. Ritchie, Lond. and
N. Y., 1893.

The Novels of T. L. Peacock, ed. Geo. Saintsbury, Lond.
and N. Y., 1895–97, 5 vols. *The Adventures of Hajji Baba
of Ispahan*, J. Morier, ed. G. N. Curzon, Lond. and N. Y.,
1895.

Works of J. and M. Banim, Dublin and N. Y., 1865, 10
vols. *Traits and Stories of the Irish Peasantry*, W. Carleton,
ed. D. J. O'Donoghue, Lond. and N. Y., 1896, 4 vols. *Handy
Andy*, Samuel Lover, ed. C. Whibley, Lond. and N. Y., 1896.

Novels of B. Disraeli, Lond. and N. Y., 1878, 10 vols. For
works of Bulwer-Lytton, see page 309. For specimens of
Mrs. Gore's fashionable tales, *The Dean's Daughter*, Lovell's
Lib., and *Self*, Harper's Lib. Select Novels. Novels of Theo.
Hook, Lond. and N. Y., 1872–73, 15 vols. Reprint of Pierce

Egan's *Tom and Jerry*, Pt. I., Lond., 1869; Pt. II., 1889. On the numerous imitations, see *The Finish*, etc. ch. i., where Egan discusses them; and *Dict. Nat'l Biog.* For Thackeray on, see essay on George Cruikshank, *West. Rev.*, June, 1840, and *Tunbridge Toys* and *De Juventute* in *Roundabout Papers*. For word *Pickwick*, see the *Finish*, ch. ii.

180. Charles Dickens and the Humanitarian Novel

On state of English society in first half of nineteenth century, see John Howard's *State of the Prisons in Eng. and Wales*, 4th ed., Lond., 1792; Sir James Mackintosh, 'On State of Criminal Law,' *Miscellaneous Works*, Lond., 1846, vol. iii.; *Social England*, ed. by H. D. Traill, Lond., and N. Y., vol. v., 1896, vol. vi., 1897; *Popular History of England*, by Charles Knight, Lond., 1856–62, vol. viii.; and Thos. Carlyle on 'Model Prisons' in *Latter Day Pamphlets*. Carlyle is corroborated by Thackeray in *Pendennis*, vol. i., ch. xxix.

On the historical connection between the humanitarian novel and the revolutionary school of Godwin, see preface to first ed. of *Paul Clifford* and *The Life*, etc. of Edward Bulwer, Lord Lytton, by his son, the Earl of Lytton, Lond., 1883, bk. vii., ch. xiii. The theme of *Paul Clifford* was suggested by Godwin.

The Novels of Charles Dickens, with introduction by Charles Dickens the younger, Lond. and N. Y., 1892–96; or the Gadshill edition, ed. A. Lang, Lond. and N. Y., 1896–99. Standard Life of Dickens by John Forster, Lond., 1872–74. The literature on Dickens is immense. See particularly *Charles Dickens*, by W. Bagehot, *Nat'l Review*, Oct. 1858, republished in *Literary Studies*, vol. ii.; and *Charles Dickens*, a critical study, by G. Gissing, Lond. and N. Y., 1898.

For novels of C. Kingsley, see p. 310. Works of E. Gaskell, Lond. and N. Y., 1897, 8 vols. The Writings of H. B. Stowe, Boston, 1896, 16 vols. For unprecedented popularity of 'Uncle Tom's Cabin,' see *Life of H. B. Stowe*, by C. E. Stowe, Boston, 1889.

197. William Makepeace Thackeray

Works of W. M. Thackeray, with biographical introductions, A. T. Ritchie, Lond. and N. Y., 1898–99. *Thackeray*, by Anthony Trollope, in Eng. Men of Letters series, 1879.

211. George Borrow

Works, new ed., Lond. and N. Y., 1888.

212. Charles Reade

The Library ed., Lond. and N. Y., 1896.

215. Anthony Trollope

The Chronicles of Barsetshire, Lond. and N. Y., 1892, 13 vols. *An Autobiography*, by Anthony Trollope, Lond. and N. Y., 1883.

224. Charlotte Brontë

The Works of Charlotte, Emily, and Anne Brontë, illus. by H. S. Greig, Lond. and N. Y., 1893, 12 vols. Contemporary criticism: 'Recent Novels' (G. H. Lewes), *Fraser's Mag.*, Dec. 1847; 'Jane Eyre' (Lady Eastlake), *Quarterly Rev.*, Dec. 1848; and 'Novels of the Season' (E. P. Whipple), *North Amer. Rev.*, Oct. 1848. *The Life of Charlotte Brontë*, by Elizabeth Gaskell, Lond., 1857, often reprinted; *Charlotte Brontë and her Circle*, C. K. Shorter, Lond. and N. Y., 1896.

234. Elizabeth Gaskell

For Works of E. Gaskell, see p. 312.

237. George Eliot (Marian Evans)

Cabinet ed. of Works, Edin., Lond., and N. Y., 1896. *Life of George Eliot*, by J. W. Cross, Lond. and N. Y., 1885. 'George Eliot as Author,' and 'George Eliot's Life and Letters,' by R. H. Hutton, in *Essays on Some of the Modern Guides of English Thought in Matters of Faith*, Lond. and N. Y., 1887. *Studies in Literature*, by E. Dowden, Lond.,

1883. *Le Naturalisme Anglais* (1881), by Ferdinand Brunetière, in *Le Roman Naturaliste*, revised ed., Paris, 1892.

252. George Meredith

Novels, revised by the author, Lond. and N. Y., 1898. 'On the Idea of Comedy and of the Uses of the Comic Spirit' (*New Quarterly Magazine*, April, 1877), republished, Lond. and N. Y., 1897.

INDEX

A

Abbess, The, 308
Abbot, The, 134
Abduction, The, 137
Absentee, The, 96–97, 169, 172, 297
Adam Bede, 238, 240, 241, 244, 246, 249, 252, 274, 298
Addison, Joseph, 24–25, 31, 49, 50, 52, 54, 58, 100, 147, 166, 179, 203, 205, 206
Adeline Mowbray, 90
Adventurers, The, 137
Æschylus, 143, 251
Æsopian fables, 5
Agg, John, 308
Ahnen, Die, 138
Aimard, Gustave, 155, 310
Ainsworth, W. H., 141–143, 147, 190, 198, 280, 309
Akenside, Mark, 65
Alan Fitzosborne, 307
Aleman, Mateo, 63
Alembert, Jean d', 41
Alexander: romances of, 1
Alicia de Lacy, 308
Almeria, 96
Alton Locke, 194, 219
Amadis de Gaula, 7, 11, 16, 57, 301, 303
Amazing Marriage, The, 252, 253
Amelia, 54–57, 63, 72, 77, 272
Amos Barton, 237, 238, 244
Anatomy of Melancholy, 69, 70
Ancestors, The, 138
Ancient Mariner, The, 163

Anna St. Ives, 88–89
Annals of the Parish, The, 169–170
Anne of Brittany, 308
Anselmo, 136
Antiquarian Romance, An, 308
Antiquary, The, 127, 131
Antony and Cleopatra, 133
Appleton, Elizabeth, 308
Apuleius, Lucius, 302
Aquinas, St. Thomas, 251
Arabian Nights, 103, 185
Arblay, Mme. d', 121. See Burney, Frances
Arblay, Mme. d', Diary and Letters of, 307
Arblay, Mme. d', Macaulay's essay, 309
Arbuthnot, John, 70
Arcadia (Sannazaro's), 8
Arcadia (Sidney's), 11, 13, 14, 19, 25, 113, 302
Aretina, 19
Argenis, 14–15, 303, 307
Ariosto, 10
Aristophanes, 10, 43
Aristotle, 31, 44 and n., 45, 273, 285
Arnold, Matthew, 269
Art of Fiction, The, 265 n., 267 n., 301
Art of Love, 3
Arthur Arundel, 140
Arthur Mervyn, 107
Arthurian romances, 1–3, 10, 57, 293
Ashton, John, 301, 302

315

Assommoir, L', 272
Astonishment ! 308
Astrée, L', 303
Asylum, The ; or Alonzo and Melissa, 151, 308
Atom, The History and Adventures of an, 66
Aucassin et Nicolette, 4
Auerbach, Berthold, 80
Austen, Jane, 82, 114–124, 125, 126, 155, 162, 171, 215, 224, 225, 231, 232, 255, 298, 309
Austen, Jane, Life of, 309
Austen, Jane, Memoir of, 309
Autobiography, An (Trollope), 313
Awdeley, John, 63, 302
Ayrshire Legatees, The, 169

B

Bacon, Francis, 61, 119, 165
Bage, Robert, 88, 90, 91, 92, 306
Bagehot, Walter, 52, 184, 309, 312
Ballad of Dead Ladies, A, 287
Banim, John, 172, 311
Banim, Michael, 172, 311
Barbauld, Mrs. A. L., 304
Barbour, John, 113
Barchester Towers, 218, 221, 298
Barclay, John, 14–15, 19, 21, 110, 135, 303
Barham Downs, 90
Barrett, E. S., 171
Barrie, J. M., 171, 290
Barry Lyndon, 198
Beauchamp's Career, 252
Beckford, Wm., 103, 161, 172, 307
Beers, H. A., 307
Behn, Mrs. Aphra, 20, 46, 92, 303
Belinda, 96, 172
Belknap, Jeremy, 151, 308
Bellamy, Edward, 281
Bentivolio and Urania, 19
Berger extravagant, Le, 17
Betrothed, The, 138

Bivouac, The, 150, 310
Björnson, B., 80
Black, Wm., 282
Blackmore, R. D., 282
Blanche the Duchess, 129, 300
Boccaccio, 300
Boileau-Despréaux, N., 17
Bolingbroke, Henry St. John, Viscount, 147
Book of Snobs, The, 198–199, 205
Border Chieftains, The, 308
Borrow, Geo., 174 *n.*, 211–212, 215, 283, 313
Boswell, James, 73, 305
Boyle, Roger, 19
Bradshaw, Mrs. M. A. C., 308
Brambletye House, 140
Bray, Anna E., 139–140, 309
Bride of Lammermoor, The, 126, 129
Brontë, Anne, 228, 313
Brontë, Charlotte, 205, 224–233, 234, 237, 255, 298, 313
Brontë, Charlotte, and her Circle, 313
Brontë, Charlotte, Life of, 313
Brontë, Emily, 166–167, 228, 232, 313
Brooke, Henry, 85, 306
Brown, C. B., 107, 109, 152, 159, 161, 307
Brown, Thomas, 18, 23, 65
Browne, Sir Thomas, 286
Browning, Robert, 253
Bruce, The, 113
Brunetière, Ferdinand, 61, 235 *n.*, 303, 305, 314
Brushwood Boy, The, 298
Brydges, Sir S. E., 308
Buccaneer Chief, The, 311
Bulwer, Edward, Lord Lytton, 10, 109, 143–145, 160–161, 172–174, 182, 186, 198, 200, 208, 209–210, 213, 215, 239, 281, 298, 299, 309, 310, 311
Bulwer, Edward, Lord Lytton, Life of, 312

Bunyan, John, 21, 22, 30, 297, 303
Burke, Edmund, 290
Burlesques (Thackeray), 205
Burney, Frances, 86, 94–95, 172, 306, 307. See also Arblay, Mme. d'
Burton, Robert, 69–70
Byron, Lord, 109, 158

C

Caleb Williams, 91, 92, 107, 306
Calprenède. See La Calprenède
Candide, 189
Canons of Criticism, 40
Canterbury Tales, The (Chaucer's), 6, 25
Canterbury Tales, The (Harriet and Sophia Lee's), 308
Carleton, Wm., 172, 311
Carlyle, Thomas, 61 *n.*, 174, 194, 197, 213, 219, 235, 253, 309, 312
Casaubon, Isaac, 304
Cassandre, 110
Castle of Otranto, The, 101–103, 307
Castle Rackrent, 97–98, 297
Castles of Athlin and Dunbayne, The, 104
Cathedral Stories, The, 218–223
Cavendish, William, Life of, 303
Caxton, Wm., 6
Caxtons, The, 209–210
Cecilia, 94–95, 172, 306
Celestina, La, 302
Cervantes, 9, 10, 43, 44, 52, 53, 63, 70, 258, 259, 301
Champion of Virtue, The, 102–103
Chapelain, André le, 301
Chapter on Dreams, A, 286–287
Charlemagne: romances of, 1, 4
Charles O'Malley, 150
Charles Vernon, 195
Chateaubriand, F. A. de, 106
Chaucer, 4, 6, 10, 25, 43, 112, 222, 292, 300, 301

Cherubina, The Adventures of, 171
Chettle, Henry, 12, 28, 302
Christie Johnstone, 213
Chronicles of Barsetshire, The, 218–223, 313
Chronique du règne de Charles IX., La, 138
Cibber, Colley, 304
Cinq-Mars, 138
Citizen of the World, The, 172, 306
Clarissa Harlowe, 31–32, 33, 57, 62, 63, 94, 274, 297, 304
Clélie, 17, 303
Cléopâtre, 110
Cloister and the Hearth, The, 88, 213, 214, 280
Coleridge, S. T., 133, 238, 279, 309
Collier, Jeremy, 36
Collins, Wilkie, 223, 281
Collins, Wm., 100
Colloquies on Society, 159 *n.*
Colonel Jack, 29
Comedy, an essay by Geo. Meredith, 254, 314
Coming Race, The, 6, 281
Comte, Auguste, 236, 243, 249, 251, 261
Condorcet, M. J. A., 84
Confessio Amantis, 301
Confessions (Rousseau's), 257
Congreve, Wm., 46, 58
Coningsby, 174–175
Conscious Lovers, The, 37, 58
Cooper, J. F., 84, 109, 137, 150–156, 280, 298, 309, 310
Cooper, James Fenimore, 310
Copland, Wm., 7
Count Fathom, 45, 63, 65, 69, 100
Country Jilt, The, 204 *n.*
Courtenay of Walreddon, 140
Courthope, W. J., 300
Cowper, Wm., 122
Crabbe, Geo., 122
Cranford, 234–235, 264
Crockett, S. R., 289

Cross, J. W., 313
Crotchet Castle, 171
Crowne, John, 19
Cruikshank, Geo., 141, 176, 312
Cruise of the Midge, The, 156
Cullen, Stephen, 308
Cumberland, Richard, 82–83, 307
Cyropædia, 32

D

Daniel Deronda, 238, 243, 244, 266
Dante, 159, 248, 251, 269
Darwin, Charles, 249, 263
Daudet, Alphonse, 264
David Balfour, 282
David Copperfield, 189, 191, 210, 286 n., 298
David Simple, 77, 305, 306
Day, Thomas, 86, 87, 306
Day's Work, The, 298
De Amore, 301
Dean's Daughter, The, 311
Decameron, The, 300
De Coverley Papers, The, 304
Deerslayer, The, 152, 154
Defoe, Daniel, 20, 27–30, 63, 66, 100, 101, 135, 147, 151, 161, 166, 182, 204, 211, 283, 285, 297, 304
Deloney, Thomas, 12
De Quincey, Thomas, 166
Deserted Village, The, 80
Desmond, 90, 306
Despotism, 308
Destiny, 168–169
Deutsche Nationallitteratur des 19 Jahrhunderts, Die, 310
Devereux, 143
Diana, 8, 11, 301
Diana of the Crossways, 252, 254, 255
Dichtung und Wahrheit, 80, 305
Dickens, Charles, 10, 40, 67, 109, 168, 175, 176, 177–193, 196, 198, 200, 209, 210, 215, 216, 217, 219, 239, 272, 298, 312
Dickens, Charles (Walter Bagehot), 312

Dickens, Charles (Geo. Gissing), 312
Dictionary of National Biography, 75 n., 300, 306, 312
Diderot, Denis, 41, 305
Disraeli, Benjamin, 172–173, 174–175, 193, 198, 218, 311
D'Israeli, Isaac, 308
Divine Comedy, The, 269
Dobson, Austin, 304, 305, 306
Docteur Pascal, 270
Dr. Heidegger's Experiment, 164
Dr. Jekyll and Mr. Hyde, 283, 285, 287
Dr. Thorne, 218
Don Quixote, 9, 25, 63, 299, 301
Don Sebastian, 308
Donne, John, 55
Dowden, Edward, 313
Doyen de Killerine, Le, 110
Doyle, A. Conan, 289
Drayton, Michael, 160
Dryden, John, 41, 61
Duchess of York, The, 308
Duke of Clarence, The, 308
Dumas, the Elder, Alexandre, 138, 147–148, 283, 288, 289
Dun, The, 96
Dunlop, J. C., 300, 303
D'Urfey, Thomas, 81
Dynamiter, The, 288

E

Earl Strongbow, 112, 308
Earle, John, 304
Early English Text Society: publications of, 301
Eastlake, Lady (Elizabeth Rigby), 313
Ebers, Georg, 138
Eclogues, Vergil, 8
Edgar, 308
Edgar Huntley, 107
Edgeworth, Maria, 86, 87, 95–98, 129, 169, 172, 213, 234, 267, 290, 297, 306
Edwy and Elgiva, 308

Egan, Pierce, 176–177, 178, 179, 207, 209, 312
Egoist, The, 252, 254, 256, 258
Eliot, George, 42, 62, 196, 233, 234, 235 and n., 237–252, 253, 255, 257, 258, 263, 266, 268, 269, 272, 274, 279, 280, 287, 298, 313–314
Eliot, George, as Author, 313
Eliot, George, Life and Letters of, 313
Eliot, George, Life of, 313
Ellis, Geo., 301
Éloge de Richardson, 305
Eloisa and Abelard, Letters of, 304
Elsie Venner, 281
Émile, 85, 86
Emilia in England, 252
Emilie de Coulanges, 96
Emma, 115, 120, 123, 224
Endicott and the Red Cross, 152
English Novel in the Time of Shakespeare, The, 302
English Poetry, A History of, 300
English Rogue, The, 19–20, 24
Englishman, The, 28 n.
Ennui, 96–97, 213
Entail, The, 170
Epic and Romance, 2 n.
Époques du Théâtre français, Les, 305
Études sur L'Espagne, 301
Eugene Aram, 186, 213
Euphues, 12–13, 14, 84, 303
Euripides, 41
Eustace Fitz-Richard, 137
Evan Harrington, 252
Evans, Marian. See Eliot, George
Evelina, 94, 299, 306
Evelyn, John, 22

F

Fabliau, The mediæval, 5 ; the line of descent from, 27 ; Fielding's relation to, 57
Fabliaux or Tales, 301
Faery Queen, 14, 113

Fall of the House of Usher, The, 162–163
Fashionable Tales, 96
Fatal Vow, The, 308
Felix Holt, 238, 243, 249
Female Quixote, The, 307
Ferdinand and Ordella, 308
Ferriar, John, 69, 306
Ferrier, Susan, 168–169, 311
Fielding, Henry, 9, 10, 25, 42–57, 58, 60, 63, 64, 65, 67, 72, 73, 76, 77, 78, 80, 82, 92, 93, 99, 108, 119, 122, 130, 136, 182, 188, 197, 198, 203, 204, 205, 206, 207, 209, 226, 241, 258, 259, 271, 272, 279, 285, 297, 305
Fielding, Henry, Life of, 305
Fielding, Miss Sarah, 61, 76, 77, 305
Fitz of Fitzford, 140
Fitzgerald, Percy, 306
Five Years of Youth, 171
Flamenca, Le roman de, 300
Fleetwood, 90, 182
Florice and Blancheflour, 4
Fool of Quality, The, 85–86, 306
Fordyce, James, 86
Forester, The, 308
Foresters, The, 151, 308
Forster, John, 312
Fortune des Rougon, La, 270
Fortunes of Nigel, The, 132, 134, 136 n., 243
Framley Parsonage, 218
Francion, 18
Frank, 87
Frankenstein, 108, 142, 307
Französischen Romans im xvii. Jahrhundert, Geschichte des, 303
Fraternity of Vagabonds, The, 63, 302
Freytag, Gustav, 138
Froissart, Jean, 112, 146
Fuller, Anne, 307, 308
Furetière, Antoine, 18

G

Galland, Antoine, 103
Galt, John, 137, 155, 168, 169–170, 171, 311
Garland, Hamlin, 310
Garrick, David, 65
Gaskell, Mrs. Elizabeth, 194–195, 234–237, 238, 244, 299, 312, 313
Gates, L. E., 211 *n.*
Gawain and the Green Knight, 4
Geoffrey of Monmouth, 2
George a Green, 227
Gervase Skinner, 175
Gesta Romanorum, 301
Gil Blas, 44, 299
Gilbert Gurney, 176
Gissing, Geo., 312
Gleig, G. R., 149
Godwin, Mary W. See Wollstonecraft
Godwin, Wm., 84, 88, 89, 90, 91, 92–93, 107, 109, 161, 163, 182, 306, 308, 312
Goethe, 40, 61, 76 *n.*, 80, 81, 159, 305
Götter Griechenlands, Die, 145
Golden Ass, The, 302
Goldoni, Carlo, 42
Goldsmith, Oliver, 10, 78–81, 172, 182, 297, 306
Gomberville, Marin le Roy de, 15, 16
Gondez the Monk, 308
Good, Mrs. V. R., 308
Gore, Mrs. Catherine, 174, 311
Gosse, Edmund, 303
Gossip on Romance, A, 301, 309
Gottschall, R. von, 309, 310
Gower, John, 5–6, 10, 301
Grace Abounding, 22, 303
Grand Cyrus, Le, 15–16
Grant, James, 149, 150, 280, 310
Gray, Thomas, 100
Gray Champion, The, 152
Greek Romances, 300
Green, Robert, 12, 13, 18, 302

Griechische Roman, Der, 300
Griffith, Richard, 83
Griffith Gaunt, 213
Groat's Worth of Wit, 12, 14
Grosart, A. B., 302
Guinea, The Adventures of a, 66
Gulliver's Travels, 30, 304
Guy of Warwick, 4
Guzman de Alfarache, 301

H

Häring, Wm., 137
Haggard, H. Rider, 282, 290
Hajji Baba, 172, 311
Hall, Joseph, 69
Hamilton, Anthony, 103
Hamlet, 37, 62, 108, 123
Handy Andy, 172, 311
Hard Cash, 213
Hard Times, 191, 272
Hardy, Thomas, 272–280, 283, 293, 298
Harold, 143
Harry Lorrequer, 150
Harry Richmond, 252
Harte, F. Bret, 155, 186, 310
Hartland Forest, 140
Haunted and the Haunters, The, 281
Haunted Priory, The, 308
Hawkins, Anthony Hope, 289
Hawthorne, Nathaniel, 27, 60, 109, 152, 162, 163–166, 268, 298, 311
Haywood, Mrs. Eliza, 20–21, 65, 110, 303–304
Hazlitt, Wm., 92, 306
Head, Richard, 19–20, 28
Hedge School, The, 172
Helbeck of Bannisdale, 269
Helme, Elizabeth, 308
Henly, Samuel, 103
Henry, 82, 307
Henry de Pomeroy, 140
Henry Esmond, 146–148, 157, 199, 205, 206, 224
Hermsprong, 91, 92

Héros de roman, Les, 17
Histoire de M. Cléveland, L', 110
Historic Tales, 308
*History of the British Kings
(Historia Regum Britanniæ)*,
2, 301
Hobbes, Thomas, 61, 84
Hoffmann, Ernst, 160, 161, 162
Holbach, P. H., Baron d', 84, 88
Holcroft, Thomas, 88–89, 90
Holinshed, Raphael, 112, 132
Hollow of Three Hills, The, 164
Holmes, O. W., 281
Homer, 26, 41, 44
Hook, Theodore, 175–176, 179,
207, 311
Hooker, Richard, 84
Horace, 273
Houghton, Mary, 308
Hours in a Library, 146 n.
House of Fame, The, 112
House of the Seven Gables, The,
27, 166
Howard, John, 181, 312
Howells, W. D., 48, 265, 299
Hugo, Victor, 138, 142, 147
Humble Remonstrance, A, 301,
305
Humphry Clinker, 63, 66, 67–68,
76, 82, 99, 169
Hunt, Leigh, 158, 163, 311
Hurd, Richard, 109
Husband and the Lover, The,
308
Hutton, R. H., 313
Hypatia, 145–146, 310

I

Idylls of the King, 2
Iliad, 44
Inchbald, Elizabeth, 87, 88, 91,
306
Indian Scout, The, 311
Inferno, Dante's, 159
Ingelo, Nathaniel, 19
Inheritance, The, 168–169
Ireland, S. W. H., 308

Irving, Washington, 109, 151,
160, 162, 166, 267, 311
Italian, The, 104, 105–106, 307
Ivanhoe, 134, 146, 198, 217, 224

J

Jack Brag, 176
Jack Sheppard, 142
Jack Wilton, 12
James, G. P. R., 141, 198, 309
James, Henry, 48, 97, 263–267,
268, 299, 301, 305
Jane Eyre, 42, 109, 227, 228–231,
232, 233, 298, 313
Janet's Repentance, 238
Jeffrey, Francis, 126, 129
*John of Gaunt, The Adventures
of*, 112, 308
Johnson, R. B., 298, 306, 310, 311
Johnson, Samuel, 40, 77–78, 80,
81, 121, 205, 305
*Johnson, Samuel, Boswell's Life
of*, 305
Johnstone, Charles, 66
Jonathan Wild, 45, 64, 198
Jonson, Ben, 24
Joseph Andrews, 18, 43–45, 47,
51, 56, 305
Journal of the Plague Year, 29–
30
Jude the Obscure, 272, 274
Jusserand, J. J., 302, 303

K

Kajütenbuch, Das, 310
Kempis, Thomas à, 251
Kenilworth, 133, 134, 298
Ker, W. P., 2 n.
Kidnapped, 289
Kingsley, Charles, 145–146, 157–
158, 193–194, 214, 219, 299, 310,
312
*Kingsley, Charles, Letters, and
Memories of his Life*, 310
Kipling, Rudyard, 290–292, 293,
294, 298
Kirkman, Francis, 19

Knight, Charles, 312
Knights, The, 308
Körting, H., 303
Koran, The, 83

L

La Calprenède, Gautier de Costes de, 15, 16, 110, 138
Lad and Lass, 80
Lady of the Lake (a prose romance), 308
Lady of the Lake (Scott's), 126
La Fayette, Mme. de, 15, 17
Landor, W. S., 186
Last Chronicle of Barset, The, 218, 222
Last Days of Pompeii, 143, 144
Last of the Barons, The, 143, 145, 299
Last of the Incas, 155, 311
Last of the Lairds, The, 137
Last of the Mohicans, The, 152, 154
Lathom, Francis, 308
Latter Day Pamphlets, 312
Lavengro, 211
Lawrie Todd, 155
Lazarillo de Tormes, 9, 12, 301, 302
Leather-Stocking Tales, The, 152
Le Breton, André, 303
Lee, Harriet, 308
Lee, Sophia, 111, 151, 307, 308
Legend of Sleepy Hollow, The, 151
LeGrys, Sir Robert, 303
Leibnitz, 81, 188, 189, 199
Leigh, J. E. Austen-, 309
Leland, Thomas, 101, 307
Lennox, Charlotte, 307
Leopardi, 277
Lesage, 43, 44, 52, 63
Lessing, 70
Lettre à d'Alembert sur les spectacles, 305
Lever, Charles, 149, 150, 172, 198, 199, 310

Lewes, George Henry, 224, 231, 232, 313
Lewis, M. G., 106–107, 159, 307
Ligeia, 162
Lillo, Geo., 304
Lindamira, a Lady of Quality, Letters of, 23
Lionel Lincoln, 136, 152
Literary Studies, 309
Littérature française, Manuel de la, 303
Lochandhu, 137
Locke, John, 61, 84
Lockhart, J. G., 144, 309
Lodge, Thomas, 13, 80, 297, 303
London in the Olden Times, 136–137
Longsword, Earl of Salisbury, 101, 103, 110, 111, 307
Looking Backward, 6, 281
Lopez de Ubeda, 204
Lord Ormont and his Aminta, 252
Lorna Doone, 282, 283
Lounsbury, T. R., 310
Lover, Samuel, 172, 311
Lovers of Provence, The, 4 n.
Loyalists, The, 308
Lucian, 10, 43
Lyly, John, 12–13, 18, 24, 39, 303
Lyrical Ballads, The, 238
Lyttelton, Geo., first Baron, 65
Lytton, Bulwer-. See Bulwer

M

Macaulay, T. B., 73, 217, 224, 290, 309
Macbeth, 108, 274
Mackenzie, Geo., 19
Mackenzie, Henry, 83, 182
Mackintosh, James, 312
MacNeil, Hector, 308
Madame de Fleury, 96
Maigron, Louis, 309
Malory, Sir Thomas, 2, 297, 301
Man of Feeling, The, 83

Manley, Mrs. Mary, 20, 65, 110, 303
Manley, Mary, Letters written by, 303
Manœuvring, 96
Mansfield Park, 115, 120, 123
Mansie Wauch, 171, 311
Manzoni, Alessandro, 138
Marble Faun, The, 165
Marcella, 269
Mare au Diable, La, 80
Margites (Homer), 44
Marianne, 35, 57
Marivaux, Pierre Carlet de, 35, 72, 228
Markheim, 287
Marriage, 168–169
Marryat, Frederick, 156–157, 195, 310
Marsh-Caldwell, Mrs. Anne, 228
Martin Chuzzlewit, 189, 190
Martineau, Harriet, 171
Martinus Scriblerus, Memoirs of, 70–71
Mary Barton, 194
Masque of the Red Death, The, 162
Master of Ballantrae, The, 282, 285, 289
Matthews, Brander, 268, 305
Maturin, C. R., 159, 161, 162, 311
Maxwell, W. H., 149–150, 310
Melmoth the Wanderer, 159, 311
Memoirs of a Cavalier, 29, 101, 151
Memoirs of a Certain Island Adjacent to Utopia, 20–21
Memories and Portraits, 301, 305, 309
Menander, 262
Menaphon, 13
Meredith, Geo., 234, 252–262, 263, 298, 314
Mérimée, Prosper, 138
Meyer, Paul, 300, 303
Microcosmography, 304

Middlemarch, 238, 243, 244, 246–248, 269, 272
Midshipman Easy, 156
Midsummer Eve, 308
Mill, John Stuart, 261
Mill on the Floss, The, 27, 235, 238, 240, 242
Milton, 279
Minstrel, The, 308
Mr. Gilfil's Love-Story, 238
Mitchell, Isaac, 151, 308
Mitchell, S. Weir, 290
Mitford, Mary, 171, 311
Modern Guides of English Thought in Matters of Faith, 313
Moir, D. M., 168, 171, 311
Molière, J. B. P. de, 17, 43, 52, 58, 262
Moll Flanders, 29, 204
Monk, The, 107, 307
Montalvo, Ordoñez de, 7, 12, 301
Montemayor, George of, 8, 11, 301
Montford Castle, 308
Moonstone, The, 281
Moorland Cottage, The, 235, 238
More, Hannah, 267
More, Sir Thomas, 6, 159, 303
Morel-Fatio, A., 301
Morier, James, 172, 311
Morley, Henry, 302
Morris, Wm., 282
Morte Darthur, 2, 297, 301
Mosse, Henrietta, 308
Much Ado about Nothing, 120
Munday, Anthony, 301
Murray, Hugh, 308
My Novel, 209–210
Mysteries of Udolpho, The, 104–105, 116, 307
Mysterious Freebooter, The, 308

N

Nash, Thomas, 12, 302
Nature and Art, 91, 306
Nature's Pictures drawn by Fancy's Pencil, 303

Ned Clinton, 137, 149
Never too Late to Mend, 213
New Atlantis, The, 20
New Landlord's Tales, 136
Newcastle, Margaret Duchess of, 22, 23, 303
Newcomes, The, 199, 205, 206, 207
Newman, J. H., 146, 211 and *n.*
Nicholas Nickleby, 183
Night Thoughts, 40
Nightmare Abbey, 171
Noctes Ambrosianæ, 171
North and South, 194
Northanger Abbey, 115–116, 117, 171
Northumbrian Tale, A, 308
Notre-Dame de Paris, 138, 142
Nouvelle Héloïse, La, 85, 306
Novel, The: historical and descriptive definition of, xiii–xv; the novel of incident and the novel of character, 26–27; relation to the drama, 57–63
Novel previous to the xviith Century, A History of the, 300

O

Œdipus, the King, 37, 44
Old Curiosity Shop, The, 183, 185–186, 189
Old English Baron, The, 102–103, 307
Old Manor House, The, 91
Old Mortality, 128, 134
Old Saint Pauls, 143
Oliver Cromwell, 140
Oliver Twist, 182–183, 184, 188–189, 190
On State of Criminal Law, 312
One of our Conquerors, 252
Opie, Amelia, 88, 90, 306
Ordeal of Richard Feverel, The, 252, 298
Origin of Species, The, 249
Ormond, 172
Oroonoko, 20, 46, 84

Orphan, The, 58
Otway, Thomas, 58, 304
Our Village, 171, 311
Overbury, Thomas, 24
Ovid, 3
Owenson, Miss Sydney (Lady Morgan), 172

P

Paine, Thomas, 88
Pair of Blue Eyes, A, 273–274
Palace of Pleasure (Painter), 300
Palmer, Miss A. T., 308
Pamela, 22, 31, 32, 33 and *n.*, 35, 36, 37, 38, 42, 43, 44, 46, 50, 75, 76, 77, 79, 94, 304
Pandion and Amphigenia, 19
Parthenissa, 19
Partial Portraits, 265 *n.*, 301
Pathfinder, The, 152, 154, 298
Paul Clifford, 182, 188–189, 198, 312
Pausanias, 143
Peacock, T. L., 171, 311
Peep at Our Ancestors, A, 308
Peep at the Pilgrims, A, 137
Peg Woffington, 213
Pelham, 173–174, 298
Pen and Ink, 268 *n.*
Pendennis, 175, 199, 204, 312
Pepys, Samuel, 22
Peregrine Pickle, 63, 65, 66–67
Persuasion, 115, 120, 122
Peter Simple, 156
Phelps, W. L., 307
Philip, The Adventures of, 199, 207
Philosophy of the Short-Story, The, 268 *n.*
Phœnix, The, 307
Picara Justina, La, 204
Picaresque Novel, The, 9–10, 11, 12, 17–18, 19–20, 28, 44, 57, 63, 66, 77, 99, 182–183, 189, 203, 212, 301, 302
Pickwick Papers, 60, 178–180,

183, 185, 186, 189, 190, 198, 280, 311, 312
Piers Plain, 12, 302
Pilgrims of the Rhine, 160
Pilgrim's Progress, 21, 25, 297, 303
Pilot, The, 156
Pioneers, The, 152, 153, 154
Pirate, The, 155
Plutarch, 112
Poe, E. A., 109, 161–163, 164, 165, 186, 268, 281, 283, 299, 311
Poetics, Aristotle's, 44 *n.*
Polexandre, 16
Political Justice, 89, 306
Poor Scholar, The, 172
Pope, Alexander, 41, 70, 99, 100, 304
Popular History of England, 312
Porter, Anna M., 308
Porter, Jane, 112–113, 126, 307, 308.
Portuguese Letters, The, 23, 304
Postl, Karl, 310
Power of Love, in Seven Novels, The, 20
Pownall, Thomas, 308
Prairie, The, 152, 154
Prairie Flower, The, 311
Précieuses ridicules, Les, 17
Prévost, Abbé, 33 *n.*, 41, 110
Pride and Prejudice, 84, 115, 119–120, 224, 232, 298
Prince Otto, 282, 287, 288
Princess of Thule, A, 282
Princesse de Clèves, La, 17, 25
Prisoner of Zenda, The, 27
Professor, The, 227
Promessi Sposi, I, 138
Prometheus Unbound, 93
Prose Fiction, History of, 300, 303
Protestant, The, 139
Provost, The, 170
Pynson, Richard, 6

Q

Queenhoo-Hall, 113–114, 308
Quevedo-Villegas, F. de, 63

R

Rabelais, François, 43, 69, 70
Racine, Jean, 58
Radcliffe, Ann, 104–106, 107, 108, 109, 126, 158, 159, 163, 225, 307
Raleigh, Professor Walter, xvi
Raleigh, Sir Walter, 158
Rambler, The, 77
Rameses, 136
Rasselas, Prince of Abyssinia, 77–78, 306
Reade, Charles, 88, 212–215, 216, 280, 313
Rebecca and Rowena, 198
Recess, The, 111, 151, 307
Reeve, Clara, xiv–xv, 102–103, 112, 307, 308
Refugee, The, 137
Reid, Mayne, 310
Rejected Addresses, 140
Repentance, 12
Return of the Native, The, 274, 298
Reuben Apsley, 140
Revenge, The, 158
Revolt of Islam, 93
Reynard the Fox, 5, 9
Rhoda Fleming, 252
Richard Cœur de Lion, The Adventures of, 112, 308
Richardson, Samuel, 3, 8, 16, 21, 24, 27, 31–42, 43, 46, 49, 50, 57, 58, 59, 63, 64, 65, 75, 76, 77, 78, 80, 84, 85, 93, 95, 99, 108, 114, 187, 188, 205, 228, 236, 266, 279, 297, 304–305, 306, 307
Richardson, Samuel, the Correspondence of, 304, 305
Richardson, Rousseau, und Goethe, 305
Richelieu, 141
Rienzi, 143

Rights of Man, The, 88`
Rime of Sir Thopas, 4, 300
Rip Van Winkle, 151
Ritson, Joseph, 301
Robert Elsmere, 269
Robert the Devil, 4
Robinson, Ralph, 303
Robinson Crusoe, 22, 27-29, 297, 304
Robinson und Robinsonaden, 304
Roderick Random, 63, 65, 66, 69, 155, 156, 297, 305
Roger de Clarendon, 112, 308
Rohde, Erwin, 300
Rojas, Fernando de, 302
Roman au dix-septième siècle, Le, 303
Roman bourgeois, Le, 18, 24
Roman comique, Le, 18
Roman expérimental, Le, 270 n.
Roman historique, Le, 309
Roman naturaliste, Le, 235 n., 314
Romance, The: historical and descriptive definition of, xiii-xv; its relation to the epic, 1-2, 25-26, 300
Romance of the Forest, The, 104, 307
Romance of the Rose, 129
Romance of War, The, 150
Romanceës, Ancient Engleish Metrical, 301
Romances, Early English Prose, 302
Romances, Early Prose, 302
Romances, English Metrical, 301
Romances in the Department of MSS. in the British Museum, Catalogue of, 301
Romances of Chivalry, 301, 302
Romances of the West, The, 140
Romances, Specimens of Early English Metrical, 301
Romania, 3 n., 300

Romantic Movement, Beginnings of the English, 307
Romanticism in the Eighteenth Century, A History of English, 307
Romany Rye, 174 n., 211
Romola, 238, 242, 243, 244, 245-246
Rookwood, 141-142
Rosalind, 13, 14, 80, 297
Rosamond, 87
Roseteague, 140
Rougon-Macquart, Les, 270
Rousseau, J. J., 41, 42, 75, 76, 84, 85, 86, 87, 88, 257, 270, 305, 306
Rousseau, Jean-Jacques, et les origines du cosmopolitisme littéraire, 305
Ruskin, John, 279
Russell, W. C., 310
Ruth, 235-237, 238, 244

S
St. Clair of the Isles, 308
St. Irvyne, 107
St. Ives, 282, 288
St. Leon, 89-90, 92, 107, 308
St. Ronan's Well, 131, 171
Sainte-Beuve, C. A., 17
Saintsbury, Geo., 127, 305, 306, 311
Salut d'amour dans les littératures provençale et française, Le, 303
Sand, Geo., 80
Sandford and Merton, 86, 306
Sandra Belloni, 252, 261
Sannazaro, Jacopo, 8
Sayings and Doings, 175-176
Scarlet Letter, The, 164-165, 166, 298
Scarron, Paul, 18, 44
Scenes from Clerical Life, 238, 241
Scenes in Feudal Times, 308
Schiller, 145
Schmidt, Erich, 305

Schopenhauer, 277
Scott, Mary A., 302
Scott, Michael, 156, 310
Scott, Sir Walter, 10, 30, 60, 70, 84, 91, 101, 104, 109, 110, 111, 113, 114, 120, 125–136, 137, 138, 139, 140, 141, 142, 143, 144, 146, 147, 148, 155, 156, 158, 160, 168, 169, 171, 179, 182, 183, 187, 188, 190, 198, 201, 205, 209, 211, 224, 243, 280, 283, 288, 289, 290, 292, 293, 298, 299, 304, 307, 309
Scott, Sir Walter, Journal of, 309
Scott, Sir Walter, Life of, 309
Scottish Adventurers, The, 308
Scottish Chiefs, The, 113, 308
Scudéri, Madeleine de, 15–17, 19, 21, 35, 254, 303
Sealsfield, Charles. See Postl, Karl
Secret History of Queen Zarah and the Zarazians, The, 20
Secret Intrigues of the Court of Caramania, 20–21
Self, 311
Senior, Henry, 195
Sense and Sensibility, 115, 116–117
Sentimental Journey, A, 69, 75–76, 108
Sephora, 137
Sermons to Young Women, 86
Seventeenth Century Studies, 303
Shakespeare, 8, 13, 43, 48, 58, 60, 62, 108, 110, 119, 120, 126, 132, 133, 134, 143, 160, 164, 205, 221, 224, 226, 237, 251, 274, 279, 288, 309
Shakespeare Jest-Books, 302
Shaving of Shagpat, The, 252
Shelley, Mary, 108, 158, 307
Shelley, P. B., 93, 107–108, 158, 161, 307
Sheridan, Frances, 78
Sheridan, R. B., 78
Sherlock Holmes, 281
Sherwood Forest, 308

Shirley, 227, 231–232, 233
Shorter, C. K., 313
Sicilian Romance, A, 104
Sidney, Sir Philip, 11, 13, 18, 25
Silas Marner, 238, 240, 249
Simms, W. G., 310
Simple Story, A, 87
Sir Charles Grandison, 16, 32, 33, 34, 35, 36, 37, 41, 228, 304
Sir Launcelot Greaves, The Adventures of, 63
Sketches by Boz, 191
Small House at Allington, The, 218
Smith, Charlotte, 88, 90, 91, 306
Smith, Goldwin, 309
Smith, Horace, 140, 309
Smollett, Tobias, 9, 10, 45, 63–69, 71, 72, 73, 76, 78, 84, 97, 99–101, 102, 112, 135, 144, 155, 156, 179, 191, 209, 240, 285, 297, 305
Sociable Letters, CCXI, 23, 303
Social Contract, The, 88
Social England, 312
Son of Ethelwulf, The, 308
Sophocles, 41, 143
Sorel, Charles, 17, 18, 63
Southey, Robert, 139, 159, 301
Spanish Fiction, History of, 301
Spectator, The, 24–25, 147, 304
Spenser, Edmund, 14, 108, 109, 147, 165
Spirit of the Age, The, 306
Spy, The, 151–152
Staël, Mme. de, 172
State of the Prisons in England and Wales, 312
Steele, Richard, 24–25, 28 n., 37, 52, 58, 147, 205, 206, 304
Stephen, Leslie, 146, 304
Sterne, Laurence, 10, 69–76, 79–80, 81, 83, 108, 130, 186, 205, 206, 209, 210, 212, 253, 258, 259, 293, 297, 306
Sterne, Illustrations of, 69, 306
Stevenson, R. L., 30, 282–289, 292, 298, 301, 305, 309

Stories of Waterloo, 149, 310
Stowe, H. B., 195–196, 312
Stowe, H. B., Life of, 312
Strutt, Joseph, 113–114, 308
Studies in Literature, 313
Studies of the Stage, 305
Subaltern, The, 149
Suckling, Sir John, 55
Sue, Eugène, 156
Süden und Norden, 310
Suicide Club, The, 288
Swift, Jonathan, 30, 41, 43, 65, 70, 304
Swiss Emigrants, The, 308
Sybil, 193
Synnöve Solbakken, 80
Système de la nature, 88
Système de politique positive, 243–244

T

Taine, H. A., 249
Tale for a Chimney Corner, A, 163, 311
Tale of Two Cities, The, 188
Tales of a Traveller, 160, 311
Tasso, Torquato, 10
Tennyson, Alfred, 2, 33 n.
Tess of the D'Urbervilles, 274–279, 280
Texte, Joseph, 305
Thackeray, W. M., 10, 139, 141, 146–148, 157, 159, 176, 196, 197–208, 209, 210, 211, 215, 216, 217, 225, 226, 230, 236, 239, 241, 254, 258, 259, 272, 290, 298, 312, 313
Thackeray, Life of, 313
Thaddeus of Warsaw, 113, 308
Theagenes and Chariclea, 26 n., 302
Thomas Fitzgerald, 136
Thomas of Reading, 12
Thoms, W. J., 302
Thomson, James, 47
Thóroddsen, Jón, 80
Three Studies in Literature, 211 n.

Ticknor, Geo., 301
Tieck, Ludwig, 160, 166
To the True Romance, 291
Tom and Jerry, 176–177, 178, 312
Tom Burke of Ours, 150
Tom Cringle's Log, 156, 310
Tom Jones, 18, 45–54, 55, 56, 57, 62, 63, 64, 82, 92, 93, 204, 224, 297, 305
Tor Hill, The, 140
Tower of London, The, 143
Tragic Comedians, The, 252
Tragic Muse, The, 265, 267, 305
Traill, H. D., 312
Traits and Stories of the Irish Peasantry, 172, 311
Treasure Island, 283, 285, 298
Treasure of Franchard, The, 287
Trelawny of Trelawne, 140
Trevisa, John of, 226
Tristram Shandy, 69, 70–75, 297
Troilus and Cressida, 6, 25, 301
Trojel, E., 301
Trollope, Anthony, 196, 215–224, 233, 236, 255, 298, 313
Troy: romances of, 1
Turgénev, Ivan, 264
Twenty-ninth of May, The, 137

U

Uncle Tom's Cabin, 20, 195–196, 213, 312
Underdown, Thomas, 26 n., 302
Urfé, Honoré d', 303
Utopia, 6, 14, 84, 303

V

Vanbrugh, Sir John, 46
Vanity Fair, 199–204, 205, 207, 230, 298
Vanity of Human Wishes, 78
Vathek, 103–104, 307
Vergil, 8, 26
Vicar of Wakefield, The, 78–81, 297, 306
Vigny, Alfred de, 138
Villette, 227, 232–233

Villon, François, 287
Vindication of the Rights of Woman, 306
Virginians, The, 146, 199, 205, 206, 207
Vittoria, 252
Vivian, 96
Vivian Grey, 172-173
Voltaire, 42, 70, 103, 189

W

Walladmor, 137
Walpole, Horace, 101-103, 163
Walton, Izaak, 22
Warbeck, 307
Ward, H. L. D., 301
Ward, Mrs. Humphry, 268-270
Warden, The, 218
Warleigh, 140
Warren, F. M., 300
Watson, John, 171, 290
Watts, H. E., 301
Waverley, 82, 126-127, 129, 130, 158, 168, 179, 243, 298, 307, 309
Way, G. L., 301
Weber, H. W., 301
Wesley, John, 49
West, Jane, 308
Westward Ho! 157-158, 299
Weyman, Stanley J., 289
Whately, Richard, Archbishop, 309
Whipple, E. P., 313

White, James, 112, 308
Wieland, 107
Wildfell Hall, 228
Wilhelm Meisters Lehrjahre, 61 n., 305
Will o' the Mill, 288
William Douglas, 137
William of Normandy, 307-308
Wilmot, R. H., 308
Windsor Castle, 143
Wister, Owen, 155, 310
Wollstonecraft, Mary, 84, 90, 306
Woman in White, The, 281
Woodstock, 129, 140
Worde, Wynkyn de, 6
Wordsworth, Wm., 223, 238, 242, 251, 269, 276
Wuthering Heights, 166-167, 228
Wyclif, John, 5

X

Xenophon, 32

Y

Yeast, 194
Yong, Bartholomew, 301
Young, Edward, 40-41

Z

Zanoni, 160-161
Zastrozzi, 107
Zola, Émile, 18, 270-272